URBAN
THEOLOGY
UNIT
210 ABBEYFIELD RD.
SHEFFIELD, S4 7AZ.

Prison Governors

*For
Elizabeth,
James, Hannah and Jemma,
and
the Governors
who are able to make our prisons
a better place in which to live and work*

Prison Governors

Managing prisons in a time of change

Shane Bryans

WILLAN
PUBLISHING

Published by

Willan Publishing
Culmcott House
Mill Street, Uffculme
Cullompton, Devon
EX15 3AT, UK
Tel: +44(0)1884 840337
Fax: +44(0)1884 840251
e-mail: info@willanpublishing.co.uk
website: www.willanpublishing.co.uk

Published simultaneously in the USA and Canada by

Willan Publishing
c/o ISBS, 920 NE 58th Ave, Suite 300,
Portland, Oregon 97213-3786, USA
Tel: +001(0)503 287 3093
Fax: +001(0)503 280 8832
e-mail: info@isbs.com
website: www.isbs.com

First Published 2007

Hardback
ISBN: 978-1-84392-223-0

British Library Cataloguing-in-Publication Data

A catalogue record for this book is available from the British Library

Project managed by Deer Park Productions, Tavistock, Devon
Typeset by TW Typesetting, Plymouth, Devon
Printed and bound by TJ International Ltd, Trecerus Industrial Estate, Padstow, Cornwall

Contents

List of tables

Acknowledgements

In addition to the 42 prison Governors who were kind enough to take time out of their busy schedules to give me the opportunity to interview them, I have a number of debts to acknowledge. To the many Governors who inspired my work over the years, and who taught me so much, I shall always owe a huge debt of gratitude. My academic supervisors, Professors Robert Reiner and David Downes, provided the sound advice and wise counsel that practitioner-researchers find invaluable. The Prison Service provided funding for part of the study, until budget cuts required the money elsewhere. The staff of the Prison Service library, and particularly the head librarian Catherine Fell, treated my hundreds of requests with good humour and worked enthusiastically to track down old texts. The European Commission and Council of Europe kindly funded study visits to look at prison management in France, Spain, Ireland and The Netherlands.

My wife Elizabeth remains as understanding as ever, and continues to provide support and encouragement. My children, James, Hannah and Jemma, kept me going by asking, on a daily basis, why I hadn't finished writing yet. My academic soul mate, Roma Walker, helped me to find clarity in the bleaker moments of thinking and writing. Dhao Wotherspoon continues to question my use of English and provided many helpful comments on the manuscript. My mother, Jean Ann Bird, deserves the credit for first getting me interested in prisons. She took me to see Dartmoor prison on one windswept and foggy afternoon, when I was a young boy, and said that if I didn't behave myself that was where I would end up. She was right; some 20 years later I was appointed as assistant governor of Dartmoor prison.

The opinions expressed in this book are those of the author, and the personal views expressed by the prison governors who were interviewed. They do not necessarily reflect the views of the Home Office or government policy.

Preface

Although other professional groups within the criminal justice system have drawn research interest, and studies of penal institutions and their prisoners have an established research record, little attention has been paid to the work of prison Governors. Since joining Her Majesty's Prison Service in 1985, as an assistant governor trainee, I have been trying to work out how Governors are able to keep our prisons functioning despite what appear to be overwhelming obstacles.

This book is an attempt to answer that question. It is an empirical study that examines the changing role and work of prison Governors, charting their historical evolution from medieval gaolers to the emergence of modern Governors in the second half of the twentieth century. It describes how the role has changed over a 500-year period by categorising the office-bearers into five historical types. The development of the modern governor is traced over its 40-year history and four ideal-typical models are constructed to characterise the Governors currently in post. Key areas of transformation in the role are identified as well as aspects that have remained relatively constant.

The focus of the book is on contemporary developments, exploring the nature of the work that Governors do, the changing contexts in which they operate and the ways in which serving Governors define their role and purpose. The book provides an analysis of how the process of change has been accomplished. It examines the role of the prison Governor in relation to significant changes within prisons and the criminal justice system, as well as broader shifts in political culture and public policy.

The book also contributes to the literature on public sector administration and management, examining in particular whether the managerial role of the Governor is *sui generis*. The book provides a detailed analysis of the role played by prison Governors as managers of complex organisations. It questions, in particular, whether there is anything unique about the managerial tasks facing prison Governors in comparison to other public sector managers.

The primary fieldwork for the book involved 42 interviews with serving Governors and 10 interviews with 'stakeholders' (comprising area managers, headquarters staff and directors of private prisons). A national survey of Governors' job descriptions was also undertaken and a literature review encompassing historical and contemporary materials on prison administration and governance. This book sets out the views of these 42 Governors on how they seek to achieve secure, safe and productive prisons.

The interviews with Governors took place in the late 1990s. The Prison Service has moved on since then and some new structures and organisational changes have taken place. While some of the Governors interviewed have retired, been promoted or moved to other governing posts, what they have to say about their work remains valid today. In the text care has been taken to prevent quotes being individually identifiable. However, I am sure that my former colleagues in the Prison Service will be eager to play 'spot the Governor'.

Shane Bryans
Ankara, Turkey
January 2007

Chapter 1

Introduction – Governors and the prison system

Why study Governors – a neglected breed?

The prison is an instrument of punishment, which constitutes the 'darkest region in the apparatus of justice' (Foucault 1979: 256). Despite calls for decarceration, tougher community penalties and greater social inclusion, the prison continues to occupy a central position in our criminal justice system as these commentators point out: 'the prison as an instrument of punishment has escalated further in importance, and solidified its position' (Mathieson 2000: 173); 'So successful has the prison been that, after a century and a half of "failures", the prison still exists, producing the same results, and there is the greatest reluctance to dispense with it' (Foucault 1979: 277).

While prisons are likely to be a key, and probably the dominant, feature of our penal landscape for the foreseeable future, surprisingly little is known about the people who govern them and what they do on our behalf.

Prison Governors are a key occupational group within the criminal justice system. On behalf of society, Governors enforce the state's most severe penalty. It is Governors who run the 137 penal establishments in England and Wales. Governors hold in custody over 75,000 citizens, deprive them of their freedom and enforce the rules and regulations that dictate prisoners' daily lives. Governors exercise considerable personal power within their institutions. Prisoners can be: physically restrained; segregated; transferred; confined to their cells; strip searched; refused physical contact with their families; and released temporarily; all on the instructions of the Governor. Governors manage a 24-hour, 365-day a year organisation which provides: various types of accommodation (for staff, prisoners and visitors); a shop; a catering service; a health service; a maintenance department; a sports centre; a college of further education; a library; industrial workshops; and possibly a small farm or laundry (West 1997).

It is a complex task in itself, even before considering the individuals who are incarcerated. Governors have to control, care for, and contain a variety of offenders. Prisoners range from the hardened career criminal, and the violent and dangerous psychopath, to the inadequate and the mentally disordered. The majority are ordinary people who have committed offences of all kinds, and who want to get through their sentence as quietly as they can. Some, however, will be desperately trying to escape; some will be permanently anti-authority; many will want to carry on the delinquent behaviour that they bring in from the streets; a number will be desperately immature and unable to control their actions; and some will want to harm themselves.

The critical contribution that the Governor makes to the life of a prison has remained remarkably constant over time:

> The governor is the keystone of the arch. Within his own prison, he is ... supreme ... (Fox 1952: 87)

> A penal institution is the lengthened shadow of the man in charge. (Conrad 1960: 245)

> It hardly needs saying that the most important person in any prison is the governor. (Advisory Council on the Penal System 1968: para. 190)

> Perhaps in no organisation is the position of general manager, and the person who fills it, of such concern to all the organisational participants as it is in the prison. (King and Elliott 1977: 149)

> The key managerial role in the Prison Service is that of Governor ... a well run prison runs more than anything else on the skill and approach of the Governor. (HM Prison Service 1997a: paras 4 and 9.14)

> It is difficult to think of a more challenging and important job than governing a prison. Prisons stand or fall by the people who manage ... them. (Lyon 2003: 3)

Surprisingly, academic consideration of Governors, and prison governance, is more limited than the importance of their role suggests that it should be. In order to contribute to filling the gap in the literature this book gives an insight into the people who run our prisons and the way in which they govern. It provides an additional dimension to the existing work on penality because it focuses on the perspective of the key manager in the prison landscape – as one commentator put it: 'adequate description and understanding of contemporary penality depends on the perspective of those who shape and administer its mission' (Lucken 1998: 108).

The nature of the work, and the environment in which it is undertaken, has led to the role of the Governor being described, in the past, as unique or *sui generis*. It has been suggested more recently that the role has undergone something of a transformation and become more managerial and less distinct as a *sui generis* profession. The Prison Service Review concluded that the role of Governor had become much more demanding. It found that Governors were increasingly seen as general managers and concluded that 'the responsibilities of governors and the demands made on them have increased enormously over the years' and that 'the role of governor is in need of redefinition and review' (HM Prison Service 1997a: paras 9.34 and 9.77). The view from outside the Prison Service is similar: 'the recent period has been an eventful one in the prisons of England and Wales ... it seems apparent ... that what governing prisons means and involves will also have changed significantly' (Sparks *et al.* 1996: 134–135). These changes to the Governor's role and work highlight the need to study Governors, and what they do, if we are to truly understand how our prisons function.

Purpose and structure of the book

The purpose of this book is not to elucidate a systematic sociology of imprisonment but rather to develop further an understanding of how prisons are managed and by whom. It hopes to contribute to the theory, policy and practice of running prisons. The book will identify who governs our prisons, discuss the work that they do, and consider whether that work is different from the work of their predecessors. It will consider whether the Governor is still the key player in a prison and whether the success, or failure, of a prison depends more on the Governor than on anything else. This book also contributes to the literature on public sector administration and management by considering the impact of a new ideology (New Public Management) on a particular group of public sector administrators (Governors) and whether it has been successful in transforming them into generic public sector managers.

This book seeks to identify the patterns and structures of prison governance primarily through Governors' discourse. Very few Governors who were interviewed as part of the study set their views within any explicit theoretical, academic or legal framework. Their discourse was grounded in experience rather than in some esoteric body of knowledge. It was derived from Governors' claims to know prisons and prisoners, gained from experience of dealing with prisoners and from running prisons.

The book has been divided into eight chapters. Chapter 1 now goes on to describe the research process that underpinned the contents of this book, explaining how the research was planned and accomplished. It also looks at ethical issues in conducting the research and reflects on being a 'practitioner-researcher'. The chapter ends by looking at the 'office' of Governor and how Governors fit into the prison system.

Chapters 2 and 3 trace the development of the role and work of Governors since the time of the first gaolers. They outline the key organisational and penal changes for each historical period and set within that context how the role, work and status of Governors has changed over the years.

Chapter 4 explores how the role of this academically neglected occupational group has changed under external pressures that have affected the use and practice of imprisonment and the treatment of prisoners. It highlights some of the factors that have been influential in changing the nature of the Governors' working environment, in particular: the changing status of prisoners with the development of the concept of prisoners rights; the increased scrutiny of the press and politicians; the 'competitive' element introduced by the privatisation of penal establishments and the introduction of risk management approaches. It goes on to discuss the introduction of managerialism (which brought with it new organisational structures and demands for monitoring and ordering of performance) into the Prison Service and its impact on the role of the Governor.

The demographic and social characteristics of the 42 Governors interviewed are described in Chapter 5. The chapter looks at their social origins, education, occupational backgrounds, level of job satisfaction and espoused ideologies. Career paths are also shown and distinctions drawn between those characteristics of direct-entry governors and those who had been promoted from the ranks of prison officers.

An exploration of prison governorship, and what it means to govern a prison, forms Chapter 6. The chapter makes a contribution to the understanding of management practices within the peculiar context of the prison and of the tensions and dilemmas that are characteristic of prison societies, as perceived by those who govern them. It identifies what the role and tasks of the Governor amount to in reality, as perceived by the persons interviewed. The chapter considers the general management tasks, as well as those that are specific to the running of a prison: maintaining security and achieving order and control; attempting to provide positive regimes; and balancing these objectives through 'ensuring legitimacy, justice and fairness'. The importance that Governors attach to leadership, personal example and 'jailcraft' are highlighted.

Chapter 7 pulls together the earlier discussion and analyses the Governors' current role. It identifies a typology of Governors based on the research, before going on to outline how a Governor's work has become increasingly managerial in nature. It emphasises the continuing significance of the Governor in achieving a balanced and healthy prison and highlights the tension that exists between control from above in the form of rules, regulations and directives, which reduce the Governor's autonomy, and the need for flexibility and personal influence in managing penal institutions. The chapter concludes by considering whether the work of today's Governors remains a form of management that is *sui generis*.

The final chapter, Chapter 8, discusses the implications of the research and its implications for prison policy and organisational practice, before making suggestions for future research. The book concludes with some thoughts about prison governance in the future.

Studying a criminal justice elite

Two major reviews (HM Prison Service 1996b and 1997a) concluded that the role of the Governor was in need of redefinition and review. As a result, the Prisons Board decided that a study into the changing role of the Governor should be commissioned. Given my previous work on the subject of governing prisons, I was asked to undertake the study. The Prison Governors Association (PGA) fully supported the proposed research – perhaps in part because 'research about the theory and practice of an occupation confers on it a measure of professionalism' (Brown 1996: 177).

One of the key issues for any researcher is deciding how to collect the primary data – in this case information about Governors and what they do. The advantages of using interviews far outweighed other options. Indeed, it has been suggested that:

> Elites need to be interviewed. The best way of finding out about people is by talking to them. It cannot guarantee the truth, especially people well practised in the arts of discretion. But it is superior to any alternative way of discovering what they believe and do. (Crewe 1974: 42–43, quoted in Reiner 1991: 39)

Given the time and resources available to interview Governors, and to analyse the data, it would not have been possible to interview all 126

5

people governing a prison at the time of the field research. It was decided therefore to select a sample of Governors to interview. A sample size of 42 interviews, which equated to one third of Governors, was manageable given the time available. A stratified random sampling methodology was adopted around the different types of prison, which is the main variable. The type of prison dictates the category, gender and age of prisoner and size of the establishment. By including the different types of establishment in the sample it was ensured that interviews would take place with Governors of male/female, adult/young offender, high/low security and large/small prisons.

Table 1.1 Interview sample methodology

Type of establishment	Number of establishments of each type*	Percentage of the total number of prisons	Number of interviews in the sample
Local/Adult remand	34	27%	11
Dispersal	5	4%	2
Category B	11	9%	4
Category C	34	27%	11
Open	9	7%	3
YOI/RC	22	17%	7
Female	11	9%	4
Total	126 (100%)	100%	42 (33%)

*Source: 1997/98 Prison Service Report and Accounts (HM Prison Service 1998).

The result of the exercise was a list of 42 prisons and a letter was sent to the Governor of each of those prisons. The interviews with Governors can best be described as a 'guided or focused interview' for which the researcher establishes a framework by selecting topics around which the interview is guided (Bell 1996: 94). As a means to give some structure to the interviews, and to ensure that relevant points were covered, an interview schedule was produced. The schedule highlighted the key topics that were to be investigated, together with broad open questions for each of those topics. A number of force-choice questions were also used to gather factual data about Governors.

The interviews were conducted over an 18-month period (between 1998 and 2000). The interviews themselves lasted between one hour and 10 minutes and three hours and 15 minutes, with an average time of two hours. All interviewees agreed to the interviews being taped, some only after reassurance that the interviews were going to be confidential and that any quotes used would be anonymous. On five occasions interviewees asked for the tape to be turned off for a short period in order to recount an anecdote or describe the actions of another named Governor.

In addition to the 42 interviews with Governors, a number of interviews were conducted with stakeholders (area managers, Headquarters staff, private prison directors) in order to obtain background information on the work of Governors. It also enabled me to identify whether stakeholders identified different 'themes' in the role of the Governor compared to the views expressed by the Governors themselves. A total of 10 stakeholder interviews were conducted: three with members of the Prison Service Management Board; four with area managers; one with HM Chief Inspector of Prisons and two with directors of contracted-out prisons.

The tapes of the interviews were transcribed and computer text files created for each interview. The transcripts were also manually examined for concepts and themes that seemed significant. All transcripts were incorporated as anonymised text files into a computer software package for qualitative analysis. The transcripts were analysed using *NUD*IST* (Non-Numerical Unstructured Data Indexing, Searching and Theory-Building), a software package specifically designed to support qualitative analysis of non-numerical unstructured data, using indexing, searching and theorising tools.

One important part of the study was identifying the key tasks and duties that the Governor was expected to undertake. Letters requesting job descriptions were sent to the Governors of the 126 publicly managed prisons. A total of 98 job descriptions were returned which represents a sample of 78 per cent. A further five Governors indicated that they did not have a job description.

Part of the context of any research study is the nature of the researcher. All researchers are subject to prejudices, cultural beliefs and values that they bring into the research process with them. My position as a researcher was unambiguous, in that I was clearly an 'indigenous insider' (Brown 1996). Indigenous insiders, or practitioner-researchers as they are sometimes known, tend to be people who hold down a job in some particular area and at the same time carry out systematic enquiry that is of relevance to the job (Robson 1993: 446).

Practitioner-researchers tend to face a number of disadvantages when conducting research. As a Governor I had a number of preconceptions about the issues being studied. I had to make conscious efforts throughout to ensure that they did not become manifest in the study. On the other hand, there was a clear danger of 'over-rapport' (Hammersley and Atkinson 1983: 98–104) with the interviewees and that the interviews would be 'contaminated with sympathy'. Practitioner-researchers are often seen as being too close to the subject matter to be objective. 'Outsiders' are considered better placed to '. . . step back from the institutional context and take a dispassionate view. They can see the organisational structure of the institution better, at least potentially, because they have no vested interests' (Sheptycki 1994: 127).

On the positive side, practitioner-researchers have the advantage of pre-existing knowledge and experience about the organisation; and work-related additional insights when it comes to designing, implementing and analysing the data. My experience of working in prisons over a 10-year period also made it easier to understand the language, processes and culture of the organisation, and this 'insider knowledge' assisted in formulating the key themes of this book.

While the external researcher's 'blissful advantages of naïve ignorance, waiting to be informed' (Reiner 1991: 46) is not a ploy available to the insider, there were some advantages of being known to be an insider. Interviewees clearly perceived at least a moderate degree of empathy coming from me due to my status as a Governor. This may have made them more willing to be honest and frank about their experiences, as these quotes from Governors reveal:

I know you will use this information carefully.

It is interesting but I wouldn't have done this sort of interview with anyone I didn't know and trust.

During the course of the interviews Governors made comments that indicated that they appreciated my status as an insider. A number of Governors believed that I would 'understand' what they meant:

As you know . . .

Again as you'll know . . .

I think you know . . .

I think you and I know . . .

Others made reference to my status as a practitioner:

You will be familiar with this argument.

You will have heard staff say, as I have . . .

I think you've probably done it yourself.

Come on, you know as well as I do . . .

I bet as a Governor you'd answer that question in the same way.

It is possible however that some interviewees were less frank and honest about the job and its pressures because I was a colleague rather than an outsider whom they would not meet again. Reiner rightly points out that 'all interviews are inevitably a form of reciprocal impression management' (Reiner 1991: 47). Some Governors may have told me what they thought I wanted to hear; a few may have been deliberately controversial in their responses; and others made comments aimed at the audience who would read the research.

There is a danger that a researcher may become captivated by the particular group being studied and come to take on their point of view to the exclusion of others. Examples abound, particularly in the research literature on prisons, of the dangers of 'going native'. (See for example, Fleisher's (1989) reflections on ethnographic research as a correctional worker.) In the case of the current research, my position as a Governor researching Governors brought with it particular concerns. Anyone looking at the research can reasonably ask whether the subject of study, the formulation of the research and interview questions, the interpretation of the Governors' answers and the conclusions reached in this book were influenced unduly by my status as a 'practitioner'. There can be no perspective-free, absolutely objective account by a 'practitioner-researcher', but what I tried to do is to be reflexive throughout, and particularly cautious when it came to interpreting the results of this research. Nonetheless, there is a need for readers to be alert to the precise position from which this book is written.

Governors and their role in the prison system

This book has at its focus the people who occupy the office of Governor and explores what they do when occupying that office. It is the Prison Act 1952 (as amended) that vests Governors with formal authority and status. Governors are appointed by the Secretary of State under Section 7 of the Act and are, therefore, holders of a statutory office. The exercise of the Home Secretary's power under the Act to appoint persons to the office of Governor has to be exercised rationally. Those making the appointment therefore have to satisfy themselves that the person to be appointed is fit and proper to hold the post and has the requisite knowledge, skills and experience to perform in the position, to an adequate standard.

As holders of the office of Governor incumbents exercise powers delegated by the Home Secretary, as well as their own statutory powers. Governors exercise power delegated by the Home Secretary in various circumstances such as transferring a prisoner or discharging a prisoner temporarily on grounds of ill health. In some cases the Governor will act for the Home Secretary, for example in relation to home detention curfew and release on temporary licence. The Act also confers on Governors some statutory powers (such as the power to conduct adjudications on prisoners) and the Prison Rules authorise Governors to take certain actions (for example, to segregate prisoners), which contribute to their formal authority and status. Governors have the freedom to use their legitimate authority and statutory powers without being unlawfully constrained or fettered.

It is the Secretary of State who has the responsibility for the administration of prisons under the Prison Act and it is the policies of the Secretary of State that determine how prisoners are dealt with. The Governor's accountability, therefore, is both to the court and to the Secretary of State. The warrant of the court, on whose authority the prisoner is sent to custody, is addressed to the Governor and requires the Governor either to produce the remand prisoner back to court or to keep the convicted prisoner in custody for the time determined. The prisoner is in the legal custody of the Governor, who is accountable to the court for that secure custody (s. 13 Prison Act 1952).

Curiously the courts do not tend to hold Governors to account when they fail to hold prisoners who escape. However, there have been a number of cases where Governors have been summoned to court to explain why a prisoner has not been produced at court on time.

Governors are required to undertake the duties and tasks as set out in their job descriptions. In addition, they have to ensure that the requirements of Prison Rules, other statutory obligations and line management are met. With the permission of the Home Secretary (under Prison Rule 8) Governors may delegate any powers or duties to another officer of the prison.

Under Section 8 of the Act, Governors, as Officers of the prison, have the 'powers, authority, protection and privileges of a constable' (*R* v. *Secretary of State for Home Office*, ex parte *Benwell* [1985] QB 554). This status is useful to Governors in carrying out their duties and gives them a certain amount of protection whilst doing so (Wasik and Taylor 1995: 127).

Unlike their colleagues in other jurisdictions (see, for example, Vagg 1994) Governors are not required to have a legal qualification, or to be a lawyer, and are not appointed directly to the office of Governor. Governors are appointed from within the ranks of existing Prison Service staff and there is no provision for someone to join the Prison Service and take up a Governor's post immediately. People wanting to be Governors join the Service as operational managers, and after suitable training and experience become deputy governors, before taking up a post as Governor of a prison, following an intensive evaluation and selection process.

Prisons are grouped for line management purposes into geographical areas, each with its own area manager. Area managers line manage Governors. The area managers are personally accountable for the performance of each prison in their area (Laming 2000: 28). Their role and relationship with Governors is discussed more fully in later chapters.

Each prison has a Governor. The type of prison, its security category and the number of prisoners that it holds will dictate the grade of the Governor and the number of other operational managers who work in that prison. The most senior Governors are in charge of high-security and larger prisons.

The Governor directly manages a number of functional heads (security, regimes, finance and so forth). Reporting to each functional head will be a number of heads of department (education, chaplaincy, catering and so forth). This group is known as the senior management team (SMT). Some of the functional heads and heads of department will be operational managers. Operational managers have duties in addition to their functional or departmental responsibilities, such as acting as 'duty' or on-call governor, incident management and conducting adjudications. Operational managers within prisons tend to be known as 'governor grades' even though this title ceased to be officially used in 1987 (HM Prison Service 1987). One operational manager is appointed as deputy governor. Administrative, finance and personnel posts are generally occupied by non-operational managers.

A sample establishment structure is shown in Appendix A. Not all establishments are structured in this way. The detail of the structure will depend on the size and function of the establishment but a similar hierarchical structure and key functional areas will be found in most establishments.

Understanding what Governors do

A 'governor' can be defined as: a steersman, pilot, captain of a vessel; one who exercises authoritative control; the officer in command; one who bears rule in an establishment or institution; and a tutor (*Oxford English Dictionary* 1985, p. 713). The dictionary also defines the detail of what Governors do, namely, govern. That is, they: rule with authority; direct, control and regulate the actions and affairs of people; command; hold sway over; influence; guide; master; lead; determine the course; prevail; have decisive influence; administer; manage; order affairs and undertakings; attend to; care for; look after; manipulate; hold in check; curb; and restrain (*Oxford English Dictionary* 1985, p. 709). As later sections of this book will describe, Governors occupy many of these roles and perform most of these tasks in their daily work.

11

The last decade has seen the nature of imprisonment undergo a number of 'relatively radical transformations in terms of its functions, organisation, and the size and make-up of the prison population' (Matthews and Francis 1996: 1). Despite these changes and ongoing debates about penal theory, Governors have to be grounded in reality and take as their focus the daily operation of their institutions. The practical issue facing Governors is how to achieve the four functions of penal confinement (Faugeron 1996): the custodial function (preventing escapes); the restorative function (providing opportunities for rehabilitation and reform); the controlling function (ensuring order, safety and justice); and the maintenance function (providing decent and humane conditions).

Assuming that prisoners are held securely, Governors then have to consider difficult and often controversial questions concerning 'the provision of humane treatment in prisons and the kind of life prisoners should lead while they are in custody' (Tumim 1996: 12). Governors therefore face the challenge of running their establishments in such ways that they are able to: keep prisoners in custody; ameliorate the potential negative impacts of incarceration; and achieve the rehabilitation of their inmates.

Very little research has been done on Governors and prison governance. While some attempts have been made to describe the work of Governors, no empirical studies of Governors' work have been published. The existing literature is in the form of autobiographies by retired prison Governors (Blake 1927; Rich 1932; Fancourt-Clayton 1958; Grew 1958; Kelly 1967; Miller 1976); practitioner accounts of their work (Bryans and Wilson 1998; Willmott 1999; Bryans 2000a, Abbot and Bryans 2001); and official Reports and Reviews of what Governors should be doing (most recently, HM Prison Service 1997a and Laming 2000).

Research in this country on aspects of the management of prisons has tended to focus on specific organisational issues such as: prison culture (Finkelstein 1993); 'prisonisation' and prisoner subcultures (Irwin and Cressey 1962; Irwin 1970; Cohen and Taylor 1972); mental health of prisoners (Gunn *et al.* 1978 and 1991); administrative decision-making in prison systems (Bottomley 1973; Adler and Longhurst 1994); maintenance of order in prisons (Useem and Kimball 1989; Sparks *et al.* 1996; Wortley 2002); absconding from open prison (Banks *et al.* 1975); race relations in prisons (Genders and Player 1989); suicide and self-harm by prisoners (Liebling 1992 and 1995); and the use of incentives and earned privileges in prisons (Liebling *et al.* 1997). Some studies have considered aspects of prison regimes, such as work for prisoners (Simon 1999) or prisoner education (Wilson and Reuss 2000). Others have focused on the needs of particular groups of prisoners, such as lifers (Cullen and Newell 1999), were written as guides to practical aspects of how a prison operates (Gravett 1999), or looked at the context in which Governors operate (Carlen 2001).

The paucity of academic interest in governing and prison management in this country is in marked contrast to Warden Studies in the USA, which has now established itself as a legitimate academic discipline. American books on the work of wardens include: comparative correctional management (DiIulio 1987); prison leadership (Wright, K. 1994); correctional organisation and management (Duffee 1980; Houston 1995; Peak 1995; Phillips and Connell 1996; Freeman 1999); analytical and critical overviews of the literature on corrections management (McShane and Williams 1993); and the examination of contemporary penality from the perspective of wardens working in the penal system (Lucken 1998). The literature on wardens also includes various articles on their work and approach, including correctional orientation (Cullen *et al.* 1993a) and job satisfaction (Cullen *et al.* 1993b, Flanagan *et al.* 1996). Various attempts have also been made in the USA to produce models of prison management (Barak-Glantz 1981).

This book now goes on to fill the gap in the literature in this country by looking at how the Governor's role and work has developed over the years.

Chapter 2

Early Governors – from gaolers to reformers

The next two chapters chart the development of the office, role, duties, recruitment, selection and accountability of Governors over the last 500 years. A knowledge and understanding of this history is critical to understanding the work of today's Governors. The manner in which the role and office evolved has had a direct impact on what prison staff, and prisoners, expect of current Governors. Many of the duties undertaken by Governors today have their origins in what their predecessors were required to do.

The role of Governor cannot be considered in isolation from the events and penal environment in which it has to be exercised. As Thomas pointed out in his study of prison officers, the role 'cannot be separated either from the social structure which forms its environment, or from other key roles from which it derives' (Thomas 1972: 13). An attempt has been made, therefore, to set the changes to the role of Governor within the context of the organisational and penal changes which were taking place. In some cases the changes to the Governor's role and duties were caused by the broader penal changes, such as a report, incident or legislation, and in others derived from a change in the broader public sector or society itself.

For the purposes of charting the changes, history has been broken down into various periods. McConville points out that such division for the purposes of study is 'sometimes helpful, but more often may mislead' (McConville 1995: 17). The boundaries drawn for the historical periods used in this book were based on an Act or Report that caused a discontinuity in the work, role or management of Governors. Another author may well legitimately adopt different points to divide the history. The time period which each section covers is not important in itself.

Gaolers and keepers (before 1779)

Historical studies of imprisonment indicate that imprisonment has existed in some form in this country since the eighth century and by 890 the word 'prison' (carcerr) first makes its appearance in a code of laws (Pugh 1968: 2). However, it was not until the Assize of Clarendon in 1166 that the first systematic approach to a national network of prisons was adopted. The Assize required all sheriffs to ensure that in counties where no gaols existed, gaols should be built (Pugh 1968: 4 and Harding *et al.* 1985: 5). In addition to the county gaols there were a small number of 'national' gaols, 'municipal' prisons and franchise gaols owned by leading ecclesiastics and lay barons.

These places of custody required custodians to guard incarcerated individuals. The sheriff, or owner, of the franchise prison, built and repaired these gaols, equipped them and accepted responsibility for securing the prisoners. The day-to-day work of running the prisons, however, was deputed to others. In some cases the 'custody' of the gaol was temporarily sold to someone willing to purchase it. In others they granted the gaolership to a 'keeper'. Sheriffs were originally unfettered in making appointments to gaolships and keeperships, which provided them with a useful piece of patronage. However, from the later thirteenth century the Crown strove to appoint its own servants to run gaols and the practice of using gaolerships as a means of providing for minor civil servants, to the detriment of local patronage, soon became the norm (Harding *et al.* 1985: 27). Whilst the public sale of 'gaolerships' was forbidden by an Act of 1718 (s. 10, 5 George I, c. 15), there was public and government acceptance that the holder of the position should be paid either a lump sum or a proportion of income by their successor.

The titles of the people appointed to run these gaols were as varied as the types of gaols themselves: gaoler; bailiff; warder; counter; porter; keeper and undermarshal. The title of the office holder would depend on the name adopted by the person holding the office, or the person making the appointment, rather than on any statutory provision (Pugh 1968: 148).

While thirteenth-century sheriffs employed working gaolers for a set annual salary, by the mid-sixteenth century all stipends for 'keepers' seem to have vanished (Pugh 1968: 166). Prisons at this time were largely self-financing operations and, where no salary was paid, gaolers had to derive their income from the fees paid by prisoners (in return for food, accommodation and so forth). Once they were inside prison a number of different fees could be exacted from them: on entrance; for better accommodation; for bedding; food; lights and fuel and finally a payment could be taken on release (Harding *et al.* 1985: 27). For example, there was graded accommodation, varying in price from room to room, and the warden would also run a kitchen and bar, where prices were likewise adjusted to the prisoner's rank (Pugh 1968: 176). In addition, avoiding the use of 'irons' and 'shackles' came to be connected with payments by the prisoner to the gaoler. Prisoners who could afford to do so were able to pay for their 'irons' to be removed or exchanged for lighter ones.

Additional income came from the profits of commercial opportunities that were organised, as the gaoler took a percentage of the proceeds made by the prisoners from the sale of their products (Pugh 1968: 332). The gaoler was often under considerable pressure to ensure that prison labour was profitable. The North Riding Justices, for example, appointed a new 'maister' in 1620, a clothier, who was paid the inclusive sum of £60. The prisoners were put to labour on the looms and if the maister could not generate sufficient funds to purchase raw materials, the justices would take £10, for every £100 worth of materials supplied, out of his yearly pay (Webb and Webb 1922: 15).

Prison finance very much reflected the reality of the times where all office holders were expected to obtain their incomes from fees. McConville argues that this should not be regarded as any more corrupt than most of the other public institutions at the time (McConville 1980: 9). Whilst it was accepted that gaolers would look to their prisoners as a source of profit, the dividing line between legitimate revenue generation and exploitation was far from clear. There were seemingly few opportunities for profit which medieval gaolers spurned and extortion and excessive charges by keepers were commonplace (Babington 1971: 53; McConville 1981: 11; Harding *et al.* 1985: 11–27).

Gaolers were expected to provide their own subordinate staff out of their prison income. Records indicate a range of people appointed to assist with the running of gaols: 'assistant'; 'deputy'; 'garcio'; 'servant'; 'yeoman'; 'clerk'; 'officer'; 'guard' and 'crossbowman' (Pugh 1968: 161). When, for example, the Middlesex Justices in 1615, opened their new house of correction they appointed a keeper at an inclusive salary of £200 a year, out of which he was directed to pay a matron, a chaplain, a porter and sufficient servants (Webb and Webb 1922: 15). As a result keepers often employed as few personnel as possible. They tended to allow prisoners to police themselves and 'tolerated a wide measure of self-government on the part of those confined' (McGowen 1995: 74) and often shared power, or at least reached an accommodation, with the prisoners.

The primary purpose of the early prisons was to detain prisoners and to 'deliver' prisoners for trial. Gaolers were not expected to reform or rehabilitate their prisoners but simply to prevent escapes and hold their charges until they paid their debts or until their sentence expired. Contact with prisoners was often prohibited and where it did occur the gaoler 'must not, at any time . . . hold unnecessary conversations with the prisoners, but must give his commands and receive their wants in as few words as possible' (Regulations for Chester Castle, quoted in Webb and Webb 1922: 103).

By the middle of the thirteenth century the post of gaoler formed a well-recognised occupation. Most were simple men, known by their occupational names, which have left their traces in the surnames of Galer, Gayler, Gaylor, Jailler, Gayle and Gale (Reaney 1958). However, a number were, or had been, minor royal officials. Keepers of the larger gaols were in some cases men of considerable property and land (Pugh 1968: 148).

The fourteenth century saw steps being taken in some of the larger municipal areas to find men of more responsible character to become keepers. Ordinances were laid down which required that only men of good character should be appointed 'keepers' and that they should be confirmed in office annually to ensure that they had carried out their duties faithfully (Pugh 1968: 185). The higher standards expected of the newer gaolers were often reflected in the regulations of the gaol. The gaoler of Chester castle, for example, had to 'guard himself against every impulse of anger or personal resentment; he must command with temper, enforce his just authority with firmness, and punish resistance without favour or partiality' (Regulations for Chester castle, 1802, quoted in Webb and Webb 1922: 103).

Keepers were expected to directly manage the prison, and, in order to do so, were often required to live in quarters located within, or adjacent to, the prison (Pugh 1968: 357), a requirement that was to remain in force until well into the twentieth century. Failing to do so often led to dismissal, as in the case of the keepers of Newgate who lost their posts in 1595 and 1636 for living outside the prison (Harding *et al.* 1985: 86).

One of the early requirements was for the gaoler to visit all parts of the prison each day; a practice later enshrined in legislation and continuing today. However, gaol fever and typhus was endemic to the early prisons and keepers were reluctant to go into certain parts of the gaol for fear of catching some disease (McConville 1981: 282–283). Indeed, living and working in close proximity to prisoners who suffered from starvation, ill treatment and disease often had a detrimental effect on the gaoler's health. In 1414, for example, the keepers at Newgate and Ludgate died of disease caught from their prisoners (Pugh 1968: 331).

An important development for the emerging profession came in 1356 when the City of London drew up regulations for the good governance of its four prisons (Pugh 1968: 186). While this move helped to ensure good conduct on the part of its keepers, it was also a first move towards clarifying the duties and level of performance required of them. The City ensured that the regulations were observed by sending in 'visitors' to inspect and report on the state of the prisons and the way they were being managed. These 'visitors' were given the power to fine, and in the last resort, to expel unsatisfactory keepers. The City codes also regulated fees and controlled the other forms of money making (hire of bedding, purchase of rights, sale of food, liquor, coal and firewood) which the gaolers participated in. The evidence for the control of gaolers in provincial towns is much more sparse than it was in the City of London (Pugh 1968: 191).

The eighteenth century saw the gradual transfer of responsibility for the gaol from the sheriff to the Justice of the Peace. The shift began with justices increasingly having control of the buildings of prisons, then being made responsible for ensuring that fees were reasonable and displayed in the gaol and finally gaining the power of inspections over gaols.

Despite the statutory foundations that enabled them to become more involved in prison management, the magistracy took little interest in their prisons and failed to lay down rules defining the keepers' authority and the type of discipline they were to enforce. The hours of unlock and locking up, the programme of work, the use of irons and punishment of prisoners were all left to the discretion of the keepers and their servants (Ignatieff 1978: 36). The reality was that as keepers continued to derive income from fees, and not from a salary from the state, they were able to remain independent from the control of the magistracy (Ignatieff 1978: 30).

Gaolers were however subject to extreme actions, in the form of fines and loss of office, if any of their prisoners escaped. Where complicity, negligence or corruption was proved to be the cause of the escape, the gaoler was himself likely to be imprisoned or subject to the death penalty (Pugh 1968: 232–236). The Statute of Escapes (1504) even set out a tariff of fines, which varied depending on the degree of culpability of the gaoler and his staff. The escape of a person imprisoned for debt resulted in the debt transferring to the keeper. A riot by prisoners in Newgate in 1450, for example, which caused considerable damage led to the gaoler being dismissed and imprisoned (Harding et al. 1985: 26).

A Select Committee inquiry into prison conditions in the early 1720s found that statutes were not being observed, wardens were conniving at the escape of prisoners and many prisoners were being maltreated and heavy fees were being charged (Journals of House of Commons, vsi. 21: 277, quoted in Harding et al. 1985: 86). In a number of cases the abuses perpetrated by the gaoler led to prisoners rebelling, resulting in the death of the gaoler (Pugh 1968: 183). Gaolers also abused their office in other ways, for example, the gaoler of Newgate was gaoled for rape of his female prisoners in 1149, as had been the gaoler of Richmond, a few years earlier. A gaoler at Newgate was condemned to death for killing a prisoner by putting him in excessively heavy and tight irons (Harding *et al.* 1985: 40 and 46).

The term 'Governor' was first introduced for independent regulators who oversaw prisons. The London Bridewell, set up in 1556, had a reformatory function and, in order to avoid the dangers of a profit-orientated keeper, was put into the hands of an independent unpaid body of regulators (O'Donoghue 1923). These 'Governors' played a part in the affairs of the prison that went beyond policy-making and inspection, and included getting involved in daily operational decisions (McConville 1981: 36).

Following the passing of a statute in 1576 (18 Elizabeth, c. 3) other towns developed their own institutions based on London's Bridewell. The Act allowed the justices to appoint 'wardens at the houses of correction'. These wardens, like their Governor counterparts in London's Bridewell, were unpaid. In order to discharge the day-to-day management functions many wardens paid people to run the houses of correction on their behalf. These paid individuals had varying titles including 'bailie', 'guider' and 'master' (McConville 1981: 38–41). The bailies were partly paid from the profits of inmate labours, the remainder of their salary funded from a compulsory levy on local inhabitants (Harding *et al.* 1985: 68).

Given the limited role that the gaolers were expected to undertake, the occupation was not highly regarded and to some extent gaolers were thought of as belonging to an untouchable caste: a group of people performing essential but contaminating work (McConville 1981: 67 and 72). Gaolers had to associate daily with the prisoners who were seen as the worst outcasts of society and with the gaol staff who came, if not from the criminal underworld itself, at least from the fringes of its economy and culture (Hibbert 1957: 59). The charging of excessive fees and other nefarious activities led to many keepers being the subject of social condemnation and suspicion. The *Gentleman's Magazine* in July 1767 went so far as to describe keepers as 'low bred, mercenary and oppressive, barbarous fellows who shrink at nothing but enriching themselves by the most cruel extortion' (quoted in Webb and Webb 1922: 18).

Gentlemen Governors (1779–1876)

It was not until the end of the eighteenth century that real attempts were made by central government to exert greater control over what happened in prisons. The Penitentiary Act of 1779 (19 George III, c. 74), and subsequent Prison Acts, set out the role of imprisonment and instructions for the management of penal institutions. Increasingly the attention of parliament turned to standardising the operation of prisons and improving conditions for those incarcerated. The impact of these changes was felt directly by keepers whose freedom was curtailed by the various pieces of legislation which, over time, abolished fees; prohibited private trading; required them to keep detailed journals of their activity; and subjected them to quarterly reports by the justices.

The Gaol Fees Abolition Act of 1815 (55 George III, c. 50), which substituted payment by the justices for gaol fees, had a crucial effect on gaolers. By abolishing these fees the reformers hoped to convert the keeper from an independent contractor into a paid subordinate of the state (Ignatieff 1978: 77). No matter how reluctant the justices had been to intervene in prisons in the past, the Act forced their involvement if only to ensure that the county's rates were being properly spent.

The term Governor was increasingly used to refer to salaried officers (as distinct from entrepreneurial keepers). As early as 1807, Robert Southey noted that the old eighteenth-century term 'keeper', with its rude connotations of animal taming, had been replaced by the more impersonal and commanding term 'Governor' (quoted in Ignatieff 1978: 190). Many authorities introduced the term in an attempt to improve the dignity of the office and, as McConville points out, it would have been unthinkable to sully the sense of moral mission and social prestige at Millbank or Gloucester Penitentiaries by giving their chief officials the title of 'gaoler' or even 'keepers' (McConville 1981: 307).

The title of 'Governor' received official endorsement in 1839 when an enactment provided that:

> If the Persons authorised by Law to appoint the Gaoler or Keeper of any Prison shall appoint such keeper by the Style of Governor such Governor shall have all the Powers and Duties of the Gaoler or Keeper at that Prison; and all Enactments made with regard to the Gaoler or Keeper shall apply to the Governor so appointed. (An Act for the better ordering of Prisons 1839, s. 24, 2 and 3 Victoria, c. 56).

Further changes to the way prisons operated, and to the work of the gaoler, came with the passing of the Gaol Act in 1823 (4 George IV, c. 64). The Act sought to achieve a measure of uniformity of practice by mandating visits by justices at least three times a quarter and required an annual report on the state of each prison to be made to the Secretary of State. Section 10 of the Act also set out, for the first time, that the Governor was required to visit each cell at least once every 24 hours and to keep a journal.

The Governor's primary task was to maintain the safe custody of prisons and to ensure that adequate control was exercised within the prison. In reality few gaols were large enough to warrant a sufficient complement of staff to remove the Governor from the petty routines of institutional life. Journals of Governors in the early nineteenth century reveal that the possibility of an escape was a source of 'ceaseless discomfort', that they had to restrain violent prisoners and correspond with the families and friends of young or sick prisoners (see for example, Chesterton 1856: 56–57).

The daily routine of the Governors depended on the type of prison system they operated under. Two systems existed: the separate system that kept prisoners apart so that they would not contaminate each other; and the silent system which permitted prisoners to be in association with each other but which prevented them speaking.

Governors of prisons operating the separate system adopted an endless military-type inspection of staff and inmates. In their report on prisons in 1837–38, the government inspectors had clear views on what Governors should be doing:

> Considering the importance of attending to the daily inspection of the cells, of making regular visits to each prisoner, and of constantly observing the manner in which the subordinate officers perform their duty, we cannot help expressing our decided opinion that the Governor's time ought not to be unnecessarily occupied with matters of detail, for instance with bookkeeping and such other business as may safely be confided to a clerk. (Quoted in McConville 1981: 267)

This reveals an early example of the tension between Governors being required to maintain a high profile in the prison and, at the same time, having to ensure that administrative duties were completed. It has been a constant theme in the subsequent history of prison management in this country.

In contrast to this energetic but intentionally remote monitoring and surveillance of the separate system Governor, a silent system Governor participated much more in the daily business of institutional life. The Governor would supervise staff and prisoners' activities in the day rooms and workrooms where they would be assembled. As a result the Governor was fully engaged in his duties until lock-up had taken place, as the 1844 journal of the Governor of Ilford gaol records:

> In the Morning I see that the Prisoners are unlocked at the Proper time, and set to Work. Afterwards I see that the Breakfast is served at Eight O'Clock . . . At 9 O'Clock the Schoolmaster brings his Books into the Office to me, with the General Report Sheet, for the Previous Day. Before Unlocking after Breakfast I see that the Turnkeys have

on the Uniform as Ordered, and I then Examine the Daily Report, and the Turnkeys' Report Books. About 10 O'Clock, I attend Chapel, and after Service is Over, make a General Inspection of all the Yards, Cells and Infirmaries, and Enquire into Reports of Misconduct, or Complaints ... I also see that my Orders of the Previous Day are executed, and write such Others in the Order Books as may be requisite. I Examine all the Commitments ... and Discharge such Prisoners, whose term of Imprisonment has Expired. I also see that the Dinner is Delivered agreeably to the Regulations. The Afternoon is Devoted to the General Duties of the Office, in which the Books are kept ... I also make out Parliamentary Returns, and Copies of all Warrants under the Game Laws, for the Secretary of State. In the Afternoon I again go round the Prison, to see that the Prisoners are properly Engaged, and frequently Visit the Prisoners at Night after Locking up. (Journal of the Governor of Ilford gaol 1844, quoted in McConville 1981: 268)

Governors were also required to supervise floggings and hangings; escort prisoners to London who were due for transportation; take prisoners to court whenever they were required to make a court appearance (which involved Governors being absent from the prison for a large proportion of their time); and keep a variety of books and journals. The Governor of Ilford gaol, for example, had to maintain 25 books (McConville 1981: 273–279).

The Gaol Act of 1823 required the Governor to reside in the prison and any absence had to be approved in advance and an entry made in the journal. This arrangement of work had a strong tendency to isolate Governors from wider social contacts and to heighten the physical and nervous strains of their work. The health of many Governors broke down as a result of the unremitting demands of duty (McConville 1981: 281). Some personal relief from the burden of governing was provided in the 1839 Prisons Act, which provided for legally authorised and responsible deputies to be appointed. However, the Governor remained accountable for the acts and omissions of his deputy.

The monitoring of Governors' activity became more intensive with the passing of the Prisons Act 1835 (3 and 6 William IV, c. 38) which introduced the appointment of government inspectors to visit prisons and make reports to the Secretary of State. The importance of the Act was highlighted by Webb and Webb, who pointed out that:

By this revolutionary statute the immemorial autonomy of the two hundred local authorities in England and Wales which still maintained prisons, was at one blow, destroyed. For the next forty years county and borough justices went on administering their gaols, and paying for men out of local funds, but subject always to ever increasing regulations made by the Home Office on every detail of prison life; incessantly watched and criticised by a staff of salaried inspectors reporting to the Secretary of State and the public. (Webb and Webb 1922: 112)

While they were not empowered to order changes in local prisons, the reports made by inspectors could create public embarrassment and often contained specific recommendations. For example, William George, Governor of Caernarvon Gaol, was the subject of an inquiry by inspectors, which resulted in his being charged with drunkenness and various abuses (Harding *et al.* 1985: 146). Inspections also led to the gaoling of one Governor after his conduct was brought into question:

He introduced of his own authority another punishment, not only utterly illegal, but most objectionable from its painful, cruel, and exasperating character, which he practised with a frequency distressing to hear of, for offences often too trivial to call for any severity of punishment at all, and upon offenders quite unfit to be subjected to it, combining with it also other inflictions and privations, and directing and witnessing their application with a lamentable indifference to human suffering, until the penal system of the gaol became almost a uniform system of the applications of pain and terror. (Quoted in Webb and Webb 1922: 174–176).

The creation of a Convict Service in 1850, consisting of prisons used to hold prisoners who had been convicted of a crime, led to a number of important differences developing between Governors of local prisons, which held prisoners on remand, and Governors of convict prisons. Unlike their colleagues in local prisons, the convict prison Governors had quite large populations, long-term prisoners with a low turnover and no escort or court duties. In addition, they tended to have a greater number of support staff, including deputies, who were able to relieve them of many of the pressures of responsibility. McConville points out that this enabled them to 'concentrate on administration, staffing and the regulation and disciplining of inmates . . . and to keep a social distance from subordinate staff' (McConville 1981: 445).

Another difference between convict prison and local prison Governors was that the former were responsible not to a heterogeneous group of magistrates but to a group of Directors with backgrounds and opinions similar to their own, and to whose rank some, at least, of their number would some day be appointed (McConville 1981: 446). In addition, they worked within a unified and uniform disciplinary and administrative system, which specified what was required of Governors and their prisons.

'Rules and Regulations for the Government of Convict Prisons' were issued in 1858 (Home Office 1858) and revised editions published in 1872 and 1886. One section of the Rules and Regulations identified the duties that the Governor was expected to undertake (Home Office 1858: 6–18). They required the Governor to have 'a general superintendence over the prison and prisoners', exercise 'his authority with firmness, temper, and humanity; abstain from all irritating language, and not strike a prisoner'; attend Divine Service in the prison whenever it was performed; visit and inspect daily the wards, cells, yards and divisions of the prison; also the kitchen and the workshops, and see every prisoner 'once at least in every twenty-four hours'; visit the Infirmary frequently; enforce a high degree of cleanliness in every part of the prison; take every precaution necessary for preventing escape (Home Office 1858: 2–11). The Governor was also required to keep 10 books and journals covering everything from prisoners' property to a misconduct book and account book (pp. 13–15). Each year the Governor was required to submit to the Directors a written account of life in the previous year.

The Convict Service Governors, in the late 1850s and early 1860s, therefore had no real discretion, unlike their local prison colleagues who continued to be able to largely operate as they saw fit. The different way the two groups of Governors operated their prisons became the subject of considerable public debate. In 1863 a Select Committee of the House of Lords on prisons and prison discipline (Carnarvon Committee) condemned the lack of uniformity that prevailed in the 193 local prisons. It also highlighted the differing standards developing in the Convict Service with regards to the severity of punishment and the treatment of prisoners, compared to what was found in local prisons. The report produced by the Committee led to a drastic tightening up of local prison administration (Webb and Webb 1922: 188) and resulted in the 1865 Prisons Act (28 and 29 Victoria, c. 126) which extended to local prison Governors many of the requirements already required of Convict Service Governors.

Schedule One to the 1865 Act contained 'Regulations for Government of Prisons' (Anderson 1878). These Regulations specified in minute detail what should happen in a prison and were unalterable except by legislative change, whatever the conditions of a particular prison. Schedule One set out 13 provisions relating to the work of the Governor. It required the Governor to 'strictly conform to the law relating to prison regulations' and 'be responsible for the due observance of them by others' (s. 69). The Governor was also required, as far as practicable, 'to visit the whole of the prison, and see every male prisoner once at least in every 24 hours' and 'at least once during the week, go through the prison at an uncertain hour of the night' (s. 71). The Governor was required to keep 10 records and sets of accounts (s. 77). These included his journal, a record of prisoners, punishment book, and visitors' book and an inventory of furniture and moveable property. The Governor was also required to 'reside in the prison' (s. 68) and to obtain written permission from a visiting justice if he required being absent from the prison for a night (s. 79).

Governors made steady and substantial progress away from the disreputability of earlier periods with the social upgrading of the people recruited to govern. The new breed of Governors came initially from the military, which reflected the view that in practice the primary objective of a Governor, just as it had been with the gaoler, was control (Harding *et al.* 1985: 168) and that 'tighter prison discipline; like tighter supervision of the streets, depended on the recruitment of men with an aptitude for the exercise of strict authority' (Ignatieff 1978: 189). This change in approach to the appointment of Governors can be seen in actions of the Gloucestershire magistrates. They wanted to replace the 'unregulated discretion' of the old keepers with 'mild government by rule' and wanted to 'make a change in the race or kind of men usually chosen for a gaoler or a keeper of a prison' (quoted in Ignatieff 1978: 104). They looked to the ranks of the military for these new disciplines:

> The humanity of the gaoler should rather be the result of coldness of character than the effect of a quick sensibility . . . He should be endowed with a patience which obstinacy the most pertinacious could not overcome; a sense of order which is method, rather mechanical than reflective and which few men obtain but by long habits of subordination and obedience. Such then . . . would be found if sought for in a profession where the passions are habitually subjugated to discipline. (Quoted in Ignatieff 1978: 104)

After the end of the Napoleonic Wars (1815), many military officers looking for alternative occupations took up posts in prison administration. This infusion of trained disciplinarians changed the characteristics of Governors as a group. The movement of gentlemen officers into positions formerly occupied by men of 'lower social standing' indicated the increasing importance of prisons as institutions. Those who specialised in prison administration came to be seen as vital and respectable public servants (Ignatieff 1987: 190).

A gentleman could take up a prison governorship without loss of self-respect. Advertisements were placed in the local and national press, seeking applicants for governorships, who could demonstrate the necessary characteristics of firmness; humanity; cool deliberation; some education; and considerable knowledge of human nature. The recruitment of Chesterton as Governor of Cold Bath Fields, in 1829, was typical of the new type of Governor appointed at this time. Chesterton had been a captain in the army of Columbia before returning to England on health grounds and was persuaded to apply for a governorship. He applied himself vigorously to the task:

> Traversing the length and breadth of the county, I visited every locality in which a magistrate resided, and, with one solitary exception, experienced the utmost courtesy ... my canvass progressed favourably, but failed to extort a single promise ... on the 23rd July 1829, I was nominated to the post by a vast majority of votes and the crowd assembled in the court and purlieus of Clerkenwell Green exceeded anything I have ever since seen, so much was the public interest excited by the contest. (Chesterton 1856, quoted in Priestley 1999: 268)

Varied prison experience had also become a recognised qualification and highly desirable in a candidate for governorships (McConville 1981: 314). Governors increasingly required greater skills, good levels of literacy and numeracy, and a higher degree of probity than their predecessors of earlier in the century.

The improved social standing of Governors, and their experience of several different systems operating in prisons, resulted in Governors having greater influence on penal policy, both at a local and at a national level. This was primarily because of the higher social standing of Governors and because they were drawn from a similar social background as the justices. Governors also had experience of the several different systems operating in prisons that enabled them to proffer informal advice about penal matters. The more established position of Governors was reflected in the extent to which they were called before parliamentary committees of inquiry (McConville 1981: 323).

Administrator Governors (1877–1945)

As a consequence of the 1865 Prisons Act, many of the boroughs and franchises decided to give up their prisons rather than face the expense of putting their prisons in a proper state, and 80 of the 193 prisons closed between 1862 and 1877 (Webb and Webb 1922: 192). In order to deal with the continuing variation in practice across the prison estate the 1877 Prisons Act vested overall responsibility for all prisons and prisoners (the 10,000 prisoners held in convict prisons and 21,030 held in local prisons) in the Home Office. The Act was seen as necessary to improve penal administration, ensure a greater measure of uniformity across the penal estate, and to placate the ratepayers by reducing costs (McConville 1995: 192). Actual administration of the prisons was delegated to a Prison

Commission, which was accountable to the Home Secretary. An Inspectorate assisted the work of the Commission.

The new Prison Commission took the view that a national prison system required fewer prisons, the restructuring of prison staff and the removal of the less professional kind of administration still found in some of the local prisons (Harding *et al.* 1985: 200). The structural changes resulted in a reduction in the number of prisons from 113 to 69 (McConville 1995: 194). The closures led to the dismissal of 41 Governors and 17 deputy Governors (Thomas 1972: 72).

The main aim of the Commission was to centralise control and enforce uniformity across the penal estate:

> The extent to which this fetish of uniformity was pushed seems today extraordinary. For not only was the uniformity to extend to all parts of the Kingdom, to all features of the regimes, and to all departments of each prison, but it was even carried so far as to ignore, almost entirely, all the differences among the prisoners themselves (Webb and Webb 1922: 204).

The Commission asserted control and imposed a new regime of regulation and standardisation on prisons. The discretion of the individual Governor was quickly eroded and uniformity was applied to all areas of the prison's activities, from discipline and labour to health, diet and discharge arrangements. The Prison Commissioners believed that it was possible:

> By a uniform efficiency of administration upon 'enlightened' principles, in which Governors ... were given precisely detailed rules with which they are required to conform, to prevent the evil consequences that had admittedly happened in the diversely administered prisons of 1822–77. (Webb and Webb 1922: 208)

Governors' discretion became so limited, and prisons so regulated by the Commission, that 'A Prison Commissioner could pull out his watch and boast that he could say at that moment what every prisoner was doing in every prison in England' (Ruck 1951: 9).

The duties of Convict Service Governors were laid down in the Standing Order for the Government of Convict Prisons (Home Office 1894). Similar regulations for local prison Governors were set out in the 1878 Rules for Local Prisons (Anderson 1878). The Governor's duties, as set out in Rules 79 to 100, constituted a blueprint for the management of the entire institution, from the broad requirement to 'see that discipline is maintained among the convicts at all times' to the detailed instruction that: 'He will not allow any dog, poultry, pigeon, pig, or rabbit to be kept in the prison, or in any quarter of a subordinate officer.' Some of the Regulations were as prescriptive of the Governor's private life: 'He shall reside in the prison, and he shall not be absent from it for a night without permission in writing from a visiting justice.'

Rules, Regulations and Standing Orders were issued which dealt with the vast majority of business, and indeed prisons became so governed by routine that unexpected events and awkward cases were comparatively rare. Where rules and standing orders failed to meet circumstances, Governors were required to make a report to Headquarters. Even where an independent decision taken by a Governor produced desirable results, the lack of consultation made it suspect. Governors kept to these rules and there were few demands to exercise initiative or assume individual responsibility (McConville 1995: 523).

While the prisons were under local government control, the surgeon, together with the chaplain, were 'superior officers', with access to the justices, acting as 'balancers' or checks on the authority and actions of the Governor (McConville 1981: 120 and 133). When the prisons were nationalised, the right and duty of routine access to the Governor and justices was removed from these 'officers'. In the governance of prisons, and in the wider structure of administration, the surgeon and chaplain were reduced to the level and function of technical specialists (McConville 1995: 303).

Governors lost the power to decide on many personnel matters. Thomas suggests that 'governors became less and less able to deal with staff problems. More and more officers had to rely on visiting Inspectors and Commissioners to help them with personal problems about pay, postings, quarters and so forth' (Thomas 1972: 102).

The reduced influence of the Governor can also be seen in the results of two major inquiries, which took place in the late 1880s and early 1890s. The Rosebery Committee was set up in 1883 by the Home Secretary to look into the complaints made by subordinate officers about pay and working conditions (Home Office 1883). Whilst the findings of the Committee did not impact greatly on Governors (the Committee found that the officers' pay was adequate and conditions were satisfactory), the consequential discussions established the right of staff to complain about their pay and working conditions. It also led to subordinate officers having security of tenure, as Governors lost the power to dismiss staff. The second inquiry, chaired by Lord De Ramsey, was asked, like its predecessor, to look at the conditions of service of the subordinate officers (Home Office 1891). Among its other findings it recommended the introduction of paid overtime for subordinate staff (Thomas 1972: 101). This recommendation, which was accepted, created an issue that would preoccupy Governors until the eventual abolition of overtime in 1987.

The 1877 Act changed the function and role of the justices. It confined their role to inspecting and reporting to the Home Secretary, and to adjudicating upon and punishing serious prison offences. Their policy making, administrative and executive powers were removed, so that direction for the work of the Governor came solely from the Prison Commission and not from any local functionary (McConville 1995: 436).

The reflections of a prisoner incarcerated during the late nineteenth century provide an insight into the approach of Governors at the time:

> I suppose [he] would be called a modern Governor . . . He was a man of the minutest detail and did his best to fulfil to the letter the prison rules and regulations. He was an official first and a man after . . . This self-important and self-satisfied gentleman ruled by fear . . . He seldom or never entered a cell if the prisoner were in it. He had a particular aversion to coming into the immediate presence of a prisoner. To be asked a direct question on any subject whatever was an offence to him. (Cook 1914: 111–113)

Others shared this view, according to the Reverend John Pitkin:

> The first Governors, appointed under this system, were a true type of the system they represented. They had a righteous contempt for the prisoners they kept in custody. They spoke to them with a harsh and unsympathetic voice. They had grown up under rigid rules, and had become rigid themselves. (Pitkin 1918: 18, quoted in Priestley 1999: 272)

The Commission adopted the recruitment and promotion policies that had applied in the Convict Service. Promotion was based on seniority, fitness and good reports, and lobbying resulted in disqualification (McConville 1995: 210). A circular was issued three weeks after the 1877 Act came into force, which made clear that promotions as well as appointments would not be influenced by political considerations:

> Prospects of promotion must depend on the report which their supervisors may make as to their qualifications for, and as to their conduct in the performance of their duties. Merit and not favour will thus be the ground of advancement, and any officer who may attempt to bring private interest to bear, for the purpose of influencing the directors to promote him, will be considered as having disqualified himself for the promotion. (Quoted in Thomas 1972: 39)

The introduction in 1877 of what Thomas calls a paramilitary structure, with uniforms for staff other than Governors and a pyramidal structure with the Governor at the pinnacle, confirmed the Governor as the clear head of the institution (Thomas 1972: 40). The Governor was the Commission's representative in the prison and was expected to exercise appropriate leadership both to prisoners and to staff.

By the mid-1890s the Commission 'had completely succeeded . . . in promoting uniformity, economy and a generally improved administration' (Ruggles-Brise 1921: 137). However, there was a strong reaction from both the public and informed opinion against the over-rigid and disciplinary approach adopted by the Commission. As a result, the Gladstone Committee (Home Office 1895) was set up to consider what changes were required. The 1898 Prisons Act which followed placed the control of local and convict prisons under one Board; gave the power to the Secretary of State to make Rules for the government of convict and local prisons, thereby allowing the Rules to be changed without the necessity for fresh legislation; and established a Board of Independent Visitors for every convict prison.

The daily operation of the prison continued to be controlled by detailed Prison Rules and Standing Orders. In the case of local prisons, by 1911 there were 1,441 Standing Orders and 313 published Rules that regulated all aspects of prison life. The Standing Orders prescribed the precise daily and weekly timetable, the exact objects (from personal clothing to books and cell furniture) allotted to each prisoner and the principles to be followed by the Governor in censoring letters, searching prisoners and the treatment of mentally ill and suicidal prisoners (Hobhouse and Brockway 1922: 64). A distinctive feature of the management of prisons at this time therefore was the continuing level of central prescription.

The day-to-day work of Governors in the early part of the twentieth century was very similar to the work of their predecessors:

> His first duty in the morning is to attend chapel and, from a seat which overlooks the whole building, observe that discipline is duly maintained. He then sits in the orderly room, hears the 'applications', adjudicates upon the 'reports', and conveys the contents of official and other permissible communications to the prisoners concerned. An inspection of the prison follows . . . In most instances the practice is for the governor to pass round the landings of one hall a day, glancing into the cells as he passes, and to walk through the workshop and yards in a similarly remote manner . . . A visit to the prisoners on punishment and in the hospital is never omitted, but even here it is in most cases little more than a matter of form. The morning's duties are concluded by an examination (generally cursory) of the food in the kitchen. The governor will sometimes pay a surprise visit of inspection during the afternoon, and the rules

require him, at least once a week, to go through every part of the prison at an uncertain hour of the night. (Hobhouse and Brockway 1922: 365)

Many Governors though did not find their duties too demanding. Major Blake, a Governor from 1901 to 1925, took the view that:

The work of a prison Governor is just as hard as he cares to make it . . . there is not very much to do. He will be able to make his inspection in something under the hour; there is very little office work, and if he is fortunate enough to have a reliable chief warder . . . he has plenty of time for golf and tennis or whatever his chosen recreation may be. From about 9 a.m. until noon is about all the actual time necessary for him to perform the purely routine duties of his office. A look round in the afternoon, with perhaps another in the evening . . . (Blake 1927: 24)

The importance of recruiting the right people to become Governors was recognised by the Commission as being critical:

The secret of good administration in a penal establishment lies in a very simple principle: if you want to exert an influence on human beings, you must call upon men capable of exerting that influence. It follows that it is necessary to exercise extreme care in the selection of such men, to submit them to a rigorous course of training and to pay them properly. (Patterson 1930, quoted in Ruck 1951: 102)

During this period a careful process of vetting suitable external applicants for the post of Governor was introduced. Social status and previous contacts continued to be important. There was an established custom of choosing a recognised 'type of man' with military or colonial experience, whose previous conduct could be clearly vouched for (Forsythe 1990: 141). Whilst there was no longer a need to canvass magistrates, and certainly no meetings attended by 'public interest' in the proceedings, the element of patronage remained strong in the system. For example, in 1901, Major Blake returned home on sick leave from colonial service in British East Africa. He happened to be having lunch with Captain Price, then Governor of Wormwood Scrubs, when the idea of Blake's applying for a job in prisons was broached. That afternoon Blake went to visit the secretary to the Prison Commission at the Home Office, who happened to be a family friend. Shortly thereafter Blake was appointed to be a trainee Governor (Blake 1927: 10–15).

Personal acquaintance played a similar role in the progress of Basil Thomson to a governing post in the Prison Service:

> Sir Evelyn Ruggles-Brise had been appointed to the chairmanship of the Prison Commission, and it fell to him to make recommendations for a number of new appointments. He knew something of me from old Eton days and he sent up my name. It chanced that the Home Secretary's private secretary, who had stayed with me when I was acting as Prime Minister of Tonga, saw my name among the others and telegraphed to me asking whether I would accept the appointment. (Thomson 1939, quoted in Priestley 1999: 269)

Of the 54 Governors in 1922, 31 had served with the armed forces (Hobhouse and Brockway 1922: 362). The Gladstone Committee however made clear that 'military and naval training undoubtedly develops capacities for organisation and maintenance of discipline, but we do not consider it to be by any means essential to the qualifications of a prison governor' (Home Office 1895: 36). Commentators took a rather negative view of Governors and concluded that:

> Governors are men of limited knowledge, disciplinarians, lacking in imagination, sceptical about new proposals, but conscientious and just. Typical prisoners' view of governors is that they are 'distant gods' who deal out punishments and privileges, stride majestically past the cell door on tours . . . and sit in lofty aloofness in the chapel. (Hobhouse and Brockway 1922: 364)

Half of the Governors at that time had been promoted from within the Department. The ability to undertake clerical tasks was taken into account when it came to appointments and promotions within the Prison Department. The need for clerical ability explains why most promoted Governors were drawn from 'clerk and schoolmaster' class of warders. Indeed, a number of civil service clerks connected with the prison system were also made Governors. These appointments aroused considerable criticism amongst warders, who complained that they had no knowledge of discipline duties. Similar criticisms were made 75 years later when a number of administrators were appointed to the Office of Governor.

One significant development during this period was the appointment of the first female Governor in 1921 (Forsythe 1990: 144).

In a variety of ways, during the interwar period, Britain became the centre of the prison reform movement, one consequence of which was a limited relaxation in the tight management exercised by the Commission. While Rules continued to proliferate, Governors were allowed some freedom in managing the detailed operation of their prisons. This was particularly true of the newly created Borstals where Governors were given discretion to create the regime which best suited the needs of the prisoner population:

Governors will have a free hand in experimental work, and will at their respective institutions work out the system as best they can, with the co-operation of an efficient staff. Details as to hours of duty etc. are matters which can generally be arranged by discussions between the Governor and his staff. (Memorandum to Governors, Male Borstal Institutions, quoted in Ruggles-Brise 1921: 244)

The general attitude of the Governor began to have a distinct influence on life in prison: 'if he be at all sympathetic in his manner towards prisoners, the subordinate officers will be likely to adopt a similar bearing. Many small alleviations of prison life, such as lectures, concerts, and the use of pencil and paper, lie within the power of the governor to permit, discourage, or prohibit' (Hobhouse and Brockway 1926: 366). Indeed, another commentator went so far as to suggest that: 'the personality of the Governor was a deciding factor in the nature of the regime, for the Prison Commissioners were often far away in London and the Inspectors' visits, although regular, were not frequent . . . what actually happened depended upon the personality of officials as much as state policy' (Forsythe 1990: 141 and 213).

The Commission also led a drive to recruit potential Governors from a variety of backgrounds and were clear about the sort of person that was needed:

Men of personality and character can be drawn equally well from among ex-army officers, doctors, lawyers and schoolmasters. The necessary qualifications are an aptitude for leadership, a desire for service, a private life above suspicion, and sufficient intelligence to understand the guiding principles and grasp the details of a penal system. To these should be added a requisite qualification for any special career, good health and a constitution above the average. (Ruck 1951: 21)

A more rigorous and comprehensive selection system was introduced, which involved a written examination to ensure that the candidates had attained a certain level of education and knowledge; a medical examination; an inquiry into the previous activities of candidates and the result of their undertakings; and a confidential report from their referees. This was followed by their appearance before a selection committee (Ruck 1951: 102–106).

All candidates selected to be Governors were sent on a training course. The course consisted of the trainee Governors performing the duties of each grade: assistant warder; warder; principal; chief clerk and store-keeper. The Commission took the view that during their training new Governors 'Ought to familiarise themselves with the history of prisons, the rules which govern them, and the principles which have dictated the choice of those rules. So far as this exceedingly subtle art can be learnt, they must learn to be leaders, and they must know how to address a prisoner firmly yet good-humouredly and without provocation' (Ruck 1951: 106). On completion of this training and more general instruction, trainee Governors were posted as deputy Governors for a number of years before being offered a Governor's post (Blake 1927: 15–16).

The decision to recruit 'direct entrant' trainee Governors, in addition to promotion through the ranks and appointment directly to a Governor-ship, was to have a long-term impact on the prison system. As Thomas points out, 'These were people who had no previous experience of prisons, but who were considered to be of a *cadre*, which would spearhead the increasing volume of changes . . . the presence of such staff has given the English governor tradition an especial, often liberal, intellectual flavour . . .' (Thomas 1972: 224).

The influence of the more liberal reforming Governors of the interwar years did much to relax the regime and encourage a more positive atmosphere in prisons. Many Governors saw their role as ameliorating prison conditions with some limited attempts at reforming the individual. Major Munn, Governor of Lewes Prison in 1932, typified this approach. He sought to engage his prisoners by 'cheering the men at football, leading them at cricket, playing shove ha'penny with them, taking part in their concerts and treating them as if they were in my company in the army' (quoted in Forsythe 1990: 211). Governors also maintained an interest in their prisoners after their release. There are many examples of Governors setting up homes for boys; employing ex-prisoners in their homes as cooks and housemaids; and visiting prisoners after release 'in order to encourage them' (Forsythe 1990: 100).

Reforming Governors (1946–1962)

By 1946 the Prison Commission had expanded and a system of six directorates (Prison Administration, Industries, Works, Medical Services, Education and Welfare) had been set up in London to oversee the work of prisons. However, postwar Commissioners continued to view the Governor as the most important figure in any establishment: 'The Governor is the keystone of the arch. Within his own prison, he is in much the same position as the captain of a ship – supreme in an isolated community, responsible for the efficiency and welfare of his crew as well as for the safe arrival of his passengers at their journey's end' (Fox 1952: 87).

Governors were able to exercise considerable power over the individual member of staff and prisoner. As one commentator put it: 'however benevolent he may be, he is in fact a dictator, being at once chief administrator and judge, capable of punishing and rewarding those in his charge' (Klare 1960: 85).

The work that the postwar Governor was expected to undertake increased in scope, as the Commission turned its attention to making prisons more effective at rehabilitating prisoners. Governors had to adjust their sights to the newly restated objective of rehabilitation and to manage more complex regimes (Conrad 1960: 245). The introduction of humanitarian and treatment goals into the prison changed the way the prison had to be managed. New personnel in the form of psychologists, psychiatrists, caseworkers and welfare officers were given primary responsibility for implementing the humanitarian and treatment goals. Governors found themselves having to manage the conflict between the new professionally trained staff and the established custodial staff, as rehabilitation efforts were often seen as compromising security and safety (McCleery 1961).

The simple single-line organisation was changed to a more bureaucratic one in which there was a multiplicity of hierarchies with specialised but overlapping functions. The Governor had to manage and integrate a range of departments (including maintenance, clerical, farms and gardens, welfare, education, physical education and healthcare) which had 'grown like Topsy and have in a truly Parkinsonian fashion accumulated power, and created their own often secret and very private lines of communication which completely side step the Governor' (Lee 1966: 13).

Governors found themselves in charge of the custodial, treatment and service subsystems and were faced with the task of directing and co-ordinating their activities. To do this without violating formal or informal expectations of the various specialists demanded considerable skill (Garrity 1964: 166–167). Some commentators have claimed that these new positions challenged the authority of the Governor, as they claimed a measure of autonomy and power of their own right by virtue of their 'professional' status (Garrity 1964: 170–171).

In contrast to earlier periods, where the Commission had created an impenetrable barrier between prisons and the community, Governors were also increasingly expected to develop an external focus, as prisons became much more part of the community. A former Commissioner noted this change in emphasis: 'The Governor is responsible for . . . 'selling' his job in private to the more important visitors to the prison and in public at a variety of local meetings and functions' (Fox 1952: 88–89).

It was not until the Wynn Parry Report (Home Office 1958) that the new role and duties of the Governor were described in an official document. The Report succinctly captured the essence of what was required of a Governor in relation to managing both the internal and external environments:

> The Governor is responsible to the Commissioners for everything that goes on in his establishment: the principal aspects of his work are the maintenance of security, good order and discipline; the leadership of those sections of his staff more closely concerned with the training of the inmates, and the direction of their efforts to this end; the co-ordination of the various departments within the establishment; the development of useful activity in work, education and recreation; co-operation with outside bodies such as the education authority and with voluntary agencies and workers; and responsibility, as Sub-Accounting Officer, for the proper use of public money and property. (Home Office 1958: 44)

The role of the Governor by the early 1960s had therefore evolved into a more managerial one. The new role was described in an article titled 'Managing to Govern', which reflected the changed emphasis in the role: 'The Governor is at one and the same time, director of punishment and treatment, prison manager, staff manager, trade union negotiator, personnel officer, publicity officer and father of his flock . . . The essential function of the Governor is that of general manager of, and co-ordinator within, the establishment' (Lee 1966: 11).

The day-to-day work of the Governor remained, however, very bureaucratic, and some expressed concern that Governors would 'soon drown in a sea of petitions, reports, instructions, minutes, requests for information, returns, amendments to standing orders, and so forth' (Klare 1960: 86) – a theme that was to recur in reports on the Prison Service over the next 40 years.

The daily routine for a Governor in the late 1950s and early 1960s has been described in a number of works (Morris and Morris 1963; Kelly 1967). The descriptions draw a picture of a hectic round of activity from the time the Governor arrives at the prison to the time he or she departs. A routine morning's activity for the Governor of Pentonville in the early 1960s involved:

> The Governor normally arrives in his office about 9 a.m. . . . He meets the Deputy, the Chaplain, the Steward and the Governor's Clerk and discusses the content of his mail, instructions from 'Head Office', particular issues relating to the prison, and so forth . . . As soon as the discussion is over the Governor and the Chief Officer go off together to the latter's room where 'call ups' take place. The 'call up' is essentially a means whereby information of a specific nature is conveyed to an individual prisoner . . . From 'call ups' the

Governor and the Chief hurry down ... to inspect the men on punishment ... This contact is seldom more than a few seconds in duration, and precedes the main business on C Wing, the hearing of Reports ... As soon as Reports are concluded, the gubernatorial cavalcade is away again, this time round the prison. First through the kitchens, with a rapid tasting of the carefully arranged specimen dinner, then on with a flourish of salutes and counter-salutes through the 'Mailbags and Tailors' to the Hospital ... It frequently happens that the number of Reports makes it impossible for the Governor to cover the whole prison on his round, and as observed during the research period the Governor returned to his office at 11 a.m. in order to have a well-deserved cup of tea. At 11.15 a.m. he would be off again to the Chief's Office where a queue of men, sometimes forty to fifty strong, would be waiting outside the door to make applications. (Morris and Morris 1963: 108–112)

Kelly, in her autobiography of life as a Governor, recounted that the 'Governor's day begins at a quarter past eight at the gatehouse' and ended after she had made 'herself available in her office each evening, so that anyone who wants to see her unofficially can do so' (Kelly 1967: 171). In addition to the routine morning work for the Governor identified in the Pentonville study, Kelly described work in the afternoon:

There are letters to dictate and reports to write, on the suitability of prisoners for various forms of treatment and on records to be of use in the event of future re-conviction ... Often there are parties of magistrates, probation officers, police-women or others, who have obtained Head Office permission to be shown the prison. Usually they are taken round by an officer, but they see the governor or deputy governor during each visit. Reception boards are held each day and new admissions interviewed. Women who are going to court the following day must also be seen ... In the evening the governor will try to visit the evening classes, to see that all is well and that the teachers have all they need. A governor is supposed to make one night visit every fortnight, going round the outside and inside of the prison, to see that all is quiet and that the night patrols are on duty. (Kelly 1967: 171–173)

The Governor's routine in a large local prison was very similar to the routine followed by Governors 50 years earlier. However, in many Borstals and training prisons, assistant Governors were employed to take on the duties of hearing 'call ups' and 'applications'. This relieved the pressure on the Governor, who could then make more focused visits to different parts of the prison and use them as a useful opportunity to keep in touch with what was going on.

Traditionally, access to the Governor constituted an important formal safeguard against victimisation by prison officers and was also one of the prisoner's few legal rights. With improved conditions and more routine inspection, the requirement on the Governor to 'tour' the prison each day and to hear personally prisoners' applications was seen by some as being anachronistic. The ability of the Governor to delegate some of these 'routine' tasks was to be the subject of some debate over the following decades.

Many Governors at the time found the job to be satisfying but one which imposed 'considerable strain, demands all one's energy and resources, requires one to learn much that is painful, and calls for considerable modification of one's character' (Kelly 1967: 173). Other Governors went further in describing the pressure that the job of being a Governor brought with it: 'It is difficult to put on to paper just what tension a prison governor experiences . . . and it is not surprising that so many of us have at one time or another almost cracked under the strain. Because, do not forget, anyone with the responsibility of a prison governor is living an unnaturally tensed life' (Fancourt-Clayton 1958: 125–126).

The development of the Governor's role and duties led to changes in the recruitment criteria. A former Commissioner reflecting on what was expected of a Governor concluded that: 'The time is long past when the post of prison Governor was a suitable niche for the retired officer with the reputation of "a good disciplinarian". The command of a large prison today calls not only for a vocation for such work but for special personal qualities and adequate educational and administrative qualifications' (Fox 1952: 87).

In the postwar period appointments were no longer made to Governorships directly: all Governors were appointed from the rank of deputy Governor. It was expected that Governors would learn the elements of the work in the junior Governor grades before succeeding to the command of a prison. The Commissioners followed the principle that vacancies in the ranks of assistant Governors should be filled by promotion from within the Service, to the extent that suitably qualified candidates were forthcoming. However, the four Staff Courses held between 1945 and 1950 had only selected 14 men and two women from the officer ranks (Fox 1952: 89). The majority of vacancies for assistant Governors were filled by direct entry candidates, despite opposition from the POA (Home Office 1958: paras 11–13). A Commissioner commented that what was needed was:

> An adequate educational background, some vocation for the work, a knowledge of the lives and background of those sections of the

community from which delinquents mainly derive, a promise of some administrative capacity – all these will help, if the candidate is the right sort of person in himself, a person of sincerity, integrity, humanity and goodwill, with at any rate one foot firmly on the ground. (Fox 1952: 89)

Chapter 3

Modern Governors – from administrators to executives

Prison Department Governors (1963–1978)

The Criminal Justice Act 1961 provided the legislative foundation for the abolition of the Prison Commission in England and Wales. The order giving effect to the dissolution of the Commission was laid in February 1963 and a department, located within the Home Office, was set up to formulate policy and manage the Prison Service. The creation of the Home Office Prison Department marked a shift in the approach to prisons. Governors, and their prisons, became part of the bureaucratic machinery of the Home Office and were subject to the civil service administrative approach and style.

There was a feeling amongst Governors that something had been lost with the abolition of the Commission. Many looked on the days of the Commission with nostalgia:

> The Commission was made up of independent members of the old school who understood what prison was all about and stood no nonsense from anyone . . . It was deeply sensitive to the feelings and requirements of those in its care . . . many more experiments were carried out under the Commission because of its direct responsibility and the courage and faith of its members. Independence has great merit. Once the Service became an integral part of the Home Office there was always a feeling that everyone was looking over his shoulder, anxious about big brother in the background. (Miller 1976: 185)

The decade that followed the abolition of the Commission was a troubled one for the Prison Department and its Governors. A series of prison escapes in 1964 and 1965, culminating in the escape of the spy George Blake in October 1966 led to the Home Secretary setting up the Mountbatten Inquiry (Mountbatten 1966). Mountbatten had much to say about Governors and their work. The Report criticised what he detected as a degree of isolation of Governors from headquarters, the remedy for which he saw in the introduction of a regional structure and a more involved and supportive inspectorial function. The Prison Service also needed, according to Mountbatten, a professional head that would be a recognisable figure, both within the service and outside it. The majority of recommendations that Mountbatten made on security were implemented and a four-fold categorisation system introduced. Mountbatten ushered in an era in which Governors and the Prison Service became increasingly preoccupied with security to the detriment of rehabilitation. This was a theme that was repeated 30 years later following the publication of the Learmont Report into the escape from Parkhurst prison (Learmont 1995a).

In response to some of the criticisms made by Mounbatten, the Government decided to carry out a wide-ranging Management Review of the organisation, functions, management and administrative practices of the Prison Department. There was general agreement at the time that too much detailed work was centralised at Headquarters; clear lines of authority and responsibility needed clarifying at Headquarters, and between Headquarters, regions and the field; inadequate provision for planning and resources management took place; an assessment was needed on the effect and value of changes in the treatment of offenders in custody (Home Office 1969: para. 230).

The Government published a White Paper, *People in Prison*, in 1969, in response to the Review. The publication of the White Paper reflected growing public concern about the state of the prisons and an attempt by the Government to demonstrate that it had 'embarked on ... a complete overhaul of the structure of the Prison Department' (Home Office 1969: para. 2). The Government announced in the White Paper that it had decided to make a number of changes in the management of the Prison Department (Home Office 1969: para. 231). A full-time Director General of the Prison Service was appointed. The day-to-day work of the Department and the Service became the joint responsibility of a Controller (Administration) and a Controller (Operations). The appointment of a Controller of Planning and Development gave one person responsibility for the direction and co-ordination of all medium- and long-term planning for the Service. The Inspector General, freed of executive responsibilities, became head of a new team to carry out a co-ordinated inspection of all aspects of the work of institutions. A new and smaller Prisons Board, chaired by the Director General, was set up which shared collectively in the formulation of major policy developments and decisions.

Serious operational problems continued to preoccupy the Prison Service into the 1970s. A series of major riots and demonstrations occurred in several of the dispersal prisons and there was widespread industrial action by prison officers. From 1974 the annual reports of the work of the Prison Department noted with growing alarm the continued increase in the size of the prison population and the consequential problems of overcrowding. The *Report of the Work of the Prison Department* for 1977 made it clear that there were 'severe practical problems' facing the service (Home Office 1977b: para. 1). These problems included poor conditions in prisons, allegations of serious malpractice against staff, prison disturbances and an increasingly militant campaign of disruption in prisons by the Prison Officers Association (POA) that included a ban on overtime and restrictions on visits, recreation and escorts. Governors warned of the immediate and total breakdown of the prison system and complained loudly of the 'deplorable lack of leadership' from the Home Office (*Times*, 30 October 1978, quoted in Fitzgerald and Sim 1982: 2). The actions of some prison officers led Governors to caution that there could be 'a serious loss of control which has to be quelled by armed intervention with the probability of both staff and prisoners being killed' (*Times*, 1 November 1978, quoted in Fitzgerald and Sim 1982: 3).

Despite the structural changes and additional pressures placed on Governors, the daily routine of a Governor after the abolition of the Commission remained very similar to that of earlier Governors. A former Governor, Alistair Miller, described his typical day as consisting of: arriving at the prison by 8.45 a.m.; holding a morning meeting with senior staff to discuss operational issues; distributing the incoming mail which required action; touring the prison accompanied by the Chief Officer; undertaking adjudications and applications prior to tasting the food in the kitchen. Some afternoons Miller spent doing office work, writing letters and making reports or wandering around the prison by himself for random inspections. Other afternoons were spent chatting with prisoners or attending formal meetings with the POA, Board of Visitors (BOV) or Prison Visitors. During the evenings Miller would visit the recreation rooms or education classes to chat to the staff and prisoners (Miller 1976: 1–7).

The hands-on approach to management in the 1960s was heavily reliant on the character and personality of the Governor. The manner in which Miller dealt with a wing protest at Parkhurst, in 1966, was typical of the way such incidents were managed and contrasts sharply with how Governors are expected to act today:

> I saw this mob of, say, 200 men in front of me just waiting to see what I'd make of it . . . Little did they know how I felt, but with my

little bunch of keys (I never carried prison keys) I walked through the lot of them to the end of the wing and back again, throwing my keys up and down and catching them many times. All eyes were upon me all the time and there was a deadly hush . . . I said to them 'Do you think that just because a mob like you refuse to do what the Chief Officer orders that I am going to reverse the order – you need your heads seeing to', or some such words. I added that I would look into the complaint but that was all that I would do . . . all went back to their cells. (Miller 1976: 102)

The monitoring of a Governor's performance underwent some important developments (Home Office 1969: para. 231). An Inspectorate was introduced in 1969 to visit prisons and report on the reality of prison life for prisoners. In the following year a four-regional structure was introduced for the management of prisons. The creation of regions, each under the control of a Regional Director who was a former Governor, led to a direct operational relationship between the Governor and Regional Director. The notion of an 'intermediate manager' between Governors and headquarters had first been suggested in the Gladstone Report some 75 years earlier (Home Office 1895: para. 155).

Each region had a deputy regional director responsible for young offenders and one or two other deputy regional directors responsible for adult prisoners. Regional offices also contained an industrial manager and supervisors of works, and the various other specialist functions – chaplaincy, medical, psychological, educational, vocational training and physical education. They were responsible to the Regional Director for the general management and operational aspects of their specialities in prisons in the region, while remaining accountable to their professional heads at headquarters. The development of regional offices, with their specialist advisors looking at all aspects of the prisons in the region, created much tighter supervision and monitoring than Governors had ever experienced before.

There was a concern in the Prison Department that prisons had sometimes changed too radically with a change of Governor. In order to reduce the ability of Governors to make fundamental changes, a definition of the role of each institution within its region, and within the system as a whole, was drawn up. Whilst it was accepted that personal initiative was still needed, efforts were made to prevent Governors from starting developments where Regional Directors believed that there was no reasonable prospect of the resources becoming available to complete them or where the continuation of experiments depended on the enthusiasm of one or two individuals (Home Office 1969: para. 234).

The work and approach of Governors began to change in the late 1960s. Changes in society and the expectations of prisoners and staff meant that Governors began to operate in a different way. As one former Governor pointed out:

> Looking back in time, I recognise now that much, perhaps too much, was invested in the person and personality of individual governors; governors who could, and at times did, exercise a despotism, not always benevolent, over both inmates and staff. Thus Prison Standing Orders setting out the statutory duties of governors clearly underlined the personal responsibility and ubiquity of governors in carrying out their command function. (Gadd 1988: 8)

Governors began to take on a more co-ordinating role. This was reflected in a Prison Department submission to the Council of Europe. The paper suggested that 'in the past the governor was regarded more as the authoritarian head of the establishment who directed his staff in the efficient running of a machine which was not complicated . . . for many years now governors have been looked upon as managers and leaders of a complex team' (Council of Europe 1969: 121). The document noted that in a traditional prison system the Governor made decisions often without consultation with those who have to implement the decisions, and the communication system is primarily seen as a vertical one, passing instructions down. Governors moved from being 'the main decision-maker based on his background of technical information and expertise' to becoming 'head of an independent staff team with five main management responsibilities: setting goals and roles; free communications; interpretation; boundary function; planning and research' (Tyndall 1969: 136–7).

The 1969 White Paper, *People in Prison*, emphasised this more inclusive approach that Governors were required to adopt:

> The Governor of a prison is responsible for the maintenance of security, good order and discipline, for the effective co-ordination of the work of all the members of his staff, for the regime of the establishment and the treatment and training of offenders, and for the proper use of public money and property. This is a formidable assignment. It requires qualities of leadership and management, allied to a continuing concern for individuals. (Home Office 1969: para. 235)

Some Governors had gone so far as to designate senior staff as part of a management group, with scope for formal and informal means of consultation between the Governor and staff of all ranks (Home Office 1969: para. 235).

A Working Party on the recruitment of Governors gave further consideration to the changing role of the Governor and concluded that 'the exercise of authority in a simple hierarchical setting, if this was ever an adequate description of a prison governor's task, it is so no longer' (Home Office 1972: para. 14). The Working Party went on to describe the work of a 'modern' Governor:

> Essentially a governor is concerned with achieving defined objectives through the resources made available to him and in managing the details of his prison's executive affairs; he needs to be competent in analysing problems, making sensible decisions and ensuring the adequacy of the prison's communications. He has a major responsibility for the organisation and direction of his prison and in this is concerned with the management of change, the resolution of conflicts and the mobilisation and co-ordination of resources. (Home Office 1972: para. 14)

The working party's reformulation of the work of the Governor is significant in that it makes clear for the first time in an official report that the Governor was required to have the ability, and desire, to exercise generic management skills in order to deal with the growing volume and complexity of available resources (people, materials and equipment).

The Prison Management Review, which took place between 1972 and 1973, reinforced the view that the Governor's role was changing (Home Office 1974). The Review team initially gave some consideration as to whether a prison actually needed a Governor, rather than 'a lay management committee appointed by the Secretary of State to make the general management decisions on the lines now developing in many other institutional fields'. This notion appeared to suggest a return to the management system used for the Bridewell in 1556 (see Chapter 2). It concluded, however, that there was still a need for 'a permanent official to carry out the function of general manager of a penal establishment' (Home Office 1974: para. 242).

The Review contrasted the tasks of previous generations of Governors with what was required in the 1970s:

> Virtually all work was codified in detail. Governors were themselves little more than high-grade operatives and supervisors of codified work . . . the range and sophistication of modern penal operations is such that the assumption is no longer tenable. The reality is that the function of the governor has evolved from a simple command role towards that of a general manager of this complex of operations. (Home Office 1974: para. 26)

The work of the 'general manager', according to the Review, was not to act as the day-to-day decision maker on normal operations but as 'a general administrator'. The job required 'hard systematic work' and the 'acquisition and judicious use of a great deal of practical data, knowledge and technique' (Home Office 1974: para. 243). The proposals contained in the Review entailed a radical change to penal governance. One Governor, at that time, suggested however that the core job remained the same:

> It does not matter what it is called: it is simply man-management and understanding which no nomenclature will alter ... That a Governor becomes a manager ... makes no difference to the basic work he has to do. Compassion, humanity and understanding always have to be there ... Rule of thumb, intuition and emotions have always had and always will have an enormous role to play. (Miller 1976: 187–188)

The Prison Department issued a Circular Instruction in 1973 to define certain operational requirements which it believed were inherent in a Governor's job and which had, until then, been the subject of custom and convention rather than explicit prescription (Prison Department 1973a). The Circular Instruction was issued shortly after publication of a Notice to Staff which introduced a five-day working week for Governors and was intended to clarify the apportionment of duties between the Governor and the second in charge (Prison Department 1973b). The responsibilities of the Governor were described as:

> He is in direct control when he is in or around the establishment, either because it is his duty day or because he has returned to the establishment outside duty hours for a particular purpose; He carries an overall 'in charge' responsibility, which remains with him even though he is not in direct control, e.g. when he goes off duty; or on off-duty days; or during an absence for an official reason or otherwise. He must at all times be ready to resume direct control if necessary. (Prison Department 1973a: para. 4)

The only occasion when Governors were considered not to be in charge was if they were on annual leave, sick absence, or it was not practical for them to return to the institution. Such absences required permission from the Regional Director and a formal handover to the second in charge (Prison Department 1973a: paras 3–5).

Miller highlighted the requirement that the Governor was constantly on call to respond to emergencies: 'For my first three years at Parkhurst I had to keep a live walkie-talkie by my bed every night in case there was any trouble in the special wing. I had to keep constantly alert in order to hear anything that was said, as in those days anything that came over it had to be interpreted as requiring action, however harmless the conversation' (Miller 1976: 117).

The level of autonomy that Governors had was severely curtailed in the 1970s and particularly in relation to staffing levels and the deployment of uniform staff. The amount of overtime paid to prison officers had for some time been causing concern to Prison Service Headquarters. Governors were able to use as many prison officer hours as they wished to perform routine tasks or some innovations to the regime that they wished to pursue. The cost of the overtime was met centrally and did not impact locally. The Prisons Board decided in 1970 that headquarters, together with the newly created Regional Directors, should play an active role in controlling spending on uniform staff. Circular Instruction 80/1970 made clear that Regional Directors would 'help' Governors to 'assess the priorities being attached to particular tasks; assess fluctuating demands on resources and quantify total staffing needs for agreed commitments' (Prison Department 1970: para. 2). The biggest impact of the Circular was that Governors were instructed that 'no work which resulted in additional posts or additional demands on officers' time might be introduced without authority of P6 Division' (ibid.: para. 9).

The issuing of this circular marked a clear shift in power from the Governor to Headquarters and Regional Directors. Following the circular, it became a Headquarters Division (known as P6 Division), and not the Governor, who controlled what type of work was done in prisons, and by whom. The circular also marked the first time that 'expert outside advice' was used to assess the strengths of a Governor's proposed plans. It was the central 'manpower management' team, set up by P6 Division in 1972, together with regionally based manpower teams, created in 1974, who rapidly established themselves as the experts on the staffing at each establishment, rather than the Governor of that establishment.

The demise of the Governor's autonomy on staffing matters was reinforced in the mid-1970s. The introduction of cash limits by the Government in April 1976 led to the Prison Department issuing Circular Instruction 24/1976. The Circular introduced a 'freeze' on task lists for uniformed staff and gave each Governor a weekly 'budget of hours' which they could use to ensure the establishment operated. Where the 'budget of hours' did not meet existing demands Governors were required to 'take such measures ... to bring, as closely as possible, the total use of staff within the budget of hours' (Home Office 1976: para. 4). Governors were also required to return to regional offices, on a weekly basis, a 'staffing resources and use' form that had been personally 'scrutinised by the governor' (ibid.: para. 7). Authorised staffing levels were set at the same time by Regional Directors for prison officer grades, which created 'manpower ceilings' for each establishment. Governors had lost control of one of the main levers in a prison, the deployment of uniform staff.

The level of autonomy in other areas also came under scrutiny. A Review of the management of individual establishments reached a narrow view of what Governors should be doing: 'The task of management at local level is to carry out HQ policies with the most economic and effective expenditure of resources and that local management is not free to add to or to reduce its designated activities according to its own assessment of penal priorities' (Home Office 1974: para. 4). This marked a low ebb in the ability of Governors to shape their institutions. According to the view expressed by the Review team, Governors were no more than functionaries expected to implement policy exactly as it was promulgated by the Prison Department. Discretion and judgement were not required, just the ability as a manager to implement set out policy. This approach was to be reiterated and strengthened some 20 years later as managerialism took hold in the Prison Service.

The 1970s also witnessed worsening relationships between prison officers and Governors and industrial unrest severely strained already difficult working relationships. A considerable amount of the Governor's time was spent in dealing with industrial relations issues. Governors, in their evidence to the House of Commons Expenditure Committee, argued that prison staff 'probably presents more difficulties for them than prisoners' (*Times*, 7 December 1978, quoted in Fitzgerald and Sim 1982: 14).

Some commentators took the view that 'it has become increasingly clear that prison officers and governor grades compete for control of individual penal institutions' (Fitzgerald and Sim 1982: 14). Examples of the level of conflict were well reported in the media. In 1972, at Dartmoor prison, uniformed staff threatened to walk out if the Governor did not reverse Home Office policy and punish prisoners taking part in peaceful demonstrations. In 1975, prison officers at Winchester unanimously passed a vote of no confidence in the Governor, and demanded that he should be replaced. They complained he was 'too soft' with prisoners, and that discipline had declined (*Times*, 31 March 1975, quoted in Fitzgerald and Sim 1982: 14). Evidence for the Governor being 'too soft' was his insistence on an independent inquiry into an alleged assault on a prisoner by three officers (*Guardian*, 2 April 1975, quoted in Fitzgerald and Sim 1982: 14).

The changing expectations of a Governor were reflected in the recruitment advertisements for assistant governors. In 1967 advertisements suggested that Governors' 'duties demand a lively interest in social problems, and a good understanding of modern methods of handling them'. This was replaced in 1969 by: 'Are you interested in social work? Could you also, with the right training, do a good managerial job?' By 1972 advertisements were describing the role as: 'Management with a social purpose ... you are primarily a manager' (Waddington 1983: 16). The recruitment criteria specified that 'a steadfast character, the ability to take decisions, often in conditions of stress, a humane and understanding outlook and an instinct for leadership must all be sought for in those aspiring to be governor grades' (Home Office 1972: para. 13).

A number of prison officers, and occasionally other members of the Prison Service, entered the governor grades, but, in the main, successful candidates continued to come from outside the Service, some direct from universities, others after experience in a wide variety of occupations. Between 1964 and 1976, 64 per cent of the 375 new assistant governors came from outside the Service (Home Office 1969: para. 207 and Home Office 1977: para. 222). A Working Party of departmental and staff representatives was set up in 1967 to examine the issue of recruitment. The Working Party concluded that recruitment from outside the Prison Service would be 'necessary for sometime to come', and 'that those selected for appointment as governors would have to be required to serve for an initial period in the ranks' (Home Office 1972: para. 120). As a result all successful candidates under the age of 24 years old were required to serve as a prison officer for up to one year.

The frequency with which Governors were transferred from prison to prison varied, but the average was about every three or four years. Transfers took place on promotion or within the same grade. The consent of Governors was not a prerequisite to transfer, but they were given an opportunity to make representations against transfer, as a former Governor recorded:

I was summoned to the Home Office, not for the first time, for an interview. The Permanent Secretary very pleasantly informed me that any rumours I may have heard, and I had, about promotion were purely fictitious and he apologised if I had ever been given that impression. But as I would expect, it was time for a move from Parkhurst since I had more than my stint in difficult places. After they offered me another prison which I declined, we eventually decided on Pentonville. (Miller 1976: 161–162)

Prison managers (1979–1986)

The May Committee was set up in 1978, at a time when there was general dissatisfaction with the way the Prison Service was organised and run, with the state of prison buildings, and with the conditions in which staff and inmates alike were required to live and work (May 1979: para. 1.1). May was particularly concerned that prisons should 'not be allowed to degenerate into uncaring institutions dulled by their own unimaginative and unenterprising routines' (para. 4.46).

The May Committee were clear in their view that 'Governing Governors must govern, which means being directly responsible for all that occurs within their establishments' (para. 5.82). In order to achieve this, the Committee had no doubt that 'the role of the Governors, and the way in which Governors themselves perceive that role, must change radically' (para. 7.23). The Report spelt out the new duties and responsibilities that it believed Governors should assume. Changes in Headquarters' organisation, the development of the role of Regional Offices, and the introduction of an independent Inspectorate followed the Report's publication.

Following the May Report's criticism of the divide between establishments and Headquarters, the Home Office asked the Office of Population Censuses and Statistics to identify the content and distribution of this dissatisfaction. A survey of the attitudes held by all kinds of Prison Service staff was carried out in 1982 (Marsh *et al.* 1985). As part of the survey 107 Governors were interviewed and asked about their work and problems. When asked what they thought were the major problems in the establishments they managed, Governors identified the key issues as staff shortages; building/accommodation; industrial relations; Headquarters; attitude of staff and overcrowding.

Overcrowding in particular was a major concern because of its impact on prison conditions. John McCarthy, Governor of Wormwood Scrubs, who wrote to the *Times* to protest about the level of prison overcrowding, expressed the view of many Governors at the time:

> From my personal point of view I did not join the Prison Service to manage overcrowded cattle pens, nor did I join to run a prison where the interests of the individuals have to be sacrificed continually to the interests of the institution, nor did I join to be a member of a service where staff that I admire are forced to run a society that debases ... As it is evident that the present uncivilised conditions in prison seem likely to continue and as I find this incompatible with any moral ethic, I wish to give notice that I, as the governor of the major prison in the United Kingdom, cannot for much longer tolerate, either as a professional or as an individual, the inhumanity of the system within which I work. (Letter to the Editor, *Times*, 19 November 1981)

In response to the 1982 survey, Governors expressed varying views of their job. When they were asked whether their 'personal' task was mainly managing staff, mainly managing inmates or about equal, 60 per cent said that it was mainly one of managing staff and 37 per cent said that the two aspects are equal. Almost two thirds of the Governors thought that there should be several different systems of management depending on the kind of establishment. Nineteen per cent were in favour of one standard system for all establishments and 16 per cent thought individual Governors should decide on their own system of management. On the question of the amount of freedom that Governors are allowed, 67 per cent said that they had about the right amount of freedom, whilst 29 per cent felt that they were not allowed enough freedom to decide how things should be done. These views from Governors in the early 1980s suggest a divergence of opinion on fundamental aspects of their job and clearly reflected a lack of clarity which existed about the changing nature of the work that the Governor was expected to undertake.

The 1980s saw further changes to the management of the Prison Service as a result of external pressures and, in particular, the Government's Financial Management Initiative (FMI). FMI provided a managerial, as well as a financial, framework for the Prison Service to plan, control inputs, allocate resources, and check effectiveness (Evans 1987, 1990). In the Prison Department, the manifestation of FMI can be seen most clearly in Circular Instruction 55/1984 (HM Prison Service 1984). The document set out a general framework in which the operation of individual establishments could be set, and created the machinery by which Governors would be held to account for the operations of their establishments. Its main principles were that: the key manager was the Governor (who was charged with the delivery of Departmental policy); and that the Governor's accountability should be defined by explicit terms of reference agreed with their line manager in a 'contract' and accounted formally in an annual report (Train 1985: 177–186).

Devolution to Governors of budgets and financial management of their establishments followed. Real budget allocations in cash terms were introduced in all establishments in 1986. This financial devolution increased Governors' flexibility and their ability to redeploy resources where they were needed most. However, it also brought a requirement to take a detailed look at how money was spent, expose uneconomic practices, make unpopular resource decisions and cut back in areas of activity that were desirable but not affordable (HM Prison Service 1986). A new costing system provided in-year monitoring of the spending of budgets, and Governors found themselves, for the first time, having to account for variance in expenditure against planned levels.

Concern was expressed by some that budget management would add to the administrative burden facing Governors: 'Traditionally, we have rightly been sensitive about a Governor being thought of, or becoming, aloof, isolated, office-bound – and yet the struggle to break free of the office, meetings, and telephones, has become increasingly fierce, and the budget, with all its ramifications, adds significantly to this' (Curtis 1987: 24).

Other management developments followed in the 1980s. The first of the new initiatives was the 'accountable regimes' project, which was set up in 1982 with the task of developing objectives at prison level and auditing available resources (Chaplin 1982). In reality this meant a redefinition of the aims and objectives at the establishment, an assessment of the resources available and the way in which they are deployed. The project aimed to improve management accountability, co-ordinate activities for prisoners, and apply resources more appropriately (Evans and Marsden 1985: 4–6). The project was particularly important, as it was the first time that process management techniques were used in prisons. Systematic management principles were explored in projects at Featherstone, Shepton Mallet and Leicester prisons. The Governors concerned were required to question what they did and how their prisons operated from a performance point of view.

The projects resulted in clear and accurate information about resources, objectives and actual performance being provided to the Regional Director (Chaplin 1986: 9). This enabled them to more closely monitor and manage the work of Governors. Whilst the projects were never extended to the rest of the Prison Service, the lessons learnt were incorporated in the management accountability structures which were subsequently introduced.

The May Committee recommended that 'in-depth' inspections of establishments should be carried out by the Regional Directors (May 1979: para. 5.62). These 'in-depth inspections' became known as 'operational assessments'. As part of the process each establishment was required to divide its work into 50 or so activity areas of equal size and one of these areas had to be assessed every fortnight. The spotlight of operational assessment moved systematically around the whole establishment. Whilst it was two internal assessors who carried out the examination, all the papers (module, examination report and Governor's comments) had to be sent to the Regional Director, thereby 'reinforcing the authority of regions' (Marriage and Selby 1983: 12). The Regional Director and his staff came to have a far more detailed insight into the workings of establishments than could be achieved by visiting and were able to have specific information to add purpose to their operational visits.

It could be argued that operational assessments brought a fresh approach to the management of institutions by making the Governor the focal point of the assessments, thereby reinforcing the Governor's role. However, there was a growing feeling amongst Governors that local discretion for decision-making was being eroded and Governors were losing managerial control and independence to the Regional Directors (Marriage and Selby 1983: 11).

The introduction of Circular Instruction 55/1984 brought with it 'functions documents' which created a formal agreement between the Governor and Regional Director on what functions the establishment would perform (HM Prison Service 1984). For a number of reasons, the development of this approach to managing delivery would have a major impact on Governors. The agreement did not automatically become nullified by change of Governor or Regional Director. For the first time a newly appointed Governor had their freedom to change the work and functions of the establishment constrained. On the other hand the agreement also prevented any third party, from Headquarters or elsewhere, intervening to modify the work of the establishment or its regime without consultation with the Governor and Regional Director. For example, no longer would workshops be created or removed without the Governor being involved and agreeing to the changes.

There had been a lack of systematic information about the performance of individual establishments, which could be collated in any meaningful way. Therefore it was not possible to know what was happening either in the system as a whole, or in different establishments. One of the impacts of the functions document was an attempt to define the services and activities by which agreed functions were to be delivered in terms of 'baselines'. These were expressed as planned levels of the operating hours and the number of inmates involved in regime activities such as education, industries, other work parties, and physical education. It was against these planned levels that the actual delivery of functions was compared.

Publication of Circular Instruction 55/1984 signalled the start of two years' work of translating the functions into specific terms for each establishment. As well as the development of the functions document itself, there had been advances in setting priorities and examining the relationship between functions and resources. A summary of budgetary and staffing information and a list of the Governor's objectives (or targets) for the year had to be appended to the functions document. The functions document gradually moved towards the status of a contract between the Governor and Regional Director. The Governor, through the annual report on delivery, had to answer to the Regional Director for the discharge of the functions of the establishment. The delivery report provided a benchmark against which the Governor could monitor the establishment's performance and which the Regional Office could use for setting objectives, evaluating performance and comparing the performance of establishments. Whilst assessment had been present for many years, in the form of the Board of Visitors and Her Majesty's Chief

Inspector of Prisons, the contract and its baselines, for the first time allowed the performance of the establishment, and its Governor, to be appraised against objective and quantifiable measures.

From a theoretical position, this was an unremarkable process of defining aims, objectives, work output, and performance criteria. In practice, however, it represented a significant development for the Prison Service and an important change for the Governor. Governors, and their prisons, had become the subject of a myriad of management tools, planning processes and detailed monitoring. Governors were increasingly being held to account for the performance of their establishments.

The work that a Governor was doing at the beginning of the 1980s was captured in a review of prison Governor grading, which had been set up to consider the relative weights of Governor posts in various establishments and to provide criteria for assessing Governor posts. The review team considered 143 Governor grade posts and looked at background material including job descriptions, interviewed Governor grades and observed them carrying out various duties. The review identified the main task of the Governor as: 'Managing his establishment in accordance with the relevant statutory rules, Standing Orders, Circular Instructions, headquarters memoranda and other legislation as it affects penal establishments and their inmates. Management in this context includes responsibility for the suitable containment of inmates and for the provision of appropriate treatment within the constraints which exist' (Home Office 1981: para. 4.4).

While identifying that all Governors had a number of specific functions in common, the Review concluded that the amount of time which each occupied, and their complexity, varied according to the nature of the establishment and the extent to which they were able to delegate to other Governor grades (Home Office 1981: para. 4.7). A total of eight functions common to all Governors was identified: command; inspection; industrial relations; inmate management; staff management; management of other resources; policy and development; and representation.

During the 1980s changes to the Prison Service began to put increasingly more complex demands on Governors. The pressures imposed by overcrowding and staff shortages had been added to those of industrial relations and the increasing interest of the outside community in what went on in prisons. A greater emphasis began to be placed on the role of the Governor, not simply as operational head of the establishment but as manager of its resources. A Home Office review reached the view that the Governor was 'both operational commander and general manager' and should 'achieve an effective balance between the different elements of this role, in which he can reconcile his traditional position as operational decision maker with the increasing managerial and representational demands he faces' (Home Office 1984a: para. 60).

There was a recognition that establishments had to be organised in such a way as to create room for Governors to be able to plan, and provide strategic leadership and direction, rather than simply responding to the immediate operational demands. The review team recommended that the Prison Department should encourage the delegation of tasks by Governors to their subordinates; review tasks laid by the Department on Governors personally; be clear who to hold to account for the discharge of which responsibilities; reduce the number of staff who report directly to the Governor on a day-to-day basis to between six and eight; change the working pattern of Governors so that they worked a five-day, Monday-to-Friday week, rather than a ten-day fortnight; and ensure that Governors have the real authority and powers they need to carry out their jobs by delegating more responsibility to them (Home Office 1984a: para. 60). Significantly, the Report indicated that it was not necessary for the Governor to visit all parts of his establishment every day and that there was no reason 'why this task – the Governor's round – should not be delegated to a "duty governor" for the day, whose responsibilities, along with certain others, might be carried out on a rota basis by any one of the senior management team of the establishment' (Home Office 1984a: para. 61).

While the tasks of the Governor came under the spotlight, the importance of the role of the Governor was never questioned. At the time of introducing the new management framework for the Prison Service, the then Director General made clear that: 'The key manager in the Prison Service is the governing Governor. The Department's policies are delivered by him and his staff in the establishment for which he is responsible. In the final analysis, that is what matters' (Train 1985: 179).

As the Governor's role developed, concern was frequently expressed about the lack of training given to Governors to prepare them for the new and more complex role. Although the police, fire service and armed services all had their command courses (see, for example, Savage *et al.* 2000: 107, for a discussion of the strategic command course for Chief Constables), there had been no concept of comprehensive training for Governors before the mid-1980s.

The May Committee accepted the evidence of the Governors' Branch of the Society of Civil and Public Servants that Governors required more comprehensive training, including specific training in public relations, management, administration and industrial relations. Elsewhere in the Report, May argued that 'the training of governors must be fuller and longer than it presently is' and concluded that 'training at all levels is neither effective nor as comprehensive as we think it should be and that it is not given sufficient priority at all levels in the Service' (May 1979: para. 7.39). The overall picture painted by the May Report was that the lack of training given to Governors on specific issues such as managing resources and industrial relations had led to some of the major problems which the Prison Service faced at that time. The Committee believed that Governors 'must in future come to terms with the fact that they are occupying responsible management positions which require a wide variety of management skills ranging, for example, from budgetary control to industrial relations, as well as an increased awareness and knowledge of the social services and penal affairs' (May 1979: para. 7.59).

The recognition that the role of the Governor was becoming increasingly complex, together with May's recommendation, led to the creation of a 'command course' for new Governors. The command course was designed to fit newly appointed Governors for their enlarged role. The introduction to the course made clear that Governors would in the future:

> need to combine leadership with a sound generalist approach. They will need to be well versed in the ethical, political, legal, and social implications of their roles. They will have to be skilled in the performance of managerial and administrative tasks. They will require a firm grasp of specialist functions so that the efforts of different disciplines are effectively applied. They will also need to bring to work a keen appreciation of a prison system operating in an increasingly public and international context. (Driscoll 1982: 1)

In order to meet the challenge of the tasks ahead, the aims of the course were to help Governors to 'consider the national and international context in which the Prison Service must function, examine the Governor's accountability for implementing aims and tasks of the Prison Department, and enable the development of essential skills' (Driscoll 1982). The contents of the first course were grouped into 12 sections: constitution of the law; finance; industrial relations; staff welfare, training and development; manpower management; security and control; disciplinary systems; public relations; regimes, works and works projects; personnel management; and general management.

The first five command courses for Governors that took place between 1983 and 1986, were the subject of in-depth evaluation (Williamson 1986). Williamson recommended that the command course, as it was then structured, should be abandoned and replaced by a senior command studies course which consisted of a set of modules providing training in discrete skills and areas of responsibility supported by a new management course. This new management course was intended to meet the needs of Governors about to take charge of an establishment for the first time.

Chief executives (1987–1997)

Derek Lewis, the private sector businessman, who was made Director General of the Prison service in 1992, described Governors he encountered as:

A colourful, varied and humorous group . . . there is the Old Etonian who commands infinite respect from his staff, managing in a gentle, polite and low-key way that few would associate with a prison. There is the mildly eccentric, like the one who sports a monocle and cane as he walks around his establishment. There are those who operate an authoritarian regime with staff, and others who allow a great deal of freedom . . . The only generalisation is that the best take an enthusiastic, almost proprietorial, interest in their establishment, knowing their staff by name and many of the prisoners too. (Lewis 1997: 24)

It was this group of Governors, who were governing in the late 1980s and 1990s, that found themselves in a period of enormous change. The Prison Service was expanding rapidly as it faced unprecedented growth in the prison population, which had increased steadily from a low of 43,200 in 1980–81 to an average of 65,298 in 1998 (Home Office 1999). At the same time as having to deal with the prison population, the Service had to become more effective in its custodial and rehabilitative work, and more efficient through implementation of a demanding cost reduction programme. The Service also faced a series of riots in the early 1990s and escapes in the mid-1990s, which came to have a significant impact on Governors and their work.

A radical reorganisation of human resource systems and management structures in the Prison Service was launched in April 1986, under the banner 'Fresh Start' (HM Prison Service 1987). The new scheme restructured the pay of prison officers, limiting overtime payments, which had been regarded for some years as demand-led and uncontrollable. Working practices were changed by reorganising staff into groups with a degree of flexible rostering and by assimilating overlapping middle management grades. Management systems were altered in an attempt to assign clear roles and accountabilities, integrate specialist staff, and co-ordinate efficient prison regimes under the Governor's unifying direction.

Before Fresh Start around 75 per cent of a Governor's week was out of their control (Barclay 1988: 5). The Governor's work was dictated by routines that had their basis in history; 'statutory duties'; managers and trade unions that expected direct access; demands from Region and Headquarters to attend management meetings; and attendance at institutional meetings. Fresh Start went some way to freeing up the Governor from these routine tasks by introducing a new management structure, which contained fewer management levels and clearer lines of accountability. As a result Governors had a span of management control of between four and six people, rather than the 10 to 14 people who had previously been reporting to them.

While it was clear that the Governor was the 'overall manager of all management operations and ultimate commander in emergencies', the changes implemented by Fresh Start resulted in the Governor only taking personal command during 'major emergencies', leaving other operational staff to deal with less serious incidents (HM Prison Service 1987: 16). This was a major change from what had been expected of earlier Governors. Fresh Start also clarified that Governors were expected to work from Monday to Friday, with only periodic attendance out of hours and at weekends.

Traditionally the Governor's rounds had been the means of keeping in touch with the grass roots of the establishment. However, in many establishments the Governor's rounds had become a combination of routine and ritual. Indeed, one former Governor suggests that '. . . this routine has been predictable to the extent that, if he visited at another time of the day, the greeting was still "Good Morning"' (Barclay 1988: 5). The management structure introduced under Fresh Start, together with the ability to delegate tasks to senior managers, freed Governors from traditional routine duties (daily 'rounds', sampling food, visiting the segregation unit and healthcare centre, prisoner applications).

One area of some controversy was allowing Governors to delegate the adjudication responsibility. Conducting adjudications is a quasi-judicial activity and traditionally accepted as a key way for a Governor to set the tone and standards in an establishment. Advocates of change argued that the Governor should focus on managing adjudications through setting standards and by scrutinising the records of adjudications that had taken place (Barclay 1988: 6). Others took the view that the Governor 'must retain direct contact [by doing adjudications] . . . to set his standards of conduct for staff, as well as for inmates, and in doing so to establish the tone of the establishment in the discipline and control context' (Gadd 1988: 8). The matter continued to be the subject of debate over a decade later (HM Prison Service 1997b).

The new approach, in which the Governor worked Monday to Friday and no longer routinely visited all parts of the prison, began to change the way operational staff viewed the Governor. The Governor began increasingly to be seen as a manager who worked the hours of non-operational staff and who was seen less frequently around the prison, especially in the evenings and at weekends.

Some Governors expressed their concern about the direction the role of the Governor was moving in and the potential pitfalls it brought:

No doubt, if released from the everyday pressure of what is now seen as routine work and problem solving, a governor may well be able to focus more of his attention on the wider strategic aspects of effectively managing a modern prison establishment. There is, however, a price to be paid for this if a correct balance is not struck between managerial remoteness and the personal involvement of the governor in relation to all his staff. That price is amorphous management, lacking in inspirational direction and personal example. If so, I gaze upon such a governor with a sense of unease . . . I do not see my role in the new era of Fresh Start as being limited to the leather upholstered chair of the managing director in the boardroom. (Gadd 1988: 7–9)

Despite the changes made by Fresh Start, a 1988 review found that most Governors were still spending two to three hours each day visiting various parts of their prison to keep in touch with staff and inmates. Some Governors involved themselves daily in adjudicating and in personally handling petitions from individual prisoners (HM Treasury 1989). The review concluded that Governors:

share broadly comparable characteristics. Postholders were charged with ensuring the overall efficiency and effectiveness of the establishments to which they had been appointed. At a more detailed level their responsibilities required them in particular to ensure that acceptable standards were achieved for the welfare and occupation of inmates. They were expected to ensure that high standards of order and discipline were adhered to, that the morale and career interests of prison staff were maximised, good industrial relations were maintained and that the establishment was adequately resourced to carry out its approved functions. (HM Treasury 1989: 6)

The early 1990s saw a major switch in emphasis from central management by Prison Service Headquarters to devolution to Governors. This was in part due to the findings of the Woolf Report, which concluded that, 'The Prison Service should aim for a situation where it is appreciated by the Service as a whole that management (and the framework of controls that have been created) only exist to *enable* Governors to govern . . . We recommend therefore increased delegation to Governors for the functions connected with the management of the prison' (Woolf and Tumim 1991: paras 12.73 and 12.79).

This view was supported by a subsequent report that concluded that, 'too often governors lack any real control over their personnel or their budget' and 'plans to devolve greater personnel and financial responsibility to governors should proceed as quickly as possible' (Lygo 1991: paras 40–41). The 1991 White Paper accepted the need to empower Governors and made clear that, 'the delegation to governors of budgetary and personnel management responsibilities should be extended' (Home Office 1991: para. 3.8).

There was a recognition that 'devolution would bring with it increased demands on Governors' as they were 'asked to take on the full role of general managers' of their establishments (HM Prison Service 1994c). Governors were required to understand specialist areas, such as finance and personnel, as well as having to think and plan strategically. Devolution continued to be a priority into the mid-1990s and the Prison Service made devolution the key strategic priority for 1994–97. The corporate plan pointed out that, 'Governors will be the focal point in delivering the Service's objectives. They will have wide delegated authority to innovate, and to manage effectively within the national policy framework and specific local plans. They will be expected to use their initiative and will be accountable for the performance of their establishments, in particular the delivery of agreed local objectives and targets' (HM Prison Service 1994b: para. 1.18).

These developments led to concerns amongst some Governors about their changing role: 'All governors are certain that the style of governing will have to change. More and more, governors will be office bound. As one governor put it: "it is not my job to care for prisoners, but to care for staff who care for prisoners." Governors must learn to delegate to survive, but the result is that they will be much less in evidence and certainly less accessible' (Selby 1994: 23). The Prison Service responded to these concerns by directing Governors to 'ensure that there are mechanisms in place to enable them to spend time "managing by walking about", this might be by the provision of secretariat, staff officer, planning, project or development roles' and to 'review their management structures' (HM Prison Service 1996a).

The training of Governors between 1987 and 1997 changed to reflect the expanded role that Governors were expected to undertake. By 1987 the command course for new Governors had been transformed into the senior command studies programme (SCS), the eligibility criteria for which had been amended to include non-Governors (for example, medical officers and general civil servants). The aims of the programme had also changed emphasis and were more focused on giving an opportunity for personal and professional development. The change in course content and language from 'command' to 'management' reflected the importation of the new public management ethos into the Prison

Service and supported the view that Governors were general managers. The course continued to change and by 1991 consisted entirely of management modules (Williamson 1991). A decision was made to contract out the provision of the programme to a university business school, who ran the programme from 1992 until 1997. The thinking behind this decision appears to have been a desire to move to a more generic approach to management training, both in terms of those participating in the training and in its content.

Given the changed nature of the programme, with little emphasis on equipping people to govern prisons, it was decided to introduce a technical prison-specific course for Governors about to take charge of a prison for the first time. The two-week course consisted of industrial relations; staff disciplinary procedures and practices; race relations; information technology; contract and corporate objectives; contingency planning; leadership style; relationships with the community; budgets; and incident management. Courses were run in 1992 and 1993 but it was terminated by 1994. It was not until 1997 that a command course was reintroduced for new Governors (Bryans 1999: 27–28).

The Management Development Project was set up in 1996 to consider, amongst other issues, the role, competencies and succession planning for Governors. One of the main changes to follow from the Project was the introduction of assessment centres for Governors. Prior to the introduction of assessment centres, the promotion to the rank of Governor had been far from rigorous. A previous Director General commented:

I had been shocked to discover how governors were appointed. Promotions were made on the basis of a short interview in front of a panel that knew little about the achievements of the individual and had no objective assessment of his or her capabilities, while the postings of governors took no account of their strengths and weaknesses, or the nature of the prison itself. (Lewis 1997: 79–80).

Assessment centres, consisting of objective critical and numerical reasoning tests, committee, advocacy and negotiation exercises, tests at written expression and problem solving and structured interviews, were developed during 1997–1998. Passing an assessment centre became a requirement for people who wanted to apply for a governing post after 1999.

The Project also expressed concern about the potential lack of good quality candidates coming forward to apply for governing posts. As a result, the Project recommended two additional entry routes to becoming a Governor (HM Prison Service 1996b, recommendation 18). The first was a new direct entry to the governor grades scheme introduced to run alongside the Accelerated Promotion Scheme. In reality this meant reintroducing the scheme that was abolished in 1985. The scheme was aimed at career changers as well as talented in-service staff, from both uniformed and administrative staff. The second scheme was a 'cross hierarchical move' scheme, which facilitated the move of administrative grade staff to Governor grade posts and Governors into general administrative posts. This scheme was reminiscent of the move of administrators into Governor posts in the early 1900s, which resulted in widespread criticism from uniform staff at the time. A key plank of the scheme was that the initial transfer to a different hierarchy had to be below Governor level and would follow a development centre. However, at least one individual moved directly from an administrative post to govern a prison.

There is no doubt that in the 1990s the Governor's role became far more complex and the need for management skills accordingly far greater. The wide range of responsibilities the Governor began to take on, including financial and personnel management, detailed strategic and business planning and target setting, would have been alien to Governors of previous decades. It was recognised that Governors could no longer do everything themselves and would in the future have to rely on senior managers and intermediate management to ensure the implementation and delivery of all policies. However, there remained some ambiguity about what tasks the Governor should delegate. The 1996 Management Development Project concluded that, 'There are many tasks historically associated with governors personally which may not need to be performed by them. There are, however, unique competencies and terms relating to the in-charge role . . . which differentiate those roles from others and cannot be delegated' (HM Prison Service 1996b: para. 1.9).

Following significant criticisms set out in the reports which followed the prison escapes in the mid-1990s (Woodcock 1994 and Learmont 1995a), a Prison Service Review was set up to take a strategic look at the management and organisation of the Service. The Review reported in October 1997 and concluded that 'the responsibilities of Governors and the demands made on them have increased enormously over the years . . . the role of the Governor is in urgent need of redefinition and review' (HM Prison Service 1997a: paras 9.34–9.39 and 3.26).

Some themes from history

Chapters 2 and 3 have traced the evolution of the office, role and duties of the Governor as they have developed over the last 500 years. This historical framework provides an understanding of why today's Governors are required to undertake certain tasks and duties, and gives the background to how the Governor came to be such an important actor in the prison. Tracing the historical development of the role is important, as the profession of governing has developed through an oral tradition. There is little written material to guide Governors on how to govern. Governors learn from their predecessors, who in turn learnt from the Governors for whom they worked. Knowledge and understanding are passed orally from generation to generation. 'Jailcraft' is developed over time and lessons learnt from peers and from previous generations of Governors – Governors all serve in establishments under other Governors before they get themselves to govern.

The work of the Governor has evolved over the years. Major changes in the role have been brought about as a consequence of crises – a social crisis outside, or an internal one such as a riot or escape. Comparisons with previous periods can be made in terms of delegated authority; independence from central control; and social standing.

The era of early keepers, gaolers and wardens was very much one of caprice. By the nineteenth century Governors were required to have a disciplinary ethos and to achieve administrative efficiency and uniformity in the operation of prisons. They were the subject of centralised control and their work directed by detailed regulation. The management of prisons was redefined as a bureaucratic task, demanding knowledge, skill and expertise. Considerations of an emotional or moral kind had no place in the work of a 'modern' Governor.

By the mid-twentieth century, Governors had a more reforming ethos and were given greater freedom to experiment and to try out rehabilitative regimes for prisoners. They possessed sufficient freedom to mould their establishments and regimes according to their personal philosophies. The development of custodial and treatment aspects of regimes increased the scope of the Governor's work. Governors became 'criminological technicians' (Garland 1990: 185) who adopted a scientific approach based on therapy, treatment and rehabilitation.

More recently, Governors have been required to adopt a more managerial ethos. Prisons have to be managed in a more passionless and bureaucratic manner. Efficiency and compliance have become the administratively defined goals. Governors are increasingly seen as general managers and held to account for the total operation of their prisons, through more comprehensive line management.

Some aspects of the Governor's work have remained remarkably constant over the years. Throughout history Governors have been required to maintain a personal presence by frequently visiting all parts of the establishment; adjudicate on at least some disciplinary matters; sample the prisoners' food on a daily basis; closely monitor prisoners in sensitive areas such as segregation units and hospitals; undertake a number of symbolic and ceremonial duties; liaise with the local community; and deal personally with major incidents.

63

Other elements of a Governor's job changed, only to have the same element reintroduced many years later. For example, early Governors were expected to act as entrepreneurs, to generate work for their prisoners and make a profit from their labours. Such activity was prohibited in the twentieth century. However, today Governors are again being exhorted to make contact with local industry and to use prisoner labour on commercial contracts in order to generate revenue for their prisons.

Some facets of a Governor's role and duties have changed significantly. The amount of devolution has increased, but this has been matched with more monitoring and greater personal accountability. The scope for individuality and discretion has been reduced and replaced with a stronger degree of uniformity and regulation. While Governors in the early nineteenth century were the subjects of as much detailed regulation as today, their implementation of the rules and instructions was not the subject of such close scrutiny as one finds currently. Governing also became more complex over the years. Governors had to learn to manage more varied regimes, increasing numbers of specialist staff, multiple hierarchies and overlapping functions. More recently, Governors took on responsibility for the general management of the whole institution, including personnel and financial aspects.

In short, Governors moved from being amateur and capricious gaolers, to military men administering their institutions according to laid-down rules, to charismatic feudal barons exercising patriarchal authority over their prisons, to being general managers bound by bureaucracy and legal rules. This book now goes on to look in more detail at today's Governors and the work that they do.

Chapter 4

Governing in a changed context

Early researchers viewed 'the society of captives' (Sykes 1958: 79) as bounded by the prison wall and marked by its own conventions, codes of conduct and isolation. While prisons remain a 'society apart', the prison system today is far more responsive to the surrounding environment than earlier commentators like Sykes suggested. The prison boundary is far more flexible than it once was (see particularly Irwin and Cressey 1962; Irwin 1970 and 1980; Jacobs 1977 and 1983; Farrington 1992). Prisons are shaped by their wider environment and react to, and are acted upon by, the broader community. As one commentator put it, prisons are 'affected by the forces of economics, politics, culture, and technology. For all their apparent autonomy, each one is situated within an ensemble of social forces and is structured by the values and social arrangements which form its effective environment' (Garland 1990: 283). Governors, and their prisons, do not today operate in a vacuum, much as some Governors may wish that they did so.

Organisational theorists have long held the view that changes in this external environment precede and lead to changes in the structure and management of organisations themselves (Chandler 1962; Wilson 1989; Desveaux 1995). The demands of the external environment on the public sector have led to a radical change in its management and organisation. This was particularly so in the case of prisons, as 'the external environment exerts an enormous influence over the mission, behavior, and structure of correctional organizations' (Freeman 1999: xiii).

The environment in which Governors operate can be described as a complex interaction between the public; politicians; the judiciary; the media; prisoners; pressure groups; and unions. Changes in society over recent years, together with other changes in the environment in which prisons operate, have had a significant impact on Governors and their work. This chapter will look at some of the most important of those developments and consider their effects on Governors.

Prisoners' rights and expectations

One of the most significant developments in recent years has been the acceptance of the concept of prisoners' rights and prisoners' ability to challenge the way they are treated in prisons. As a consequence of the introduction of the Human Rights Act 1998 (which came into force in October 2000), developments in case law, and the creation of the Prisons Ombudsman, Governors' decisions are increasingly being scrutinised and challenged.

Before 1979 the courts took little interest in ensuring the rights of prisoners. The courts were clear that the Prison Rules did not give prisoners any rights and, as a consequence, if the Rules were breached that did not of itself give prisoners a cause of action against those who had breached them. Judges took the view that if the courts were to 'entertain actions by disgruntled prisoners' the Governor's life would be made 'intolerable' (Lord Denning in *Becker* v. *Home Office* [1972] 2 QB 407). Prisoners were effectively prevented from accessing the courts by such rulings and Governors took advantage of this limited scrutiny:

> I'm not proud of it but in the past I've manipulated adjudications to find a prisoner guilty. You knew back then that you would not be challenged. There were no lawyers, no real appeals . . .

> I remember when we used to turn a blind eye to things even if you sometimes thought that there may be something in it. The interests of the prison sometimes had to outweigh the individual prisoner.

Following a series of judgements (most notably *R* v. *Board of Visitors of Hull Prison*, ex parte *St Germain* et al. [1979] 1 All ER 701, and *R* v. *Deputy Governor of Parkhurst Prison*, ex parte *Leech* [1988] 1 All ER 485) the courts have increasingly shown a tendency to review how Governors exercise their discretion. By 1992 all decisions made by Governors in the discharge of their functions were reviewable by the High Court (*R* v. *Deputy Governor of Parkhurst Prison*, ex parte *Hague and Weldon* [1991] 3 WLR 340). The courts have intervened in transfers, segregation, medical consent, drug testing, tariff setting for life-sentence prisoners and categorisation (Creighton and King 2000; Cheney *et al.* 2001; Lennon 2003), all of which has added to the complexity of decision-making for the Governor.

These days none of us would dare ignore a complaint as we know that they [prisoners] will be on the phone to their brief as soon as they walk out of the office ... Just look at all the adverts in *Inside Time* [a prisoners' newspaper] for solicitors who are encouraging prisoners to take action.

Life has become more complicated. Adjudications are more complicated. Even these trainees [young prisoners] will ask for legal representation. Ten years ago they were wheeled in, wheeled out, if they didn't plead guilty they were going to be found guilty, and the appeal system was pretty much that the Secretary of State can find no grounds for interference. You didn't write to solicitors. Life is more complex.

The increase in the level of judicial and legal interest in the operation of prisons led the Prison Service to issue an Information and Practice Guidance Note to Governors titled *The Judge At Your Gate* (HM Prison Service 2000d). One of the underlying reasons for issuing the document was the number of errors that Governors were making in their decision-making. The Note concludes by stating: 'We hope that this booklet will encourage you to take legal advice before committing the Minister or the Prison Service to a particular decision if there is any doubt in your mind' (HM Prison Service 2000d: 30).

The level of judicial examination of Governors' decisions has increased significantly and is likely to increase further in both domestic and European courts (see Lennon 2003 for a detailed description of the many recent cases). On some occasions the courts have removed powers from Governors. For example, the 2002 decision of the European Court in *Ezeh and Connors* led to the removal of the Governor's ability to award additional days for disciplinary offences (HM Prison Service 2003b). Governors now have to give prisoners reasoned explanations for their decisions (*R (Angle and Angle)* v. *Governor of HMP Ford and Home Secretary* [2002] Prison Law Report 218) and all decisions made by Governors in the discharge of their duties can be reviewed by the High Court (Lennon 2003: 449).

A further development which reinforced prisoners' rights and therefore had an impact on Governors was the establishment in 1994 of the Prisons Ombudsman (Prisons Ombudsman 1996). The Ombudsman looked into 3,132 complaints made by prisoners in 2002–03 (Prisons and Probation Ombudsman 2003). These complaints were in relation to the full breadth of a Governor's work: adjudications; conditions; security; regimes; pre-release; contact with families; property; religion; segregation; transfers; and allocations. The Ombudsman has pointed out that his inquiries look at minor matters, as well as bigger issues: 'I am sometimes criticised for investigating apparently minor matters. But nothing is trivial in prison when you have so little autonomy, so few possessions, so little influence, and when every aspect of your life is ordered for you' (Prisons and Probation Ombudsman 2003: 10).

Prisoners are today also able to challenge a Governor's decision through a formal Request and Complaint system. This system allows prisoners to write directly to the area manager to appeal a Governor's decision (see PSO 2510).

The increased scrutiny of Governors' decisions has added to the complexity of the work. Governors today need to be able to ensure consistency in their treatment of prisoners and justify their decisions, or find their actions overturned or criticised. This has made Governors more wary and, some have argued, more conservative in their approach.

> I am very careful these days in dealings with prisoners. I know that if they do not like what I said they will be on the phone to their brief or the ombudsman. I make sure the evidence is there to support what I decide or else I will lose it. But it makes it more difficult to treat them as individuals. If I do something for Joey on C wing, then I know that Charlie on D wing will want the same, and if he doesn't get it there will be a CARP [a request and complaint form] or a letter to his MP.

The prisoner is now regarded, 'to a much greater extent than thirty or forty years ago, as a person with rights' (Bottoms 1995: 8). Prisoners have also come to be seen as consumers whose opinions need to be taken into account in the management of institutions (reflecting the 'consumerist management' element of managerialism). For example, prison surveys (such as Walmsley *et al.* 1992) have raised prisoners' expectations, and the Citizen's Charter set out the standards of service towards prisoners required of the Prison Service (HM Prison Service 1993f). Governors therefore have to be far more conscious of the 'judge at the gate' and the 'Ombudsman at their elbow' when making decisions and exercising their discretion. They need to ensure that prisoners' rights are not denied, that prisoners are treated consistently and that their decisions are fair and reasonable.

Politics, the media and prisons

An organisation has a high degree of legitimacy in a society when its actions are perceived as 'desirable, proper or appropriate' (Suchman 1995: 574). The Prison Service, like other public institutions, must therefore operate in a manner that ensures the confidence of politicians and the public.

Until the last decade, politicians and the public had, in the main, left direction and control of penal policy under the auspices of penal bureaucrats within Government, who took their lead from research findings (Pratt 2000b: 138). Throughout the 1990s issues of law and order increasingly captured 'public attention and, in turn, became one of the most compelling social issues for politicians' (James and Raine 1998: 4). A different set of relationships took shape whereby politicians and public sentiment seemed much more closely in tune, with penal experts shifted to a fringe role. Governors were no longer seen as penal experts who needed to be consulted on matters of penal policy. As the PGA put it: '. . . [the] Conservative Government played the law and order card. Our views became less important to Michael Howard than those of editorial writers' (Prison Governors Association 2000).

The relationship between ministers and Governors became a troubled one in the 1990s. Clear differences on issues of policy and operational matters emerged. While Governors accepted that ministers should develop policy (even if Governors did not agree with the policy being developed), Governors maintained that day-to-day operational matters and management of individual prisoners should be left to them. Some commentators shared this view: 'Within the law, and the policy as approved by Parliament, the treatment of individual prisoners should be a matter of professional and managerial, and not political, judgement' (Faulkner 2001: 301).

The creation of the Prison Service Agency in 1993 was generally welcomed as providing protection from political interference in operational matters. Indeed, one of the underlying reasons for the creation of agencies was to separate out the policy-making functions from operational concerns and hand over the 'murky plain of overwhelming detail' to managers (Power 1997). The then Home Secretary conveniently re-emphasised the divide between 'policy' and 'operations' at the time of the escape from Whitemoor prison, which allowed him to argue that the escape was an operational matter and that it was the Director General of the Prison Service, and not ministers, who should bear responsibility for the failure.

This managerial and operational autonomy was rather short-lived. Despite the creation of the Prison Service Agency, the Prison Service never did get effective operational independence from the main Home Office and ministers. The reality is that it is 'inevitable that Ministers will be interested in and wish to influence the executive functions of the Prison Service, ie: its operations' (HM Prison Service 1997a: 34). The Home Secretary, who argued so strongly for a divide between operations and policy, was quick to intervene in operational matters, ranging from the dismissal of the Governor of Parkhurst prison after a security lapse to demanding more austere regimes (Ryan 2003: 99). Since then the 'independence' of the Prison Service on operational matters has slowly been eroded. The Government now recognises that 'the Prison Service has, in practice, been a Next Steps Agency in name only for some time' (Home Office 2004) and has brought the Service back within the Home Office in creating a National Offender Management Service. Governors now find themselves firmly back under the control and influence of the Home Office, its ministers and civil servants.

There has been an increasing trend in recent years for ministers and MPs to comment publicly on what should, and should not, be happening in our prisons. In that sense the world of the Governor is becoming increasingly politicised. It cannot be disputed that the Home Secretary has a legitimate interest in the operational performance of the Prison Service, not least as he may be called to account in Parliament for it. Parliamentary Questions about the Prison Service are today answered by a Home Office Minister and not by the Director General or another senior Prison Service official, as they had been for a number of years prior to 1997. A parliamentary statement made clear that this was to enable 'ministers to answer personally to Parliament for what is done in our prisons' (*Hansard*, 31 July 1997, Written Answers 91). Given their level of accountability it is understandable that ministers will want to take an active interest in what is happening in prisons.

Governors, as a result, have had to develop a clear insight into the essentially political dimension of their work. They have to be aware that all their actions will be judged against whether they fit with ministers' policies. Governors have to respond to changes in ministerial views about prison conditions, such as the 1993 'Prison works' speech by the then Home Secretary, which marked a change of direction towards a more austere view of prisoners' entitlements (Dunbar and Langdon 1998: 29). A number of Governors commented on the growth in political interest in their work. For many this political interest reached its peak during Michael Howard's tenure at the Home Office:

> Undoubtedly in my experience, it is necessary in prisons to be aware of the political dimensions that apply and that was never more evident than under Michael Howard, when it was certainly like walking a tightrope, but also being able to cope with the issues in the press on political matters.

Governors who failed to respond found themselves subject to public chastisement by ministers, as the Governor who proposed to build a pitch-and-putt course in his prison found out. The then Home Secretary did not consider that it had a place in 'decent but austere' prison regimes and had the decision overturned after much embarrassment to the Prison Service, ministers and the Governor himself. The then Director General commented: 'A governor's ill-judged decision to provide his inmates with a pitch-and-putt course caused a massive political and media reaction, distracting the management for weeks on end as inquests were conducted and policy re-examined' (Lewis 1997: 63).

The need for Governors to adhere to ministerial views, and to avoid embarrassing ministers, is not without its critics. Carlen, for example, comments that:

> The injunction that "the 'minister' must never be embarrassed" is one of the least questioned of the rules of which governors are expected to be mindful, even at times when, as during the last couple of decades, the ministers themselves have fashioned con-stantly-changing prison policies to appease populist punitiveness rather than to further the objectives of any principled and long-term penal policy designed to address the causes of recidivism. (Carlen 2001: 5)

While some Governors support such a view, the reality is that increased political interest, or at least the willingness of politicians to castigate Governors when things go wrong, has resulted in Governors taking fewer risks in their decision-making. For example, when the Home Secretary tightened the rules on the use of Release on Temporary Licence (ROTL), by which Governors authorise prisoners to work or spend time outside prison, Governors were told that they would be held personally responsible for any future ROTL failures. As a result Governors 'became so nervous about releasing anyone that its use virtually dried up' (Ramsbotham 2003: 161). Governors made a similar point:

> I think politicians have got in the way. We are still suffering from the influence of Michael Howard, I think, in terms of, you know, he wasn't prepared to defend the Prison Service, or justify things. We have this tabloid journalism rules okay. And the problem with that I think is that we have now internalised it into a form of self-censorship. And we don't, as Governors, take risks that we would have taken before.

Penal policy-making and operational delivery is now less free from political influence. The shaping of the prison by the external environment has not however always resulted in positive changes. (For example, in the Dutch case the broader community has had a harsh effect on prisons as the penal climate has hardened. See Pakes 2004.)

Widespread media coverage of prisons has always taken place in response to operational failures. A number of high-profile escape attempts, riots and disturbances, rooftop protests, deaths in custody, and instances of racism and brutality have all rightly received extensive media coverage. In addition to 'big issue' media coverage, there is also today an ever-increasing media desire to expose instances of what is seen as poor judgement by prison officials ('luxury foods in prison'; 'cells to be painted pink to calm prisoners'; 'prisoners to be given karaoke machines to improve their self-confidence'; 'prison orders takeaway for prisoners') and more routine failures of the workings of our prisons ('prisoners visit Tescos to buy alcohol'; 'prisoners run businesses from inside'; 'mobile phones in every prison'; 'more drugs in prison than outside'). Given the level of media interest and willingness to 'expose' perceived shortcomings, Governors have to be more mindful that the result of one of their decisions will find its way (via staff, prisoners or an investigative journalist) into the public domain, where it will receive the full glare of publicity.

Privatisation and market testing

One of the most controversial changes in the penal environment in recent decades has been the decision to use the private sector to provide custodial services. The privatisation of prisons has entailed changes in structure and organisation of the Prison Service, policy-making, management and operation of prisons (what Stolz 1997 refers to as 'correctional subgovernment'). If nothing else, when a private-sector company is contracted to run a prison, the profit motive gets introduced into the spectrum of existing multiple goals (Shichor 1999: 230).

For the purposes of the current discussion, the presenting issue is whether the character and process of private-sector involvement has influenced Governors and had an impact on what they do. Governors took the view that the introduction of private prisons had little impact on their approach:

> Far too much attention has been wasted on the debates about the contracting-out of prisons. What difference has it made to [a training prison]? None, that's how much.

> One of the original reasons for going for privatisation was that the public-sector prisons would learn from the private sector. To be honest, that just hasn't happened.

> The DCMF [Design, Construct, Manage and Finance] or PFI [Public Finance Initative] prisons . . . haven't really made much difference to what we do or the way we do it.

> . . . don't tell me that privatisation has had a big impact on the state sector because it hasn't.

The National Audit Office report on the Operational Performance of PFI Prisons took a similar view: 'there is little available information on . . . whether the use of PFI has brought wider benefits to the Prison Service . . . we found only limited evidence that good practice from the private sector was being incorporated into public sector prisons' (National Audit Office 2003: 5 and 34).

Since 1992, the Prison Service has permitted the public sector to compete directly with the private sector for the management of some existing prisons. (See Bryans 1996 for the detailed early history.) This 'market testing' of prisons has, it is argued, improved the competitiveness of the public sector. The spur of competition has generated bids that represented levels of performance and value for money that had not previously been seen in the public or private sector. Having to compete with the private sector has pushed down costs and made Governors leading in-house bid teams think creatively about how to provide services. The National Audit Office concluded: 'The success of in-house management teams in bidding against private sector teams for the operation of prisons has been seen as an example of how performance has improved to the point that the Prison Service can now compete successfully on operating costs' (National Audit Office 2003: 5).

Governors, on the other hand, did not think that market testing had had a broader impact, other than at the individual prisons which were being market tested:

> We all kept a beady eye on what was going on with market testing but it was something that other people were going through not us. After all, what are we talking about, wasn't it only two, or was it three, prisons that were market tested in the end? That was not going to change the rest of the system. Just because the POA at Strangeways lowered their staffing levels my lot weren't going to do the same.

Today 'market testing' has been replaced by 'performance testing' whereby poorly performing prisons are publicly identified and given six months in which to improve their performance. A failure to improve means that the prison faces closure or being contracted-out to the private sector, without the opportunity to do an in-house bid. Governors suggested that this form of performance testing did have a direct impact on them. First, as a matter of professional pride Governors did not want to appear at the bottom of a performance table, and secondly, Governors did not want their prison to be identified as a poorly performing prison and subjected to performance testing:

> It's been much more about league tables, performance levels and internal competition than about private prisons. All Governors, even

73

if they don't admit it in public, try and keep off the bottom of the tables. That's not about being privatised. Exactly how many state prisons have been privatised? Well, none, that's how many and all that crap about market testing of open prisons, nothing happened – it's not the privatisation bit but professional pride. Who wants to be at the bottom of division three and heading for relegation?

I use the league tables to assess my performance against other comparable prisons and then use that to speak to staff about what we need to do to catch up. I find it a helpful tool because it's not [me] telling them to do better but other prisons' performance.

The impact on Governors has therefore been more to do with competition than with privatisation, which reflects findings elsewhere (Donahue 1989 and James *et al.* 1997: 175). Governors find themselves today operating in a more competitive, and less collegiate, world. More than ever before, their focus is on how their prisons are performing relative to other similar prisons.

Risk management and actuarial approaches

Late-modern Western society has seen a shift from 'penal welfarism' based on the rehabilitation of offenders to a 'new penology' focusing on the management of crime and risk (Garland 2001). The criminal justice system's preoccupation with risk has been well documented (Douglas 1986 and 1992; Giddens 1990; Beck 1992; Hay and Sparks 1992; Ericson and Haggert 1997; Hudson 2003; Kemshall 2003). Risk management has increasingly tended to view offenders as members of specific categories and sub-populations (Cohen 1985; Reichman 1986) or as 'aggregates of dangerous groups' (Feeley and Simon 1992: 449). The emphasis is on managerial processes dedicated to classifying offenders into risk groups, and then managing them in groups (rather than as individuals), as a means of maintaining the system at minimum cost (Feeley and Simon 1994).

This 'actuarial approach' (Bottoms 1995 and Young 1999) has been reflected within the prison walls and there has been a 'gradual infiltration of risk management principles into prison administration' (Sparks *et al.* 1996: 93). In the period from the mid-1990s Governors became less concerned with the diagnosis, intervention and treatment of individual prisoners and more occupied with aggregate classifications to ensure secure confinement and control. Less attention was given to the elimination of future crime than to minimisation of the risks of escape, suicide and of self-harm, loss of order, and 'embarrassing the minister'.

Decisions were made '. . . based not on study of the character of the offender or the nature of the offence, still less on any consideration of rights or due process, but on profiles of risk and dangerousness and on actuarial predictions of future behaviour, and danger to the public' (Faulkner 2001: 95).

Formal systems of internal rules and procedures for risk assessment have replaced Governors' 'professional' judgement of risk. This more mechanistic approach has little need for human relationships or individual judgement, and decision-making has become more automatic and impersonal (Jones 2000). A Governor described the change in this way:

> I see much less of prisoners these days and certainly make most decisions about them based on paper. I remember when I would see a prisoner before making a decision about his category or temporary release. I would interview him and reach a judgement about his suitability. It was all very subjective mind you and partly based on the cut of his jib, if you see what I am getting at. But it was much more personal and you would use your experience and judgement.

Professional assessments are increasingly seen as unimportant when compared to actuarial assessments based on factual information. Individual treatment needs have been replaced with group treatment needs, as individuals assume the shape of their diagnosed problem (Duguid 2001: 61).

New public management

Managerialism has, it can be argued, been the most significant development in the operation of our prisons in recent years. Managerialism has changed the Governors' world in a number of ways: the work they undertake; the way they are managed; and the level of discretion they can exercise.

The Conservative government in the 1980s, as part of its commitment to lowering public expenditure and redefining the role of the state, launched a major reform programme that affected the Prison Service, like other central government departments. The reform programme was based on the importation of a number of private-sector management techniques. This set of tools, ideas, beliefs and behaviours, when applied to the public sector, became known as New Public Management (NPM) (for a discussion of NPM see Ferlie *et al.* 1996). What has taken place has been described as an 'ideological process of managerialisation' which has transformed relationships of power, culture, control and accountability in public services (Clarke *et al.* 1994: 3). Managerialisation (defined here to mean the implementation of NPM) has been an incremental process in the Prison Service.

In the early 1990s Governors had limited devolved power over areas such as finance and personnel. Governors were unable, for example, to move resources from one area to another, as a former Director General pointed out: 'Governors were apparently unable to make basic decisions about such critical matters as how many people worked in their prisons, who they were, and what money was to be spent on' (Lewis 1997: 6). Managerialism emphasised 'decentralising management responsibilities' (Pollitt 1990: 55) and by the 1990s there was a clear view that 'Governors must be given the discretion to exercise their own judgements and to make a reality of their position as managers of the prison' (Home Office 1991: para. 3.7). The work of Headquarters was redirected to help Governors govern their establishments, within policies, strategies and objectives established by ministers, and subject to the resources available. The role of Headquarters was to be transformed into one that would provide 'the advice, assistance and instructions necessary to achieve those ends' (Home Office 1991: para. 3.8).

As a result, responsibility was devolved to Governors in the key areas of finance, personnel and prison regime. With devolution came increased responsibility as Governors were held to account for a range of matters over which their predecessors had no control:

> Certainly there is the whole area with devolution of responsibility for budgets, and for recruitment, selection, and promotion of staff, and a whole other range of purely devolved responsibilities. But I think probably the biggest issue has been the emphasis on actually managing the whole of the establishment in a much more cohesive kind of a way. I think, certainly going back to when I joined, it felt very much as though the Governor kind of managed almost the ethos of the establishment, and little else, and that other professionals managed other professional groups within the establishment, whereas I think it is much more now a question of the Governor managing the establishment, and all the groups of professionals in it.

The devolution of financial management gave Governors the freedom to respond flexibly to changing needs and demands. They were able to move money (and hence staff) from one area to another, and fund new initiatives locally.

> Increased devolution of financial management and accountability dramatically increased the Governor's ability to manipulate the budget to meet the strategic needs of the establishment.

With increased control over budgets came greater accountability for ensuring that the budget was not exceeded and an expectation that 'efficiency savings' would be delivered. For example, in 1995 Governors were told that they had to reduce costs by an average of four to five per cent per year, or 13.5 per cent in three years from April 1996 (HM Prison Service 1998). For the first time each Governor was required to achieve financial savings at his or her own prison.

The devolution of responsibility for personnel matters also had a major impact on Governors' work. Governors found themselves dealing directly with staff recruitment, selection and discipline. In the past, all these areas had been the responsibility of Headquarters or regional offices. Provided that Governors were able to find the funding from within their budgets they were able to create new posts, select and appoint staff, conduct promotion boards, and discipline or dismiss staff on performance or health grounds:

> With devolved personnel, you have much more freedom than you used to, but when I first took over as Governor . . . it was difficult to get rid of staff, it was difficult to manage staff, because of personnel systems, you were stuck with a staff which you didn't really have control over. Even though it takes up a lot of my time, I can now manage staffing properly.

Devolution took place in other areas such as regime development. Governors were given the freedom to provide, and manage, prisoner work at their prisons. By 1993 Governors were 'free to find local sources of work' for their prisoners (Simon 1999: 63) and some Governors embraced the 'entrepreneurial spirit' (Osborne and Gaebler 1992) with great enthusiasm:

> It was an exciting period as . . . it was suddenly up to you to decide what regime and work you wanted in your prison.

> Once we got the freedom, we could go outside the Service and look for local work opportunities. It was a bit like being a businessman and looking for local markets. We came up with some very innovative work schemes.

Governors were clear in their view that the scope for individuality increased significantly in the early 1990s, as Governors were given more devolved responsibility:

> In the days of Derek Lewis [Director General of the Prison Service 1992–95] much was devolved to Governors, things like budgets and

staffing levels. We could pretty much do what we wanted with the money as long as it was within the rules . . . It really did feel like we were running our own businesses.

Governors made good use of their devolved powers, often did not fully implement directions from Headquarters, and in some cases increasingly disregarded the centre. A significant variation between prisons in what they were delivering emerged as a consequence of Governors deciding which policy to implement and where to use their financial resources. One commentator put it this way: 'If not restricted . . . the field administrations may *de facto* become more or less independent from central headquarters or even turn their prisons into fiefdoms' (Boin 1998: 68).

The mid-1990s also saw a number of organisational failures: six exceptional-risk prisoners, including five IRA terrorists, escaped from HMP Whitemoor using firearms; a pound of Semtex was discovered in the false bottom of an artist's paintbox belonging to an IRA prisoner; guns were found at HMP Manchester and in the process of being smuggled into HMP Durham; Fred West hanged himself in Winson Green prison; and three prisoners (two of whom were category A) escaped from HMP Parkhurst, a maximum-security dispersal prison (see Lewis 1997: 150–165). This degree of organisational failure undermined political and public confidence in the Service and led some to the view that devolution had gone too far and some fundamental changes were needed.

Senior Prison Service officials came to the conclusion that the use of managerialist tools would be the most effective way of achieving the much-needed change, as these quotes from senior officials indicate:

Something had to be done . . . Some Governors were simply not implementing Orders, others were, quite frankly, not up to it. We had lost public and political confidence and things had to be changed. So we tightened up line management, built in a bit of competition and got rid of some crap Governors.

We looked at how we could make sure that things changed . . . we all knew that performance across the estate varied hugely and that some area managers were not doing their job. They were not sorting out failing prisons. Part of the problem though was a lack of data to compare prisons and when we got that we could see where things were going wrong.

We were all adopting what had previously been private-sector management tools . . . we had to improve our performance some-how, and the new management approach had started to work so we kept going with it.

I attended a few meetings around then and there was a good consensus about what we should do. To start with we needed to be clear about what was needed, set standards, tell people what they should be doing and then police them to make sure that they did it. Simple stuff really but not something that the Service had really done before.

The Prison Service had to decide how to co-ordinate, control and direct potentially 'recalcitrant' Governors. Managerialism presented itself as a strong and authoritative approach that would solve the problem. It called for strategies for the future, rational and effective use of resources, consistent delivery and vigorous pursuit of the achievement of targets.

Every organisation finds itself confronted with 'the same basic constitutional problem' of deciding what level of control is necessary to ensure minimum levels of performance and adherence to organisational requirements (Selznick 1957). The Prison Service responded to the large-scale organisational failure by opting for a more cohesive and integrated service organisation, adopting managerialist tools, and shifting power from Governors to the centre. This move to a more 'rational–legal bureaucracy', in which the central administration formulates policy, develops comprehensive rules and regulations and unceasingly monitors the prison's day-to-day activities (Jacobs 1977: 73) has had a number of consequences. A former Chief Inspector of Prisons commented: 'The numbers working in the "faceless monolith" that was Prison Service Headquarters had grown from 168 in the days of the Prison Commission to more than 1,800. From it spewed an endless stream of rules, regulations, operating standards, operating instructions, orders, targets and performance indicators . . .' (Ramsbotham 2003: 76).

In terms of Mintzberg's model of organisational design configurations, the Prison Service developed into a 'machine bureaucracy' within which the technostructure (analysts and central office administrators) became dominant, and exercised increasing control through standardisation of rules and procedures, and data collection and analysis (Mintzberg 1983). This bureaucratisation has created an organisation whose 'structure and operations are governed to a high degree by written rules' (Mann 1984: 28). A priority is now placed on prisons carrying out strictly defined tasks that produce determinable, impartial and impersonal operations for a whole range of functions within the prison. What has emerged as a result is an ever-increasing level of cohesion and uniformity in practice, with a concomitant sacrificing of local diversity and discretion.

From the point of view of Governors, there was a clear recomposition of previous modes of power within the Prison Service. Managerialism became synonymous with the demise of Governors' organisational power and a clear shift in power from Governors to the centre (defined as Headquarters and its field representatives, the area managers). Governors pointed to the way in which devolution increasingly became a fiction:

> Actually the area manager can take any bit of their budget away at any time of the year, and give it to somebody else.

> So much of my budget is ring-fenced by Headquarters for specific purpose it's hardly worth being in charge of the budget.

Other areas, which were initially devolved to Governors, were returned to central control:

> ... the contract for catering and contract for education are not signed by me, and that irritated me and it weakened my ability to effect the delivery locally of kitchen and education.

> I have seen it go back to something that is very centralised. I think they are trying to pull it back to a very centralised way.

Restrictions were placed on what Governors could deliver within their prison regime. For example, the programme accreditation process (whereby the Correctional Services Accreditation Panel authorises which offending behaviour programmes can be run in prisons – Joint Prison/ Probation Accreditation Panel 2002) is seen by some Governors as 'a further, and not entirely benign, limitation on the range and content of the programmes and courses which they can offer' (Carlen 2001: 6):

> I must admit to some niggling concerns about the current push to only deliver 'What Works' programmes. We have been doing some good interventions over many years and we are now being forced to dump them in favour of the 'What Works' programmes. I honestly question whether some of them will actually work. But the worst bit of all this is that I can no longer run what I know does work for my prisoners.

The desire to control Governors, and to improve the level of each prison's performance, manifested itself most clearly in the adoption of a performance management framework. The framework consisted of minimum standards; targets; performance indicators; and a clearly set-out personal accountability framework for Governors. The introduction of a number of these performance-regulating tools into the Prison Service has had a significant impact on Governors.

In April 1994 Minimum Operating Standards were first published. The covering letter, by the Director General, made clear that 'meeting the operational standards will be a line management responsibility' (HM Prison Service 1994e). Governors were, for the first time, made personally accountable for their establishments' achieving these defined standards.

Standards were set initially for security and later for all aspects of the prison regime. The last decade has seen the introduction of 72 standards with which each prison must comply. Standards now cover everything from accommodation and hygiene to industrial relations and regimes (HM Prison Service 2000b; Leech and Shepherd 2003: 28–32). The development of mandatory minimum standards has increasingly constrained and directed Governors in what they can and cannot do, as Governors pointed out:

> I sometimes feel that my hands are tied. We are increasingly getting to a point where every minute detail of a prison will be the subject of a standard. I have very little discretion to move away from the prescribed standards.

> It's much more like McDonald's than it was. There are huge manuals setting out standards and how to do things. We must comply with these central directives and all be the same.

> My professional judgement and skills are not needed as much these days. It's about following detailed instructions and doing what we are told.

A constant theme that caused friction between Governors and their line managers during the 1990s was whether Instructions to Governors were mandatory. This culture of non-compliance was most famously exposed by Sir John Woodcock in his report on the escape of prisoners from HMP Whitemoor: 'It could be said that what the Prison Service needs to do most of all is to comply with its own written instructions' (Woodcock 1994: para. 9.27). A similar theme was found in the Learmont Report which pointed out that 'the rules are in place. What is now needed is the resolve to abide by them' (Learmont 1995a: para. 6.15).

In response to this criticism, a new system of Prison Service Orders (PSO) and Instructions (PSI) was introduced in 1997 that made clear which elements were mandatory. These documents created comprehensive and detailed directions on how to implement policy and exercise discretion. PSO and PSI now cover all aspects of prison life and have increasingly specified what Governors should be doing. There are now 147 PSO (Leech and Shepherd 2003: 518–524), compared to only 27 Standing Orders, which they were introduced to replace. Some Governors expressed concern that their discretion had been severely curtailed by the new system:

> We have rather gone back to this tying it down on paper and you know, I mean look, two manuals came in today, when in God's name am I going to read those but there's whole pages of it that says 'the Governor will'. So I think that Headquarters has gone back towards centralised control.

> Today everything we do is specified in a manual. Do this, do that, don't do that and so on and on and on. It gets to me sometimes. Things were much simpler when the Governor just decided things. It is getting so bad that it won't be too long before there's a manual telling me what I should be wearing!

The introduction of business plans for each establishment in 1993, along with a new-style contract, further embedded a performance management approach. The 'development of new forms of contractual relationships' (Clarke *et al.* 1994: 24) was a common feature of managerialism as it was adopted in the criminal justice system. At the end of each year, the completed business plan showed the performance that had been achieved and formed the annual report for the establishment. It also contained the level of achievement against local targets. Governors were no longer able to produce subjective and anecdotal reports of the activities of their establishments, which had been the norm previously.

The new output-based quantitative annual reports allowed the area manager to assess the performance of a Governor through a detailed examination of the performance of the prison. Governors described the changes in this way:

> It came as rather a culture shock for people from the old school like me. I used to quite enjoy writing my annual report on the performance of the prison. I would wax lyrical about what had happened and what we had achieved and say what my plans were for the future.

> It all became much more visible and explicit if you know what I mean. You said at the beginning of the year what you were going to deliver and the area manager said at the end whether you had or not based on the figures.

Contained within the business plans were Key Performance Targets (KPTs), which were based on the national Key Performance Indicators (KPIs), and reflected the level of performance expected from each prison. Each prison has around 48 KPTs. The underpinning purpose of KPTs was to drive up the performance of Governors and their prisons, and to contribute to the achievement of the Service's KPIs. The then Director General pointed out to the 1997 Home Affairs Committee: 'It is irrefutable that our performance has improved enormously over this period. I think the biggest contributor has been the establishment of key performance indicators and targets. This has focused people's attention on improving performance' (Home Office 1997: vol. 1, para. 133).

The introduction of KPTs created a number of issues for Governors. It led Governors to focus on a narrow range of areas – the areas covered by the KPTs. A number of Governors were quick to point to the dangers of focusing on areas that could easily be measured, rather than on more qualitative but important aspects of the operation of a prison. As one Governor put it:

> It is easy enough to measure simple things such as escapes and drug tests through KPIs but what about other areas which are just as important like justice and fairness. The danger with the current KPIs is that they distort what a Governor focuses on. I am as guilty as the next man, I put all my efforts into hitting my KPIs and sometimes I am sad to say it is at the expense of other things.

A focus on narrow measures may therefore 'inhibit and deflect managers' (Newell 2002: 12) from more fundamental changes such as attitudinal change, how staff and prisoners relate to each other and legitimacy issues.

Governors, like managers elsewhere, were tempted to distort the data to present a 'rosy picture of their achievements' (Boyne et al. 2003: 33). Governors were quick to point out that performance levels could be 'adjusted' as KPI data was collected and 'interpreted' locally:

> I don't think KPIs have got a great deal to do with being a good prison and I say that simply on the grounds that we can massage almost any of the figures we have to meet KPIs.

> It is easy to spin the KPI data, believe me. If you want to play games with it you can. I have heard of Governors logging staff meetings and POA meetings as staff training, backdating request/complaints, reducing the frequency of PPM [planned preventative maintenance], removing people from offending behaviour courses early to get new starters; I could go on but you know what I mean.

The National Audit Office also highlighted the problems with the data collection systems and accuracy of the data collected: 'the internal monitoring of data varied considerably as did the validity of the data' (National Audit Office 2003: para. 2.6).

One of the effects of this strand of managerialism has been to direct Governors' attention to the internal functioning of their prisons and away from the social purposes of imprisonment. The Prison Service's KPIs are centred on process and outputs rather than outcomes – they are about the number of offending behaviour places and education qualifications rather than reconviction rates and crime reduction. As Feeley and Simon point out, 'the importance that recidivism once had in evaluating the performance of corrections is now being taken up by measures of system functioning' (1992: 456). This 'decoupling' of performance evaluation from external social objectives makes it more difficult to evaluate whether institutions are achieving their substantive social ends. One Governor emphatically made this point: 'we must be careful not to believe everything we see as performance improvement affecting desired outcomes: despite all our efforts the standard reconviction rate for prisoners remains the same' (Newell 2002: 10).

Governors soon found that not only were they required to provide detailed information returns but that a Standards Audit Unit had been set up to assess their level of compliance. Prisons are now faced with a barrage of internal and external audits and inspections. Many Governors expressed concern over the amount of time that has to be put into preparing audits and dealing with their aftermath:

> I think we are over-audited. There are too many people looking at what you are doing. We waste so much time preparing for audits and inspections, then doing them and then of course we have all the action plans in the reports. By the time you have read them someone else is at the gate wanting to have another audit.

> We have got more inspectors and auditors than you could shake a stick at, you know. I think really that they are great wedges of managerialism being injected into prisons.

Prisons are today measured against KPTs, audited against standards and inspected by an independent inspectorate. Yet it is possible to pass an audit, deliver the KPT performance and yet be severely criticised by the Chief Inspector on an inspection: 'High and improving scores on the indicators would still be combined with an overall performance which would be perceived as harsh, oppressive or unjust. A prison . . . may well perform well on its key performance indicators, but still be the subject of public criticism or an adverse inspection report' (Faulkner 2001: 85).

Unfortunately for Governors each monitoring mechanism has different baselines and approaches. KPTs have a narrow focus and are about delivering numbers. Audits are about systems and processes, with little or no attention to quality. If procedures are in place, documents filled in and notices displayed, then an establishment is likely to be compliant (Newell 2002). Whereas the Chief Inspector deals in a subjective appraisal of establishments based on key values and principles and focuses more on outcomes. A former Chief Inspector put it in this way:

> The Inspectorate and the Prison Service appeared to be working to two different agendas. Our parliamentary remit required us to concentrate on the treatment of and conditions for prisoners. Prison Service management concentrated on exact compliance with rules and regulations, and the achievement of a myriad of targets and performance indicators. These were more to do with process in prisons than outcomes for prisoners. (Ramsbotham 2003: 218)

From the Governor's point of view the difference of approach can produce mixed messages about an establishment's performance: 'I am sitting at my desk contemplating two reports which have arrived on my desk almost simultaneously. The Inspectorate report says I am a decent bloke trying to run a prison on tuppence ha'penny. The report of the security audit basically says that I am the handmaiden of Satan' (Prison Governors Association 2001b).

Whatever the criticism of these arrangements, Governors are today far more closely monitored against standards and plans, and have to account for what their establishment delivers. Governors believe that their work is subject to greater scrutiny, and that they are far more accountable for the detail of their work than their predecessors.

> Everything is measured and there is much more accountability.

> It's clearly a much more, or it's expected to be a much more accountable role, there's much more scrutiny over everything . . .

One of the most far-reaching developments in recent years has been the strengthening of the line management of Governors. These changes have had a major impact on how Governors operate and on their level of accountability. Until the late 1980s the organisational structure failed to provide clear and effective line management of Governors (HM Prison Service 1989b) and there was confusion as to whether Headquarters and regional offices existed to advise or to direct, as one Governor reflected:

> I used to work for a wonderful Governor. He was a delightful man and people would phone from Headquarters and his first question was 'to whom do I speak?' and I think if they were anything below about senior principal, he would tell them to go away and find somebody who had the proper rank to address him and then they would clearly ask him to do things and you would hear him say no, no, no, and they obviously would say at the end why and he would

say, because I am too old, I am too tired and I am too rich, good morning ... He shouldn't really have done it but he actually got away with it and he wouldn't anymore.

The main weakness of the structure was that the management of Governors was in the hands of only four regional directors and their teams. Many regional staff regarded their role as being to provide support and advice rather than manage their Governors. The span of command for each regional director was between 25 and 39 Governors, which was regarded as 'impossibly wide'. As a result, there was 'no clear and effective management chain between the top of the Service and Governors' (HM Prison Service 1989b). A number of Governors spoke of the distant management exhibited under the regional structure:

There was nobody to say nay or question it and, as I think you know, there was never any contact, or very minimal contact, with regional office.

Regional directors ... didn't visit too regularly and Governors very much did as they wanted.

A decision was taken in 1991 to restructure the management of Governors, with the creation of geographical groupings of nine or 10 establishments under 15 area managers. These changes fundamentally changed the way Governors were managed. Governors were, for the first time, closely monitored and supervised. There was some sensitivity over the impact that the area managers would have on Governors, which led the Service to make clear that 'strengthening management should not be seen as a threat to the position of the governor as the person in charge of the establishments' (HM Prison Service 1989b: 20). However, the creation of this 'new managerial strata' (McLaughlin and Muncie 1994: 120) resulted in a redistribution of power and resources from Governors to area managers.

Governors pointed out that there was still some confusion in the early 1990s as to whether the area manager existed to support, advise or direct Governors.

One of the things that struck me forcibly about being in Headquarters and seeing a number of area managers operate, both from their own offices and in area managers' meetings, is that there is no agreed structure for the way area managers operate. Each area is managed as a function of the personality of the individual, very much so. There is no real sense of what exactly the area manager should be doing.

The inability of the area manager to fetter a Governor's statutory discretion added to the ambiguity, as a Home Office review noted:

> ... neither the area manager nor anyone else can give instructions to governors on the matter on which they have statutory discretion. In accordance with the general principles of administrative law, no one may fetter the governor's discretion in exercising such powers. The current arrangement is, therefore, somewhat of a contrivance. Moreover, it sends a signal to the service about the degree of independence which governors enjoy which is not completely compatible with effective line management, and which is undesirable in an organisation with no established culture of following instructions. (Home Office 1995)

The then Director General had no doubt about the role of area manager:

> Some governors claimed that the 1952 Prison Act gave them the freedom of action and immunity from instruction by their bosses, and some area managers behaved as though they believed that to be the case ... Time and time again I had to drive home the message that operational directors, area managers and governors were all line managers with both authority and responsibility for results. (Lewis 1997: 78)

By 1996 it was clear that Governors had lost the internal power struggle and an assessment of the role of area managers concluded that they were the essential mechanism for the supervision, control and development of an operational Prison Service (HM Prison Service 1996c). The transfer of power to area managers was completed in 1997, when all policy formulation responsibility was removed from them in order to enable them to focus solely on line-managing their Governors.

As a result of these developments, there is now much closer supervision of a Governor's work than has ever been the case. Area managers now supervise around eight prisons each, compared to previous arrangements where one regional director managed between 25 and 39 establishments.

> The area manager is able to see his or her governing Governor at least every month ... to visit each of their establishments at least monthly.

> I don't think you, as a Governor, now feel so autonomous as previous Governors did. The introduction of area managers changed that.

Each area manager now has a significant area office that includes analysts; auditors; senior investigating officer; and specialist advisors (works, personnel, security, equal opportunities, regimes, drugs, resettlement):

> It sometimes feels that the area manager has more admin staff than I've got to run [a small training prison]. She has more bag carriers and experts than the old regional director had to run a huge region. I guess she is only protecting her back and keeping an eye on what her Governors are doing but it does seem excessive.

There has been a transformation of the relationship between Governors and Headquarters. Supportive supervision has been replaced with taut and robust management. The introduction of contracts and Service Level Agreements has reinforced the contractual and performance-based nature of the relationship:

> Governors are just managed much more than they ever used to be, so that has affected very much the approach to the job.

> Governors feel that they have less freedom in terms of the line management that came in under area managers – we are less autonomous.

> My new area manager did pay a lot more attention to detail and did want to be involved a fair bit in what was happening with the place . . . she said what I will want is to be assured that you are delivering and when I come round I will expect to see certain things.

> I think some area managers are more into audit mode, Mr Clipboard, going around ticking the boxes, asking where are the cleaning schedules, where's this, where's that, and that . . . What they all have in common, and it's increasingly becoming quite clear, is the drive for them all to get their Governors to achieve the targets that are set for them . . . They are not particularly interested in why you haven't achieved it, it's how well you have achieved it.

One of the consequences of managerialism is that it tends to 'relocate professionalism up the hierarchy' (McWilliams 1992). Changes to line management arrangements led some Governors to raise the issue of who was really governing prisons. The level of involvement, and direction of day-to-day matters, suggests that a number of area managers have interpreted their role as being that of 'super' Governor:

I worked for one area manager, who would basically just shout at people and tell the Governors what he expected them to do in minute detail on just about everything in the prison.

Some of these area managers see themselves as 'super Governors' and try to run your prison for you. Always phoning and faxing wanting some stupid bit of information or asking you why you did this and that, or more often why you have not done something. You might not mind as much if they were actually any good at running their own prisons. Many of them were crap at it or only governed for a short while.

The more performance-based, hands-on approach adopted by area managers has led some Governors to question the legitimacy of area managers:

They are always bloody interfering. If it is not difficult enough governing, you have now got to keep looking over your shoulder as the bloody area manager is second-guessing you all the time. It has changed the way we do the job. You ask any of the Governors you are interviewing, they will tell you that you spend most of the time doing stuff for area office rather than running the prison.

At first Governors generally welcomed the new approach that NPM brought, as it resulted in increased devolution and greater freedom from the centre. However, it soon became clear that the introduction of various managerial tools would increase Governors' accountability. The late 1990s saw the development of various forms of competition (private-sector involvement, market testing, performance testing and league tables); the setting of clear standards of performance; the creation of key performance indicators and targets; development of robust line management to monitor and assess delivery; and the construction of an audit infrastructure to ensure compliance. Middle management (area managers) has been redeployed to rationalise and regulate the daily operation of the prison system – what Foucault presciently called 'supervising the process of the activity rather than the result' (Foucault 1979: 137).

Managerialism has not been without its critics. Governors have suggested that the danger with over reliance on performance data is that it 'can mislead us into thinking we are achieving something we are not' (Newell 2002: 10) and the Prison Service will become 'an organisation that is cynical, overshadowed by managerialism and which values people less than statistics' (Wagstaffe 2002: 4). A former Chief Inspector of Prisons expressed his own reservations about managerialism:

Managerialism includes the fallacious belief that you can achieve [the Prison Service goals] by demanding and measuring exact compliance with budgets, targets, performance indicators, orchestrating the process with a plethora of rules, operating standards, operating instructions, orders, visions and mission statements, all backed up by frequent reports and returns on everything you can think of, often reporting the same thing in different ways to a variety of different people. (Ramsbotham 2001: 43)

As a result of these managerialist changes some at the centre began to see Governors as managers whose role was to manage a 'service unit' and ensure that it met targets, delivered services according to laid-down standards and kept within budget. The then Director General of the Prison Service was robust in his defence of the introduction of a performance culture:

The year [1999–2000] saw a greater emphasis on firm and effective line management based on the need to deliver on our targets. Detailed monthly meetings between the DDG and area managers closely examined the performance of all their establishments against key performance targets and were followed up with focused line management by area managers of Governors. This process has allowed poor performers to be identified and the issues addressed and dealt with at an early stage. (HM Prison Service 2000c: 28)

While it can be argued that the managerialisation of Governors was a necessary 'corollary of the dismantling of the structures of bureau-professionalism' (Clarke *et al.* 1994: 25), some suspected a more sinister motive. By creating managers out of Governors, it was thought that they could be more easily controlled.

Chapter 5

Today's Governors – origins, career paths and ideologies

There is little information in the public domain about the background and characteristics of prison staff. This is particularly the case with Governors, where media representation has added little clarity. Information on Governors' origins, career paths, motivation and ideologies can provide an important perspective on why they operate in the way that they do, and give an opportunity to identify common features amongst Governors, as well as highlighting significant differences.

Demographic and family background

Of the 42 Governors in the research sample 86 per cent were male, which is similar to the figure reported in other studies (Cawley 2001 and Liebling and Price 2001). While the percentage of female Governors has increased to 14 per cent, from the two per cent recorded in a 1997 study (Bryans 2000a: 16), females remain under-represented within the ranks of Governors. A similar gender imbalance is replicated in other jurisdictions (for example, in the USA 86 per cent of wardens are male, Flanagan *et al.* 1996: 388) – and is found at senior levels in all criminal justice agencies and services (Home Office 2001: 43–47).

No Governors in the sample were from a minority ethnic group. At the time of the research, there was only one Governor from a minority ethnic group. Only 0.9 per cent of assistant and deputy governors are from a minority ethnic group (Liebling and Price 2001: 18). This again reflects the situation in other criminal justice agencies and services where minority ethnic representation is low amongst senior staff (Home Office 2000: 62–64).

Governors in the sample were born in the range 1939 to 1963, but nearly half were born between 1944 and 1948, as Table 5.1 shows. The majority of Governors (67 per cent) in the sample were over 50 years old.

Table 5.1 Age Profile

Year born	Percentage (%)
1959–1963	14
1954–1958	9.5
1949–1953	9.5
1944–1948	48
1939–1943	19
Total	100
N = 42	

Governors were asked to identify their fathers' employment status at the time that the Governors joined the Prison Service. As Table 5.2 shows, just over a third (37 per cent) of Governors had a father who was in manual work and just over a third (38 per cent) came from intermediate and junior non-manual backgrounds. These origins are similar to the current socio-economic group distribution of the population as a whole, where 44 per cent are in the manual group, and 35 per cent in the intermediate and junior non-manual group. A slightly higher percentage of Governors (25 per cent), compared to the general population (22 per cent), come from a professional and managerial background (National Statistics 2001).

Table 5.2 Socio-economic origin

Socio-economic group	Percentage (%) at time of joining Prison Service
Professional	7
Employers and managers	18
Intermediate and junior non-manual	38
Skilled manual	22
Semi-skilled manual	10
Unskilled manual	5
Total	100
N = 42	

Many Governors (61 per cent) regard themselves as having been socially upwardly mobile, compared to their family origin. This is particularly true of Governors who joined as prison officers, where 86 per cent considered that they had moved significantly from their family's socio-economic group.

Few Governors come from Prison Service family backgrounds. Unlike chief constables, (where between 10 and 20 per cent have a father who was a police officer – Wall 1998: 289), only one Governor had a family connection to the Prison Service:

> My father was then in the Colonial Prison Service; my sister in the Women's Prison Service. And so, there was a family background to it.

However, this may be changing as five per cent of Governors in the sample indicated that they had a son or daughter working in the operational Prison Service.

Education and previous occupation

The type of education received, and the level of qualifications obtained, are important indicators of the social worlds from which someone has emerged (Stanworth 1984: 251). As Table 5.3 shows, 72 per cent of Governors went to grammar or private (non-state) schools. This is a much higher percentage than is to be found in the general population of similar ages to the Governors (Halsey *et al.* 1980). Governors have therefore tended to be drawn from the educationally more successful strata of the intermediate and junior non-manual and skilled manual socio-economic groups. The number of Governors who had a private education has declined in recent years, to the current position where all the Governors in the sample who attended private schools are over 50 years old.

Table 5.3 Schooling

Type of school attended by Governors	Percentage
Grammar	48
Private	24
Comprehensive	16
Other	12
Total	100
N = 42	

Not only have Governors achieved more educationally than the norm for their socio-economic background, in terms of the type of school they attended, but they also performed well at those schools. Over 90 per cent of Governors have some educational qualifications, as shown in Table 5.4. A large number of Governors (41 per cent) in the study have university degrees, which compares to 25 per cent of chief constables (Reiner 1991: 59). A similar situation exists in the USA where just over 50 per cent of Wardens have a degree or similar qualification (Flanagan *et al.* 1996: 388).

Table 5.4   Highest educational attainment

Highest qualification obtained	Percentage
None	7
O level/GCSE	26
A level	26
Degree	41
Total	100
N = 42	

Attainment of a degree should not be mistaken for full-time attendance at university. A quarter of those Governors in the sample who had a degree obtained that degree whilst working in the Prison Service and studying part-time. Of particular interest is the relatively large number of Governors in the sample who have a degree that is occupationally linked. The most frequently occurring subjects for the degrees are psychology (24 per cent); law (18 per cent); sociology (18 per cent) and criminology (12 per cent). All of the Governors who completed their degree whilst employed by the Prison Service studied a work-related subject such as criminology, management or law.

The majority of Governors (81 per cent) had some experience of outside employment between leaving school and joining the Prison Service. Those recruited directly from university account for only 19 per cent of Governors. Governors in the sample had a diverse range of pre-Prison Service experience, as Table 5.5 shows.

A number of Governors (19 per cent) had been in the armed forces and of these three quarters had held a commission. The small number of Governors with an armed forces background contrasts sharply with earlier periods where ex-armed forces Governors were the norm, and with chief constables where half had completed military service of some sort (Wall 1998: 273).

Table 5.5 Occupation prior to joining the Prison Service

Occupation prior to joining Prison Service	Percentage
University student	19
Armed forces	19
Police	12
Teaching	12
Management	10
Social work	7
Other	21
Total	100
N = 42	

Career paths

The Governors in the sample joined the operational Prison Service between 1961 and 1993, with half the sample joining before 1975. The period in which they joined is shown in more detail in Table 5.6.

Table 5.6 Year entered Prison Service

Year of entry	Percentage
1960–1965	14
1966–1970	26
1971–1975	14
1976–1980	24
1981–1985	19
Post 1985	3
Total	100
N = 42	

Governors entered the Service at a variety of ages, which reflects the different modes of recruitment. The overall pattern is shown in Table 5.7. Over half the Governors (64 per cent) entered the Service when they were 25 or younger.

Earlier chapters have described how modes of entry have changed over the years. A third of Governors in the study joined the Service as prison officers. Of these, 64 per cent were promoted through the various uniformed grades, and the others (36 per cent) were promoted directly from prison officer to assistant governor, on a fast-track scheme. The majority of Governors in the sample (65 per cent) joined on a direct-entry assistant governor scheme.

Table 5.7 Age entered Prison Service

Age joined	Percentage
21–25	64
26–30	17
31–35	19
Total	100
N = 42	

Table 5.8 Mode of entry to Prison Service

Mode of entry	Percentage
Prison officer	33
Assistant governor	65
Other	2
Total	100
N = 42	

Governors who joined as direct-entry assistant governors before 1972 were not required to serve a period of time as a prison officer. Of the sample of Governors, 26 per cent fell into this category and have never served in uniform as prison officers, as Table 5.9 indicates.

Table 5.9 Period served as a Prison Officer grade

Period as a prison officer	Percentage
None	26
Fewer than six months	29
Six months to one year	14
More than one year	31
Total	100
N = 42	

A number of Governors (29 per cent) in the sample were required to serve a period of up to six months as prison officers. The amount of time varied with the requirements of the scheme in the year in which they joined. The experience as prison officers was generally welcomed:

> I got to spend a few days doing each officer job in the prison, from courts to bathhouse. Because they knew that I was going to be an AG [assistant governor], I got all the worst jobs like supervising the

collection of shit parcels from the yards and supervising Cat A exercise in two foot of snow. It was bloody hard at the time but helped me to understand how a prison works. It also helped me realise that the job of an officer is very routine and monotonous but things can blow up at any moment.

A further 14 per cent, who were under 24 years old when they joined, were required to spend a longer period (of up to 12 months) as an officer:

I did a year as a prison officer at [a small local prison] which is very useful. Learnt a lot about the job which has helped me through the years. You got to know about the Spanish practices, how the POA worked and where staff hide in a prison. I learnt how to handle prisoners – to see the tricks they get up to . . . it was worth doing the time in uniform.

Spent nearly a year as an officer. The first few months were very useful but after that it was a waste of time. Didn't learn much, just wanted to get on and be an AG [assistant governor]. But it has helped my street cred with staff as I can point out that I have done their job – I just don't tell them for how long.

Governors who joined as prison officers (33 per cent) spent between 18 months and 24 years in the prison officer grades before joining the governor grade. The average period spent in the prison officer grades for those promoted directly to assistant governor was seven years. Those who served as a prison officer, senior officer and principal officer took an average of 20 years to achieve promotion into the governor grades. An indication of the range of experiences that those Governors who joined as prison officers went through before becoming assistant governors can be seen in the following quote:

I was posted to [a large local prison] initially as an officer in 1966. Promoted to senior officer in July 1972 to [a category C training prison]. Promoted to PO [principal officer] in July 1977 back to [the large local prison]. Sideways move in April 1980 to Region to work on what was then the old manpower teams. Nineteen eight-four moved to [a small remand centre for young offenders] as Chief Officer. Mid-1987 came across into the governor grades with Fresh Start.

At some point in their career, regardless of mode of entry, all Governors in the sample (with the exception of one individual who was part of a cross hierarchical move scheme) have served as assistant governors. The number of assistant governor posts that the Governors in the sample occupied varies, as can be seen in Table 5.10.

Table 5.10 Number of assistant governor posts occupied before being appointed a Governor

Number of assistant governor posts	Percentage
None	3
1	5
2	14
3	38
4	26
5 or more	14
Total	100
N = 42	

The majority of Governors (83 per cent) had occupied a deputy governor post at some point in their careers and of these 40 per cent had been deputy Governor at two prisons. However, as Table 5.11 shows, 17 per cent of the Governors in the sample had not occupied a deputy governor's post.

Table 5.11 Number of deputy governor posts occupied before being appointed a Governor

Number of deputy governor posts	Percentage
None	17
1	43
2	40
Total	100
N = 42	

In order to establish their breadth of experience before their appointment to a governorship, Governors in the sample were asked how many prisons they had worked in during their careers. The results are shown in Table 5.12. The majority (98 per cent) of Governors had worked in four or more prisons. This high level of mobility amongst Governors has tended to reinforce the perception held by officers that Governors are transitory and are only 'passing through' a particular prison (see Chapter 8). The number of prisons that Governors had worked in was not related to their mode of entry.

Table 5.12 Number of prisons Governors had worked in during their careers

Number of Prisons	Percentage
1	0
2 to 3	2
4 to 6	62
7 or more	36
Total	100
N = 42	

The Governors were also asked about the types of prison in which they had served. There are five main types of prison (local/remand, dispersal, training, young offenders and female – see Chapter 3). While only seven per cent of Governors had worked in all five types of prison, 74 per cent had worked in three or more different types.

Table 5.13 Number of different types of prisons Governors had worked in during their careers

Number of types	Percentage
1	2
2	24
3	43
4	24
5	7
Total	100
N = 42	

A number of assistant governor and deputy governor posts are non-operational and exist outside of prisons. These posts deal with policy matters or prisoner management issues (such as population or incident management) at Prison Service Headquarters, or are in the training organisation. Only a small number (12 per cent) of Governors in the sample had not worked in a non-operational post. This compares to 98 per cent of prison officers who had not worked in a post outside a prison (Marsh *et al.* 1985: 112). The Governors who had joined as prison officers accounted for the majority (80 per cent) of those whose experience was limited to operational prison-based postings. A large number (31 per cent) of Governors had experience of more than one type of post outside an establishment, as Table 5.14 indicates.

Table 5.14 Experience in posts outside a prison

Type of post	Percentage
Policy	19
Prisoner management	19
Training	19
More than one type	31
None	12
Total	100
N = 42	

The data suggest that prior to being promoted to the rank of Governor, not only were assistant governors required to work in a number of prisons, they were also required to work in different types of prison and in non-operational roles.

Governors in the sample had spent between seven and 33 years in the Prison Service prior to their appointment to the office of Governor. (Only one Governor had been in the Service for a shorter period.) A third had been in the Service for more than 20 years, with a further third having served between 16 and 20 years, as Table 5.15 shows.

Table 5.15 Number of years in the Prison Service before being appointed a Governor

Number of years	Percentage
Fewer than 10	5
11 to 15	26
16 to 20	36
More than 20	33
Total	100
N = 42	

The age of the Governor on first appointment to the office also varied, as Table 5.16 shows. Just under a third of the sample were 40 or under at the time of their appointment, compared to half who were in their forties and 19 per cent who were over 50.

Governors also varied in the amount of governing that they had done, as Tables 5.17 and 5.18 show. A third of the sample had been a Governor for 10 or more years, and over half had been a Governor of more than one prison. On the other hand, 40 per cent of the sample had been a Governor for three years or fewer and 45 per cent had only governed one prison.

Table 5.16 Age when first appointed a Governor

Age when appointed Governor	Percentage
40 or under	29
41 to 45	26
46 to 50	26
51 to 55	19
Total	100
N = 42	

Table 5.17 Number of years as a Governor

Years as a Governor	Percentage
Fewer than 1	7
1 to 3	33
4 to 6	22
7 to 9	7
10 or more	31
Total	100
N = 42	

Table 5.18 Number of posts as a Governor

Number of posts as a Governor	Percentage
1	46
2	26
3	24
4	2
5 or more	2
Total	100
N = 42	

At the time of interview around a third of the sample had been in post for fewer than two years, a third in post for two to three years and a further third for four or more years, as Table 5.19 demonstrates.

Motivation and job satisfaction

Sociologists have developed the concept of an 'orientation to work', referring to the wants and expectations which people bring to their

Table 5.19 Time in current post

Time in current Governor post	Percentage
Fewer than six months	5
Six months to one year	24
2 to 3 years	36
4 to 5 years	19
More than 5 years	16
Total	100
N = 42	

employment, and the interpretation which they thus give to their work. A person's orientation to work is seen therefore as a key factor, which shapes an individual's attitudinal and behavioural patterns at work. It is reasonable to assume that Governors' initial expectations were a contributing factor in the explanation of their subsequent perspectives and practices at work. Their original mindset and motivation for doing the work was what Reiner refers to as 'the primary grid for constituting subsequent experience' (Reiner 1991: 62).

This section explores what attracted Governors to join the Prison Service at the outset of their careers. From a methodological point of view, establishing retrospectively Governors' original reasons for joining the Prison Service is somewhat problematic. Subsequent events, maturation and experience may well have led Governors to reinterpret their reasons for joining. It has also been suggested that 'memories are reconstructed in the light of present concerns and that people will be vague about the events of years ago' (Sapsford and Jupp 1996: 5).

The reasons given by Governors in the sample for joining the Service can be grouped into 'instrumental' ones (extrinsic, material aspects of the job such as pay, status, security and career prospects) and 'non-instrumental' ones (intrinsic to the work itself such as the interest or social utility of the role). Some Governors expressed mixed reasons for joining, which were both instrumental and non-instrumental.

The vast majority of Governors in the sample (76 per cent) expressed a non-instrumental reason for joining the Prison Service. A smaller percentage of Governors who joined as prison officers (26 per cent), compared to those who joined as assistant governors (50 per cent), expressed a non-instrumental reason for joining. This perhaps reflects the original job expectations of prison officers and assistant governors. People joining as assistant governors were anticipating doing more rehabilitative and managerial work, whereas people joining to be prison officers expected to be doing more routine custodial work.

The reasons for joining also varied with the period in which the Governor was recruited. Recruitment advertising in the 1960s was focused on the ability to change offenders. By the mid-1970s the emphasis was more on 'management with a social purpose' and in the early 1980s the job of assistant governor was being described as that of 'manager'. Over 80 per cent of Governors joining as assistant governors in the 1960s did so for vocational reasons (social utility, reforming prisoners, 'doing good'), compared to only 27 per cent who joined after 1976.

The primary non-instrumental reason given was a vocational one (33 per cent), and in particular the desire to work with offenders.

> Quite simply, I'd always wanted to work with offenders. And that was the beginning and the end of it.

> It was sense of a vocation, no doubt about it . . . the attraction was being involved with offenders and trying to effect some change.

For 17 per cent of Governors the mixture of social work and management was the challenge of the role:

> I wanted to do something of value to society generally. I wanted to do a job in management, I wanted to do something in the public sector . . . It was the combination of managing in a social work environment that made me do the Prison Service.

> It was two things together. Advertisements at the time billed it as management with a social work purpose. I was a social scientist, I was actually going to be a teacher but was also interested in doing a management job.

The variety and excitement of the work, rather than the nature of the work itself, encouraged a number of Governors (14 per cent) to apply:

> I think it was the notion of doing something different, doing something that was potentially quite challenging, doing something that was slightly out of the norm.

> Essentially, I just wanted a job, a job which would interest me. It did interest me, not because of any need or desire to reform people or to be a manager or what else. I just wanted an interesting job.

There were a small number (seven per cent) of Governors who were interested in the job because of its managerial nature:

The advert was very managerial and that is what attracted me. I wanted to be a manager rather than a Borstal housemaster and change people. I am a bit dubious about people who join with this great desire to reform people, because usually they fail miserably at doing it . . . But that's about it really, I mean there was no great desire to do good.

For a few others (five per cent) it was the disciplinary and regimented environment that was the attraction:

I thought, well, this is quite interesting and the administrative tasks appealed to me – I like order. I had been in a Service, military background, and to me the Prison Service seemed a reasonable chance of maintaining service to the Crown, working in a disciplined environment and doing something useful for the community.

Only 14 per cent of Governors in the sample expressed an instrumental reason for joining the Prison Service. The reasons were varied but included career structure, job security and salaries, as the following quotes indicate:

I wanted a second career because I was 33 at the time. I wanted a career that gave me an opportunity of getting in at a management level. The Prison Service was the first one I saw like that.

I joined the Prison Service for money, because I couldn't afford to pay the mortgage and my wife was pregnant. People told me I could double my pay overnight, which I did.

Other reasons for joining included:

There were hardly any women governors, that did it, and that is really what hooked me. I wanted to show that women could do the job.

Joining the Prison Service genuinely was for a bet and I was in the mess and the barman was reading a newspaper and I could see an advert that said join the Prison Service and he said, 'Bet you won't do that.' I said, 'OK then, I will', and then when my Dad said I couldn't, I thought bugger you and did.

A number of Governors in the sample (10 per cent) offered mixed reasons for joining the Prison Service, in which intrinsic attractions were inextricably linked with more instrumental considerations of money or security.

It looked like quite an interesting job and I didn't have any great technical skills. My strength was mainly dealing with people, and I thought, Prison Governor, sounds like a nice thing to aspire to. Seemed a safe job, and money was good.

To be honest the main reason was because there was good pay and accommodation. It also met my need to work with people.

Many people joining the Prison Service as assistant governors do not go on to become Governors. Some decide that they do not want the responsibility that the role of Governor brings; others discover that their knowledge, experience or competence is judged not to be sufficient to merit promotion to Governor.

For one interviewee, the reason he wanted to be a Governor was self-evident:

That's why I joined. I joined to be the Governor.

Other Governors suggested a range of different 'instrumental' and 'non-instrumental' reasons for wanting to be a Governor, rather than a single source of motivation. These reasons tended to focus on the 'intrinsic' nature of the work such as achievement, responsibility and self-esteem; factors that have been described as the higher-level moti-vators (Maslow 1954). There was less mention of lower-level motivators and 'extrinsic' factors such as job security, pay and social status.

Promotion to the Office of Governor was regarded by some as a natural step from the deputy governor role. The Prison Service is a hierarchical organisation and personal success is often measured by promotion, and particularly appointment to the role of Governor. People regard becoming a Governor as the pinnacle of their career. For these Governors the motivation was about career path, achievement and the desire to be head of a prison:

I suppose it's just about the next challenge, it's just about the next logical career path . . . The ultimate achievement is becoming the Governor.

The ability to control what happens in, and to exert a personal influence on, the operation of a prison was the underpinning motivation for a number of Governors. This was described in a variety of ways but the central theme was around the Governor being the key person in the prison:

I wanted to stamp my own sort of hallmark on what was delivered. You see yourself as the number one with the opportunity of influencing the way the institution runs, beginning to put into it some of the things which you feel are important, the values that are important.

One Governor seemed to be have the job pushed upon him, without any particular desire on his part to be a Governor:

It was thrust upon me. I was quite happy being the Dep and my Area Manager wanted me to take over. I had had no thoughts. I mean, I thought about progressing up through the ranks, yes, but I had no burning desire to be a Governor.

Another was more cavalier in his motivation:

[I had] a kind of vague sense that I'd got an understanding of how this needed to be done, so I wanted to have a go.

Governors in the sample were also asked, having been appointed to a governorship, whether the role gave them job satisfaction. The aim was to look at the broad domain of a Governor's satisfaction with his or her overall job, rather than with any specific facets (Brayfield and Rothe 1951). Job satisfaction is a subjective, individual-level feeling reflecting whether a person's needs are or are not being met by a particular job (Lambert *et al.* 2002: 117); the challenge presented by work; the level of autonomy; the sense of achievement; recognition for effort or quality of work; and also the earnings and other rewards obtained (Culley *et al.* 1999: 21).

Of the sample of Governors, 87 per cent stated that they were satisfied overall with their job. Previous research indicates that job satisfaction is positively related to occupational status (Gruenberg 1980). One would expect therefore that Governors would have higher satisfaction levels than other prison staff. The current research supports this view, as Governors' level of satisfaction exceeded the level found for prison staff, which was 64 per cent in a 2001 study (HM Prison Service 2001b: 11).

Governors might be expected to be generally unhappy with their work if commentators were correct in their claim that prisons were dehumanising to staff and prisoner alike and that Governors were in a beleaguered profession. These perspectives do not seem to be borne out by the data. The 1998 Workplace Employee Relations Survey found that job satisfaction amongst managers was 71 per cent (Culley *et al.* 1999: 22). Governors seem to derive satisfaction from their work at a similar, or indeed slightly higher, level to that found among managers as an occupational category. Many Governors indicated that they would take the job again without hesitation, felt the job measured up to the expectations they had when they first became a Governor, and would recommend their job to a good friend.

Governors gave a variety of reasons for their high level of job satisfaction. A number of Governors pointed to their involvement with people as being the most satisfying element of their job. For many their ability to impact in a positive way on the lives of prisoners was the most rewarding aspect. There is a close link between the sentiments expressed and the credo three ideology discussed later. The following quotes typify the sentiments expressed by Governors:

> I suppose at the end of the day it's dealing with people which gives job satisfaction. It's the dealing with prisoners however difficult and however complicated their problems are, and somehow ameliorating their pain and their misery.

> It began to offer me what I particularly wanted from my working life. It was primarily dealing with people. Seeing those people out there succeed gives me a sense of achievement.

The nature of the job itself was at the heart of their job satisfaction for other Governors. In particular, Governors spoke of the variety of work that they undertook, and the fact that no two days were the same. They enjoyed the daily challenges and having to deal with complex issues:

> I think it's a very fulfilling job. Many jobs are, but I think in terms of daily challenges, the beauty of being a Governor is the fact that it is so varied . . . Nowhere else do you get the complete variety and complete responsibility that you get within a prison environment.

> I think it's the best job in the world, being a prison Governor . . . I think you would be hard pushed to find a job that has got so much interest, so much variety and so much fun in it. It really is enjoyable.

A number of Governors spoke of job satisfaction in relation to their ability to do the job well. For them it was a sense of personal achievement in running an effective prison that they found most worthwhile:

> It's the satisfaction of trying to do what I now know to be an incredibly difficult job, to do it well, that I find the most rewarding.

During the interviews, Governors did however point to a number of things that reduced their level of job satisfaction. In particular, Governors spoke of the lack of resources and increased bureaucracy as being the most frustrating and least satisfying elements of their job, as the following quotes suggest:

I still want to be in a position where I can influence for the good and that is why I've found the last four years very frustrating. I have felt unable, because of various constraints, to change anything radically for the good. [A large local prison] for the past four years has made very little progress regime-wise . . . We've had no success – I've had no success during my time as Governor in changing that.

There are times when I could just throw my keys away, when the frustration gets too much. You're not asking for a lot of money but you just can't get through the red tape, or you're stuck with an intransigent group of people and feel as if you're just knocking your head against a wall.

The other main factor leading to reduced job satisfaction was a loss of autonomy (see Chapter 6), as these quotes reveal:

I don't enjoy the job as much as I did. Things are different now than they were when I first became a Governor. As Governor of [a training prison] I have less freedom than my predecessor did, less discretion and more interference by reptile towers [Headquarters]. It is starting to feel like I am not in charge of my own prison any more.

They don't want Governors like me any more. They want managers who do KPIs and manage a budget. Governors are being screwed down these days – there are hundreds of bloody orders and instructions all wanting me to do something, or to stop doing something . . . Some of the fun has gone out of the job.

As no previous data exists on the level of job satisfaction amongst Governors, it is not possible to assess whether job satisfaction levels have changed as a result of contemporary developments in prison administration. The Prison Service staff survey found a nine per cent reduction in the level of staff satisfaction between 2000 and 2001 (HM Prison Service 2001b: 11). One might extrapolate from these findings that the level of satisfaction amongst Governors may also have fallen, as they are being caught in the uncomfortable nexus of increasing problems (overcrowding, reducing budgets, serious incidents) and shrinking administrative discretion.

Ideology – values, beliefs and goals

While Governors work within specified formal procedures, and are constrained by numerous rules, orders and instructions, they retain a considerable amount of discretion. How Governors exercise this discretion is shaped, at least in part, by their underlying ideologies and value sets. The nature of the relationship between ideology and practice is, however, both 'complex and unpredictable' (Rutherford 1994: 2). Governors may not make decisions with explicit reference to their ideological preferences, but those preferences underpin and influence their decision-making. This was made clear by a number of Governors during the course of the interviews:

> From my point of view, and from my observation, I have seen lots of Governors who have had 'a bee in their bonnet' about certain things, and that might be based on their own feeling, their own political, religious and moral beliefs.

> I think that many of the people that I have worked with have shown strong ideals, if you like, of where they wanted to go. And I think that has underpinned everything they've done, particularly if you are someone who comes in with a strong moral belief, and a strong religious belief.

Little is known about the values and beliefs that shape the work of criminal justice practitioners. One study did however look at the orientation of criminal justice practitioners (Rutherford 1994). Rutherford hypothesised that the values and beliefs that shaped the daily work and professional careers of criminal justice practitioners fell into three credos or clusters: 'The first of these embraces the punitive degradation of offenders. The second cluster speaks less to moral purpose than to issues of management; pragmatism, efficiency, and expediency are the themes that set the tone. Third, . . . there is the cluster of liberal and humanitarian values' (Rutherford 1994: 3).

Given the importance of Governors' underpinning ideologies to their approach to governing, the current study looked to generate a narrative that explored Governors' working credos. In order to obtain that data Governors were asked about their values, beliefs, motivations and levels of job satisfaction.

Few of the Governors in the sample expressed a precisely formulated working ideology when asked about their values and beliefs. Governors are not encouraged to articulate their beliefs and values in their daily work, or to discuss such issues with colleagues:

> The Prison Service is a very macho organisation – we don't speak about what we feel and not many people go on about what they believe . . . It is usually only after a few pints that Governors open up and talk about what they believe in.

You know, this is the first time that I have been asked to speak about my beliefs and values since finishing the AG's course [initial training course for assistant governors]. It is not something we talk about much.

Governors' values and beliefs tended to emerge when discussing operational matters, rather than when asked to focus on their belief systems.

Some Governors indicated that they had changed their values and beliefs during their career, reinforcing Polkinghorne's view that 'self . . . is not a static thing or substance, but a configuration of personal events into an historical unity which includes not only what has been but also anticipates what we will be' (Polkinghorne 1988: 50). The reasons for changing varied: for some it was the maturation process; or the experiences they had gone through as governor grades; others had been influenced by what had occurred in the wider environment.

While Governors indicated a variety of ideological perspectives, there was a common theme running through all the interviews. Governors had a fundamental belief that the Prison Service and its Governors should exemplify the values of humanity and compassion. This sentiment is captured in the following quote:

For me probably humanitarian values and compassion are some of the strongest attributes that civilised human beings can have and I think a well-run Prison Service or a well-run criminal justice system has those attributes in its people.

This widely held view supports Rutherford's conclusion that 'the expression of humane values within criminal justice ultimately resides with practitioners' (Rutherford 1994: xii). The majority of Governors in the sample (73 per cent) expressed values and beliefs that were closely associated with Rutherford's credo three: 'empathy with suspects, offenders and the victims of crime, optimism that constructive work can be done with offenders' (Rutherford 1994: 18). Terms such as 'social imperative', 'social conscience' and 'social purpose' populated the Governors' discourses, as these quotes indicate:

I have a very clear orientation towards rehabilitation of prisoners. The advertising was actually slanted that way . . . A large number of aspiring Governors still held that sort of value and I think still do and I think the vast majority who come in now even hold something of a social imperative in terms of the role.

I would find it difficult to understand someone coming to this sort of job without some sort of social conscience and a view that they are both serving society and have some sort of interest or concern about crime in the community and reducing it. There must be some elements of that motivation for the majority of people.

For many Governors the belief that prisoners have the capacity to change is key to their approach. These Governors want to provide regimes that will deliver these changes and return prisoners to their communities having been rehabilitated. 'Rehabilitation orientated' Governors believe prisons to be constructive and purposeful places, which will reduce reoffending.

> I firmly believe that in a prison we need a culture of hope, and that's hope for the staff and the prisoners, where it's clear people are treated fairly and justly, that inmates can respond . . . I think if the Prison Service loses that reforming, moral sort of stance, then it will lose much of what's really good about it . . . I would not want just to lock people up, I mean, even if they had TV in the cell and association all the time and they were treated justly, and good food, and clean and safe and everything else. I just think the Prison Service has to have in its vision, in its purpose, in its aims, the ability to facilitate people to stop from offending.

> Ultimately I believe in the ability of human beings to change. That's my underpinning philosophy of life. I also believe that prisoners change from being treated with respect and with understanding, and being given opportunities to actually get themselves sorted out.

Other Governors adopted a more pragmatic approach. While espousing the principle that prisoners can change, they believed that prisoners themselves must decide that they wanted to change and be motivated to take up the regime provided (what has been referred to as opportunities for 'facilitated change' – Morris 1974):

> I take the view that people change when they are ready and that you give them the facility to make that change when and if they are ready, and in the meantime you do your utmost to make them decent towards each other and show them that there is another way, and a lot of that is personal example. So I suppose my motivation, I suppose, is more about the humanitarian bit, but it is a pretty robust humanitarian bit. I am not a bleeding heart.

The remaining Governors (27 per cent) tended to define their values and beliefs in more managerial terms. These Governors fell within Rutherford's credo two, in which practitioners 'dispose of the tasks at hand as smoothly and efficiently as possible. The tenor is one of smooth management rather than moral mission' (Rutherford 1994: 13). To some extent this may reflect a more general trend in that 'positive sentiments have been increasingly marginalised in official discourses and replaced by more utilitarian objectives and expectations' (Garland 1990: 183).

A number of Governors in the study adopted a clear managerial perspective. For them the role was about running an efficient operation that focused on delivering core services to prisoners, meeting KPIs and adhering to Prison Service Orders, rather than pursuing any 'moral mission'. These Governors tended to adopt a more dispassionate bureaucratic style of management that sought procedural fairness rather than any more elevated commitment to substantive justice, reform or rehabilitation.

> There seems to be a group of people who joined just to be managers, and it could have been managing a different sort of organisation and I guess that I am probably one of them.

> I did just want to manage, actually, it's not about changing people ... I still regard myself principally as a manager.

> The end result to me is that the prisoner on the landing gets his food, gets his bedding, gets his visits, and we pull all these bits together and now somebody has got to do that and it's my job to try and help the people that are doing it, or enable them. If I have to set a priority then it would be this hotel function – I don't really believe we can do too much more.

A small number of Governors adopted an actuarial approach (Bottoms 1995 and Chapter 4) to prisoners. They valued systems and procedures over the needs of individual prisoners:

> I see prisoners as an essential part of the job, but I don't see them as individuals as being particularly important individuals. And, as a result, I'm not particularly interested whether or not we're doing wonderful personal officer work on the wing or anything like that; all I'm interested in is do we have a system and as long as we have a system and there are ways of monitoring that system's working, that's what I'm interested in.

> Somebody's particular individual problems as a prisoner do not interest me. I am here to look at the bigger picture. I do not get

involved with individual prisoners. For me it's much more about looking at the needs of groups of prisoners.

Some Governors spoke of their belief that the role was about treating prisoners decently and fairly rather than trying to achieve the broader goal of reform and rehabilitation:

I think it's containment and I don't think that we're doing anything – we may play at other things . . . I don't believe for a moment that in a local like this that a three day anger management course and a two-day anti-bullying course and a one-day taking and driving away course do any good – I mean, these get us brownie points from people who don't really understand what we're doing. It would be insane of me to think that these are going to have any lasting impact on anybody's life at all.

I suppose without getting too grand an idea, I just like to see people being treated right. Now, by that I mean, if a guy needs to go in a special cell, then I'm quite happy to put him in, sign the piece of paper. If he needs to get a phone call while there, then I'll want to make sure that the process is there for him to be able to get one. So it's just about treating people right, and maybe then getting them on the road to recovery. But there's no grand plan. I'm no social reformer.

Others adopted a 'normalising' discourse (King and Morgan 1980) and were keen to prevent or obviate the negative effects of prisons so that prisoners did not become worse during sentence:

I know a lot of Governors, and I respect that they are motivated to rehabilitate prisoners. My bit about prisoners is actually about wanting to ensure that they don't get brutalised. I don't have very big expectations about what prison does to prisoners because partly I believe prison is just such a weird environment. But I do believe that prisons can be profoundly negative and damaging places and I am quite attracted to playing my part in minimising that. It may sound quite an odd motivation but it's real.

My agenda, which I think, if I'm honest, is most strong for me, is about contributing to changing the culture of prisons. I'm very attracted to that. I want to make sure that people do not come out worse than when they went in. I am not sure that we can change many of them.

Rutherford's credo one focused on practitioners who had a 'powerfully held dislike and moral condemnation of offenders . . . who, when caught, should be dealt with in ways that are punitive and degrading' (Rutherford 1994: 11). No Governors expressed credo one punitive sentiments or beliefs during the interviews. There was a widely held belief amongst Governors that imprisonment should be used as a punishment, not for punishment. Whether they adhered to a reformist orientation or to a more managerial one, Governors believed that prisoners should be treated fairly and with humanity. No Governor suggested that prisoners should be further punished for their offence. As Garland points out:

> Prison officials, in so far as they are being professional, tend to suspend moral judgement and treat prisoners in purely neutral terms . . . prisoners will be treated not as evil or wicked persons on account of their offence, but as good or bad inmates on account of their institutional conduct. (Garland 1990: 183)

The following quotes typify the line taken by the Governors:

> I mean punishment never enters my head. I'm sure that sounds awful but it really doesn't and punishment is a matter for the law. I keep saying to people and I think it's true, my job isn't about imprisonment it's about freedom. I really am a Gladstone believer, you know, so actually, the law does the punishment. By the time we get them the punishment is dealt with.

> I know it is a euphemism but prisoners are sent to prison as a punishment not for punishment. Their punishment is the loss of liberty and we are here to keep them inside not to inflict punishment on prisoners.

Prison Governor culture

An organisation can have a distinct culture. Research has shown that parts of organisations can also have distinct subcultures, which may be different from the culture of the parent organisation. The Prison Service has a distinct culture, as do individual prisons (Leggett 2002). The notion that occupational groups can also possess a distinctive subculture has been the subject of considerable research and theorising (for example, on police culture see Waddington 1999, and on the differing cultures between managers and professionals see Raelin 1986). The literature on occupational culture defines culture as including accepted practices, rules and principles of conduct that are situationally applied, and which resides in the minds of group members (Hofstede 1996). For a group to have a shared culture, their culture should be reasonably homogeneous with regard to these characteristics (Hofstede 1998).

There was some evidence from the interviews that Governors shared an occupational culture and that their occupational culture was different to that of prison officers and administrators at Prison Service Head-quarters. One Governor put it this way:

> It was confusing when I moved from being an officer to being an AGT [assistant governor trainee]. The language changed, the think-ing changed and I guess that I changed. It was not just about having a bigger picture, there really is a different culture. It's more about treating prisoners as people and doing something positive with them. As an officer it was about 'happiness is door shaped' and banging them up; as a Governor I am more about human rights and that dictates what I do . . . Most Governors do the same, we all share the view that we are here to protect people.

Unlike some occupational groups, however, the prison Governor subcul-ture did not come across during the interviews as being particularly strong. Governing is an oral tradition, rather than a written one, with stories, myths and anecdotes conveying culture metaphorically. Gov-ernors learn their trade by watching and listening to other Governors, and by discussing professional issues with each other. Today, however, there are few opportunities for Governors to come together as a group to develop cohesion and establish a shared culture. The 'Governors' annual conference has been replaced with a 'Prison Service' conference to which administrative, as well as operational staff are invited. Governors spend less time together training today than they have done in the past. A strong collective identity and culture is also undermined by being isolated in their own individual prisons and by focusing on their own establishments. Modern management methods, such as league tables and competition, also go some way to undermine collective identity.

The professional association of Governors, the Prison Governors Association, works to create a shared view amongst its members on penal matters. Even though the Association has steadily grown in membership, since it was formed in 1987, to its current level of over 1,000 members, it has only limited impact on penal policy matters and has not sought to issue advice on professional issues to its members. Unlike its police equivalent (the Association of Chief Police Officers – ACPO), the PGA has always struggled to speak with one voice and to unite its membership behind specific policies. It has published two documents on penal policy matters: *A Manifesto for Change* (1995) and *A Manifesto for*

Effective Correctional Policy (2002) but neither have had the impact that the PGA sought. The changes to the role and work of Governors, discussed later in this book, took place without any real input from the PGA, and the PGA has had no significant impact on shaping the role of the modern Governor.

There are a number of reasons why the PGA has not played an active role. For many of its members the PGA is seen solely as a trade union that exists to defend the terms and conditions of employment of its members. They do not see the Association as being a professional association that should have an influence on broad penal policy matters. The PGA membership is also more diverse that that of ACPO. The PGA represents all ranks of governors, from assistant and deputy governors to in-charge Governors. The views of the various grades do not always enable the PGA to speak with a single voice or to develop advice on professional issues. In-charge Governors as a group may often have a different perspective on matters compared to their more junior colleagues. Attempts to create a 'Governors group' within the PGA, to speak for in-charge Governors, have always failed, as have attempts to make one vice-president responsible for professional issues and the other responsible for trade union matters.

Today's Governors

The majority of Governors in the study were male, white, over 50 years old and came from a skilled manual or non-manual socio-economic background. Governors are educationally more successful than their peer group and nearly half hold degrees. Most Governors had a previous occupation before joining the Prison Service and joined mainly for non-instrumental reasons. While the majority entered the Prison Service on the 'fast-track direct-entry' scheme, over three quarters have served a period as a prison officer. Prior to being appointed Governors, most of the sample had been assistant governors in a variety of prisons and had also undertaken at least one non-operational posting. A majority had also been deputy governors in one or more prisons. The training that the sample received prior to governing varied and depended on the date they joined and the period in which they were promoted. The Governors in the sample have considerable experience in the role of Governor. Over half of them have been Governor of two or more prisons. A similar number have also been a Governor for four or more years.

The data suggests that the Governors in the sample are distinct from the people that they manage – prison officers – in a number of ways. Governors joined the Prison Service at a younger age, are older, from a different socio-economic background, have attained higher levels of education and have worked in a number of different prisons (see Marsh *et al.* 1985, for demographic information on prison officers).

Two distinct groups of Governors emerged from the data: those Governors who had been 'promoted through the ranks' and those Governors who were direct entrants. This split in the Governor rank is a relatively new phenomenon, as, until relatively recently, few Governors had been promoted from the uniformed prison officer grades. One effect of this change is that it is no longer the case that all Governors share the same demographic and social profile. In the early 1980s it was still being suggested that '... the occupation of Governor, like some professions and the military, is not only a role, it is also a status which means that incumbents of the Office are not simply required to perform certain duties, but ... be a certain type of person' (Waddington 1983). Governors who had been promoted through the ranks tended to have a different profile compared to their direct-entry colleagues. They were generally older, came from manual working backgrounds, had lower levels of school education, and joined the Service for more extrinsic reasons. While they had occupied fewer assistant governor posts than direct-entry Governors, all 'promoted through the ranks' Governors had been deputy governors at some point. This group had received less in-service training, but many had obtained a degree whilst working in the Prison Service.

Governors who were promoted from the uniformed grades also tended to be more managerial in their expressed ideologies than Governors who were direct entrants. The trend amongst direct-entrant Governors is, however, changing. The more recently recruited direct-entrant Governors adopted a more managerial ideology than their predecessors. A typology of Governors linking their background, career and management approach can be found in Chapter 7.

Most Governors indicated that they took on the governing role in order to make a difference to prisoners' lives and to provide opportunities for reform. Others wanted to be good managers who ran efficient institutions. The interviews revealed high levels of job satisfaction amongst Governors and suggested that this was due to the varied nature of their work and the ability to achieve the goals that they set out to achieve.

While few Governors made explicit reference to their ideology, the interviews did reveal that Governors tended to ground their approaches and decision-making with reference to values and beliefs. This can be seen in many of the quotes used later in this book and supports Miller's assertion that ideology shapes the daily work of criminal justice practitioners: 'Ideology and its consequences exert a powerful influence on the policies and procedures of those who conduct the enterprise of criminal justice' (Miller 1973: 142).

The interviews took place in the late 1990s and should be placed in that historical context. The beliefs and language used by interviewees no doubt reflected the politically correct line at that time – a focus on performance, delivery and managerialism. Earlier generations of Governors would probably not have adopted such managerial language and perspective. In addition, had the interviews taken place in the mid-1990s, the levels of job satisfaction may well have been lower, because of the negative publicity generated by prison escapes, the emphasis on security and the political desire for austere prison regimes.

The new optimism that emerged by the late 1990s, associated with the 'decency' agenda, was reflected in the interviews. If the interviews took place today, levels of job satisfaction might well be lower. The growing managerialisation and 'bureaucratisation' of prison administration, with steadily increasing oversight, direction, and control exercised by Headquarters, may augur poorly for maintaining the job satisfaction associated with being a Governor. Highly centralised, hierarchical authority may have organisational benefits, but may also produce the unintended consequence of diminishing Governors' satisfaction with their work as their autonomy is reduced and organisational goals become more managerial and less in line with Governors' personal ideologies.

On the other hand, the new generation of Governors appointed since 2000 may have a different perspective on what they want from the job. These new Governors may share a more managerial orientation and want to be managers focusing on administration, budgets and performance targets rather than doing work more traditionally associated with prison governance. In which case, their level of job satisfaction may be increased as the Prison Service adopts a more managerial approach.

Chapter 6

Governing prisons – the reality

The Governor's role and duties

Role can be defined as: an actor's part; one's function; what a person or thing is appointed or expected to do (*Oxford English Dictionary* 1985); the part or character which one undertakes, assumes, or has to play (*Shorter Oxford English Dictionary* 2002); and a socially expected behaviour pattern usually determined by an individual's status in a particular society (*Webster's New Collegiate Dictionary* 1973). In short, role is not only about what a Governor does, but also about the patterned expectations attached to the office of Governor.

> I see role as a sort of wider and more kind of rounded definition than tasks and duties. Or to put the point another way, I would see tasks and duties being an element, or two elements in a role, but I think role embraces such concepts as status, I mean status in the kind of sociological sense rather than in the lay sense. So I suppose a kind of snappy definition, sort of working definition of role would be the position of the Governor in the totality of the organisation – in this case the Prison Service.

The interviews with Governors revealed that they perform generic roles and duties, which managers and leaders in all organisations undertake. In addition, there are a number of prison-specific roles and duties that are unique to the custodial environment. The roles themselves are not easily separable and form a *Gestalt* – an integrated whole – which defines the overall gubernatorial role. No role can be pulled out of the framework if the Governor's job is to be left intact.

The current study set out to identify the Governor's work and determine what duties and tasks must be carried out, regardless of who holds the office of Governor. This is often referred to as a 'practice description' (Whitemore 1995: 58). Information was gathered about the Governor's key tasks and duties in two ways: the Governors of 126 publicly managed prisons were asked for a copy of their job description: and the 42 Governors interviewed were asked to describe their main duties and tasks.

A total of 98 job descriptions were received in response to the written request, which represents an overall response rate of 78 per cent. The job descriptions contained a variety of output descriptions mixed with distinct duties and tasks (processes) that Governors were required to undertake. The most frequently described outputs are shown in Table 6.1.

Table 6.1 Main output statements in Governors' job descriptions

Prison management	Ensure the actions of the establishment comply with the policies of ministers and the law
	Hold prisoners in safe, decent and healthy environment
	Provide constructive regimes that promote law-abiding behaviour
	Protect the public
	Maintain order and discipline
	Ensure that prisoners are treated fairly and justly
General management	Deliver key performance targets
	Deliver establishment contract
	Ensure standards of behaviour conform to PSO/PSI
	Ensure value for money
Leadership	Provide the vision and direction for the establishment
	Foster effective public relations
Command	Ensure the successful resolution of incidents

General management and leadership

The notion that Governors have a general management role is not a new one. As early as 1974 the Governor was talked about as a 'permanent official carrying out the function of general manager of a penal establishment who should be managing a number of parallel operational activities, each of which deals with its own operative problems within predetermined guidelines and delegated authority' (Home Office 1974: 65–66).

More recently Governors were exhorted to take on the full role of general manager of establishments and to understand specialist areas, as well as the need to think and plan strategically (HM Prison Service 1994c). Governors today see themselves performing many general management tasks:

I mean, my view, and it's just a personal view, is that the Governor is broadly responsible for carrying out a managerial role, for seeing that arrangements are in place and that systems are in place for these procedures to be carried out properly. I suppose the Governor is like a general manager in any company in that sense.

The Governor is the appointed official who runs the prison and I guess that you could call him the general manager. He is responsible and should be accountable for all that happens to the prisoners and the staff that are employed to look after the prisoners in that establishment and, at that level, it's a simple managerial task.

All the job descriptions set out specific general management tasks. These relate to finances, planning, human resources, auditing and monitoring. Governors made clear that they were responsible for seeking, utilising and maximising resources for the establishment.

The Governor is the resource getter. So the job is to explain and make sense of this thing in a way that's meaningful and significant enough to enable funding to be secure for the purposes that would make sense in this organisation.

I've canvassed Headquarters, I've canvassed area managers. I've bid for this and I've bid for that and I've got visitors down and rammed it down their throats so they go away and try and find us resources.

Governors are responsible for drawing up and implementing business and strategic plans for their establishments. This involves looking into the future and bringing together various initiatives, as well as planning the allocation of resources. Governors highlighted the planning aspects of their work:

The head of custody should be the sort of operational day-to-day head of the prison. The Governor should be able to step back and to get more involved in policy work for his or her establishment. To actually look and plan and see where it needs to go, where we want it to go and how it's managing at the moment.

Increasingly now I think that it is the strategic planning of the establishment . . . [which is] key to a Governor's work . . .

While Governors do not have responsibility for setting pay levels, they are responsible for industrial relations, staffing numbers, recruitment, selection, discipline and training of staff. Governors dealt personally with the more difficult aspects of personnel management including conducting disciplinary hearings and deciding on appropriate action against poor performers:

> We have got rid of a fair few staff because they simply have not been performing and we have had to sack a couple for improper relationships. We sacked one for fiddling, two for not performing. And I will always do that myself, I mean the manager will deal with it but at the stage when it gets messy I will always sit with the manager and then I will take over and actually do the really nasty bits.

For many Governors effective personnel management was important because if they looked after their staff, and treated them properly, that would influence the way staff treated prisoners:

> I have a simple management philosophy which I tell my people when I go to any jail, that it is my job to look after them and their job to look after the prisoners, and I believe if I look after staff, and by looking after I don't mean just being kind, I actually mean shoving and pushing sometimes, I use that as a euphemism for the whole range of discipline and control, but caring as well. If I give them a quality service then I can expect and demand that they give a quality service to prisoners.

Governors increasingly see creating and nurturing the senior team and ensuring that they adhere to a collective way of working as key to their role:

> You have to manage a prison through a team and part of the Governor's responsibility is to make sure that each member of that senior team knows and understands what the objectives are, what the team working is all about, understands what cabinet responsibility is all about, which may or may not be about agreeing what has been decided but taking that decision collectively with the Governor overriding it if necessary.

Managing, or in most cases responding to, the latest industrial relations crisis with the Prison Officers Association (POA) was a dominant feature in a Governor's work in the 1990s. As a former Chief Inspector of prisons put it: 'Dealing with the POA has taken up far too much of prison governors' time . . .' (Ramsbotham 2003: 234). The industrial relations climate in the Service improved following the implementation of the Criminal Justice and Public Order Act (1994). In addition, a new industrial relations procedural agreement with the POA was agreed, which made clear that disagreements should be resolved wherever possible at establishment level (HM Prison Service 1993g). The Governor was given the crucial role in ensuring effective local industrial relations. Governors believed that by the late 1990s they were in a position to more effectively manage relations with the POA:

> The position is so different today on the IR front. I actually feel that I am managing what is going on. Gone are the days of being held to ransom by the local POA ... If I want to change something then I can. As you will remember for a long time it was the other way around. The POA could block any change. Now I can change staffing levels, attendance systems and the regime if I think it best for the prison. Yes, there will still be a battle and I will get yet more 'votes of no confidence' but I will eventually get there.

Governors audit and monitor their establishments as part of their routine duties. To do so they seek information from a variety of sources including reading reports and memos and attending meetings and briefings. Most information gathered is analysed to discover problems and opportunities. These are then fed to the appropriate manager to deal with. Many Governors pointed to the need to do personal monitoring, as well as managing the audit process. In order to do this they emphasised the need for the Governor to conduct observational visits.

> I think it's fair to say I tried to get out to some part of the prison every day. I even tried, at one stage in my career, to offer to carry out the checklist sheets on a daily basis where I visit and follow up notes I'd made for myself so the next time I visited, I'd mention something from last time and could say 'What did you do about that?' or 'Have you done something about that?' So the visits aren't just a social delight but are actually a piece of work and I think at times, where you might lose sight of that, it is work. You have to check, monitor, congratulate or refuse people.

While much has been written about the concept of leadership in recent years, reaching a consensus about the nature of leadership has proved elusive. It has been pointed out that leadership in the prison context relates to deliberate efforts aimed at building and maintaining an organisation, and defining what an organisation is about, clarifying the core values and promoting and inculcating those values into the organisation (Bryans and Walford 1998). Prison leadership has been described in this way:

> This leadership approach does not focus solely on such managerial activities as planning, organising, staffing, directing, coordinating,

reporting and budgeting. Institutional leadership goes beyond management. Leadership pertains to the domain of crucial decisions with regard to long-term organisational survival, effectiveness and legitimacy. These are decisions which shape the dominant goals of the organisation and define the means by which to achieve them. Leadership is, ultimately, about determining the core values which drive the organisation (Boin 1998: 212–213).

Nearly all the Governors interviewed as part of the current study spoke of their leadership role.

I believe that the key word is leadership. Leadership means to me that there is somebody in charge who is making it very clear what is to be done, which includes persuading people to do what they don't necessarily want to do, but is there – and everyone knows that they're in charge – and they know that, if they have got problems or concerns, there is somebody who will take an interest in them.

It is perhaps not surprising that Governors were keen to speak of leadership in the context of their role, given the emphasis placed by the Prison Service on the importance of leadership in recent years. Many of the reports written about the Prison Service (often in the wake of escapes, riots or industrial relations problems) have suggested that if Governors had demonstrated leadership then the problem would not have occurred in the first place (Learmont 1995a: recommendation 61; HM Prison Service 1997a: para. 9.4).

Based on what Governors said in the interviews, their leadership role includes the representational and figurehead elements of the Governors' work; the part Governors play in creating meaning; and how Governors develop and maintain the vision of the prison.

As a consequence of their formal authority as holder of the office, Governors are required to undertake figurehead and representative roles. These roles involve the Governor undertaking certain duties inside the prison and in the wider community. Governors are the public face of prisons to the external world. It is Governors who represent establishments in the community, to the media and at official functions with local dignitaries.

I think the Governor's job is to represent the prison to the world . . . speaking on what goes on in the prison to public meetings and to groups and associations and virtually anybody that will invite you, any non-political group that will invite you, and generally be the persona of the establishment, the embodiment of the establishment.

Governors are expected increasingly to represent the Prison Service on local criminal justice and other bodies (partnership meetings with National Health Service/Primary Care Trusts, public protection strategy groups, Youth Offending Teams, crime and disorder committees, judges and magistrates training, drug action teams, local criminal justice boards, joint working with probation and voluntary sector groups):

> Trends in regionalisation of government have meant that the prison Governor as a local player has become more significant – if you look towards drug action groups and criminal justice liaison committees, the whole business of bringing together the criminal justice agencies, puts this sort of ambassadorial role, as I call it, representative role much more firmly in the Governor's work.

Governors also have figurehead responsibilities within the prison. This involves them participating in rituals and ceremonies such as attending funerals, commemorative ceremonies and making presentations to staff and prisoners:

> I think one of the bits of learning for me . . . has been the value that staff put to some of the ritual bits. Somebody said recently . . . that as a Governor one of the most important things I do is go to staff funerals, so I think it may sound a slightly odd starting point but I think that the symbolic aspects of the job are not to be ignored. The most important thing I do is go to staff funerals. I think that has a resonance. Probably at other points along the way, I would have thought silly bugger, but I think I have probably come to the view that those kinds of things are important.

Governors believe that they are the people who have a total overview of their prisons and the place of prisons within the wider framework of the criminal justice system. This brings with it a distinct role – that of interpreting and making sense of the external environment for staff and prisoners. Governors see their role as reconciling the conflict between the various penal objectives, political expediency, humanity and expectations of various stakeholders (both inside and outside the establishment), as these quotes indicate:

> We've got an oddity insofar as we've got these organisations which deliver the most serious sanctions against citizens in peacetime on behalf of the state and yet we don't have an agreed clarity about what prisons are about . . . I firmly believe that that means that that ambiguity finds its focus in the Governor, because the only person you can really pin the tail on in legalistic terms, in organisational

terms, in public relations terms, in proximity terms, is the Governor and actually the Governor holds that ambiguity. That's the role of the Governor.

To be the interpreter or sense-maker, of the external change in the outside world, in a way that interprets the meaning and the significance of that establishment. What he is interpreting is the meaning of the establishment in terms of the meaning and significance of the outside world.

Governors indicated that they contribute a 'strategic vision' (Kotter 1990; Crainer 1996) aspect of leadership for their prisons and, as strategic leaders, aim to stimulate and sustain the shared acceptance and achievement of the strategic vision:

To me the main role is first of all to be the generator and keeper of the vision.

The vision, the strategic direction, the selection of that direction and the maintenance of it – that rests with the Governor and cannot be given to anyone else to do. It wouldn't be credible.

Governors need to provide a clear personal vision of what is to be achieved, how it is to be achieved, and communicate that to staff and prisoners.

I suppose really it's setting the strategic direction for the prison.

Vision sounds a bit grand but that is what it is about. If the Governor does not create the vision and sell it no one else will. I have got to keep at it all the time, over and over again, using every newsletter, staff meeting and walkabout to tell them about where we are going as an establishment and how they contribute to that.

Incident command

Prisons are institutions that are particularly vulnerable to a range of incidents. The type of person held, and the coercive nature of the environment, will lead, on occasion, to situations that are not routine and which potentially threaten the order or security of the establishment. Once they begin, incidents in prisons can quickly 'spiral out of control' (Boin and Rattray 2004: 54). In order to deal with incidents and prevent them from escalating, Governors indicated that they must be effective incident commanders (acting in a 'command role') during incidents such as fires, riots, demonstrations, escapes, hostage-taking and rooftop protests.

The notion that 'command' differs from 'management' is now widely accepted (see for example, Brunacini 1985; Keegan 1987; Larken 1992). In referring to their 'command role' Governors spoke of this difference between 'management' and 'command' and highlighted that they needed to be able to shift from one role to the other:

> When the bells go, you change from running the production line at Ford's, with all its problems, and it is very much like that, you move from that into the command role where you've actually got to sit in the chair in the command post.

> There is the operational role of the Governor. We can function in broad terms in management, in managerial principles, but when the phone goes and the security girl says, 'Sorry to bother you, Governor, but there is a slight problem in the yard, 38 of them have refused to come in and seem to have blankets and food with them', you have to change.

Incidents are often characterised by ambiguous and conflicting information; shifting goals; time pressure; dynamic conditions; complex operational team structures and poor communication. The complexity of the command role requires certain command skills (Flin 1996: 42–44). While many of these individual traits and skills are required in general management, commanding an incident requires a different approach.

> It's like the command–management spectrum. In an emergency – there's not going to be very much flexibility about what they do, and there's not very much debate in certain circumstances. Whereas in normal circumstances you are really discussing something much more openly and long term, then people have very much more space to express their own ideas.

Most Governors accepted that they will have to act in a command role and that moving into a command role is not a concern for them:

> I don't worry about the next incident. I think they're just part of the job that you do. That's what we're experienced at handling. If it comes, you know how to handle it. So, in a sense, you've got confidence. The majority of us as Governors have confidence in our ability, our staff, our planning to handle incidents . . . it can be messy at times.

127

In responding to incidents Governors have to make key operational decisions, which range from launching a 'paramilitary' counter attack on riotous prisoners to evacuating a burning prison wing or engaging in protracted negotiations with hostage takers.

> Dealing with incidents is an important part of my work now . . . We have a lot of incidents here – the youngsters tend to be more volatile and are unpredictable. I spend a lot of time in the command post. [This YOI] has had the lot recently, roof tops, hostage incidents, passive demos.

> Dispersals have more incidents than other prisons. The staff are good at handling all sorts. The duty governors do most of the incidents, so I only get involved if it is a big one – you know, sort of hostages and sit-downs that last a long time. Oh, and I always do the hostage incidents.

Prison-specific roles and duties

Governors pointed to four main prison-specific areas of activity that Governors undertake: maintaining a secure prison; achieving order through effective control; providing positive regimes; and regulating the prison.

Prisons contain people who would rather not be incarcerated and Governors have a duty to 'keep in custody those committed by the court' (HM Prison Service 2003b). Most prisoners accept their sentence and make no attempt to leave before its expiry. Some prisoners are opportunistic and will attempt to escape if they see what they think to be an opportunity to do so. A small minority of prisoners are determined to escape and will make numerous concerted attempts until they have gained their freedom.

Prison security became the central concern of Governors and their managers after a series of high-profile escapes of high-security prisoners in the mid-1990s (see Woodcock 1994 and Learmont 1995a and 1995b). Governors were given a clear message that security was paramount and that it was their responsibility to prevent prisoners from escaping (Lewis 1997). As a result, managing security to prevent escapes is a core element of a Governor's job and explicit reference is made to maintaining security in over 90 per cent of job descriptions.

The specific duties and tasks that Governors must undertake in relation to security are set out in some detail in Prison Service Orders and Instructions, and in the Prison Service security manual. In particular, Governors are required to ensure that effective security intelligence systems are in place, that security is regularly reviewed and monitored through a security committee, and that physical and procedural security are maintained. Governors made clear in the interviews that delivering on these areas required a significant effort and took up a considerable amount of their time:

> I expected a good report on the security because I actually put a lot of work in and set up an internal audit team and we went round cracking heads to make sure that it was right.

> I've put a lot of my time and effort into getting security right and following the manual.

Governors pointed out that maintaining a secure prison involved having the right physical security measures (fences, razor wire, perimeter movement detectors, bars, gates); ensuring that effective procedural security measures were in place (searching, surveillance, security intelligence systems, categorisation and assessment, accounting and control systems) and nurturing 'dynamic security'. Governors attached great importance to this concept of dynamic security, which involves 'individualism, relationship and activity ... coming together through the relationship between staff and inmates' (Dunbar 1985: 23):

> I am a great believer in dynamic security, which I think is far more effective than some of the modern technology. For me security is about keeping prisoners occupied and staff engaging them in constructive relationships. As you know, nothing is secret in such a closed environment as a prison. If prisoners are planning to escape someone outside of the circle is bound to know about it. If the dynamic security is right, my staff will get to hear about it and we will be able to prevent the escape.

Ensuring that prisoners do not escape remains a central, if not the central, concern of Governors. It is not a one-off activity but something that permeates a Governor's daily work on an ongoing basis and requires 'constant vigilance, maintenance and improvement' (HM Prison Service 2004b: 20).

Security and order are inextricably linked, as a disorderly prison creates the potential for a breach in security. A Governor's duty therefore extends to ensuring that order is maintained in the institution, both as a contribution to effective security and to provide a safe environment for staff and prisoners. Over 85 per cent of job descriptions required the Governor to 'create an environment in which order and control is achieved'.

Order is taken here to mean the absence of violence, overt conflict or the imminent threat of the chaotic breakdown of social routines (Sparks *et al.* 1996: 119). Governors have been faced, since the introduction of modern prisons, with the fundamental problem of how to prevent disorder. Despite the appearance of pervasive control, most prisons offer prisoners ample opportunities to misbehave. In 2002–03 the Prison Service recorded 28 hostage incidents; 26 acts of major concerted indiscipline (including one riot); seven roof climbs; and 6,479 assaults (HM Prison Service 2003b). Governors emphasised the need to ensure order and control in their prisons:

> It's always struck me as being open to the most major criticism, if the offenders are in a highly unsafe environment, where people are assaulted and scared. I think that's horrendous. That comes back again to my point about control. I don't think you can do any of the good things you want to do unless you have structure and control.

Governors indicated that they adopted a number of broad strategies to achieve well-ordered prisons. The first broad strategy Governors used focused on 'situational control' (Sparks *et al.* 1996 and Wortley 2002). Situational control methods aim to tackle precipitating factors that generate control issues and to reduce the opportunity for disorder to take place. Governors gave examples of where they had successfully used situational control methods:

> One of the big problem areas was always the canteen [prisoner shop]. Prisoners would line up and wait their turn, then buy their stuff and take it back to their cells. Well, you can imagine what happened. There was a lot of bullying in the queues, prisoners were forced to buy things that they did not want and hand them over to stronger prisoners, or they were mugged on the way back to their cells. Fights were always breaking out. Today, prisoners order their stuff on a shopping list which they hand to staff and their goods are then delivered to their cells. A lot of hassle has been prevented and it is much safer.

> The bloody design of this place is crap – dog legs and blind alleys everywhere. Bullying was going on and staff no-go areas were starting to creep in. There wasn't a lot we could do about the building, so we went for the camera option. This place now looks like something from *Big Brother*, but it worked.

In reality, Governors indicated that they used both 'hard' and 'soft' means of situational control and, as one researcher suggested: 'the issue for prison control ... is to find the appropriate balance between these interventions' (Wortley 2002: 219). A Governor put it in this way:

> Let me give you an example of what I mean about which levers to pull. We recently had a problem with the food here – SIRs [security information reports from staff] were telling me that there was going to be trouble, there were lots of CARPS [complaints and request forms from prisoners] about the food and wing staff were reporting that lots of food was being dumped. So we had to take action to prevent the trouble – in this case it meant doing something about the food and at the same time sending messages that we would not put up with trouble. That was about lifting [removing from normal location] the ring leaders and making sure that there were lots of staff around at meal times.

The temporary removal of prisoners (either to a different wing, to the segregation unit or to another prison) was an approach that Governors used to prevent trouble happening or to deal with an existing problem. They pointed out, however, that using this option was only a short-term 'fix', that it could only ever be used for small numbers of prisoners, and that at some point the prisoner would need to be reintegrated back into the prison:

> If you walk around the seg [segregation unit] like I did this morning you will find a mixed bag of prisoners. Most are under punishment but a few segregated under Rule 43 GOAD [Good Order and Discipline]. They're down there in most cases because of intelligence they're dealing, bullying, about to do [assault] someone or stirring up general trouble about the food or regime or something, and we don't have enough evidence to nick them. But to be honest putting someone in the seg is easy. The difficult bit is getting them out again. Someone cannot stay down there for ever so we need to work out a way to get them back on normal location.

Governors gave other examples of how they dealt with potential control problems. Examples included regulating situational factors: increasing staff patrols and visibility (formal surveillance); increasing time in cell; only unlocking a few prisoners at a time; limiting the numbers of prisoners permitted to gather in one place; and transferring troublemakers:

> When I arrived in this place it was out of control. The prisoners were running the place. Staff were hiding in their offices, there were 'no-go' areas. The place stank of fear. Everyone felt unsafe. There was violence, intimidation, bullying, no-go areas, taxing [prisoners

demanding goods from other prisoners] . . . I called a staff meeting and told them that we were going to sort the place out together. It was a slow process but we got there in the end. It took about six months, I suppose . . . To begin with we did controlled unlocking [only letting a small number of prisoners out of their cells at any one time], searched the whole place, and I was pretty tough on adjudications. As staff got more confident I relaxed things a bit and we took things from there.

The second broad strategy Governors used to achieve order is based on social controls. This approach involves attempts at socialisation and strengthening social relations: having the right balance of prisoners; changing prisoner culture; attempts at consultation and participation with prisoners; strengthening relationships; ensuring that the exercise of power was seen as legitimate by most prisoners most of the time; and developing mutual trust. A number of commentators have highlighted the need to get the 'right' relationship between staff and prisoners in order to negotiate the peaceful operation of a prison (see, in particular, Liebling and Price 2001).

The challenge for Governors is to decide what is the 'right' relationship within their prison and how to develop and sustain those relationships. Governors emphasised the importance of getting the right staff–prisoner relations:

For me keeping order is about relationships and dynamic security. In my experience there is less violence, less bullying and it's a whole lot safer where there is a healthy relationship between staff and prisoners. My job is to make sure the relationships are right.

Well, prison officers are the primary relationship in any prison. How prison officers interact and relate to prisoners is the primary relationship. My role as Governor has to be to ensure that that relationship is as positive and appropriate as possible.

Governors also pointed to the advantages of being able to use other social control means such as rewards and punishments to manage prisoners' behaviour:

IEP [Incentives and Earned Privileges scheme] was one of the best things to have happened in the Prison Service in my career. There is a clear set of carrots and sticks, or should I say costs and benefits in management speak. They are applied more or less the same across prisons and prisoners know where they are with it. You know – if you behave then you get a TV. If you don't, you lose it.

To some extent Governors were able to choose which elements of control to adopt. However, their choice is often constrained by factors such as the architecture and function of the prison. For example, the high turnover of prisoners in old local prisons makes it more difficult for staff to use 'social' control methods by establishing positive relationships. More recent prison designs keep prisoners in smaller groups and bring officers into contact with them, thereby emphasising 'social' control methods:

> The advantage of this place is that it's new. The units are small and self-contained which helps with control but that also means that my staff get to know the prisoners better. Staff felt a bit isolated to begin with but since we put the cameras in that's not such a big issue. But as I told you earlier, I'm not a great believer in cameras and all this modern technology. For me it's more about dynamic security and relationships than it's about cameras and geophones.

In addition to the physical environment, Governors pointed out that funding was often not available to introduce situational control measures, such as CCTV, or to make structural changes.

Governors emphasised that maintaining order is not a one-off event but something that they had to continually focus on:

> It's something which we have to keep on top of all the time. It's not something you achieve and then forget about. You can lose control in the blink of an eye unless you keep at it. You need systems and routines but most of all you need good intelligence so that you can nip things in the bud . . . If your intelligence is good you know in advance that there is going to be a demo or protest or escape attempt and then you can prevent it.

In order to identify potential control problems before they develop into disorder, Governors used a variety of means to monitor the stability of their prisons:

> In my last place there was a sticky period when I could see that things were not right. We were starting to lose control of the place after an overcrowding draft of scousers came in. There were some of the usual signs: increase in adjudications, more request-complaints than normal, people banging themselves up rather than going on association, staff and cons staying in groups, high levels on sick parade, increase in requests for Rule 43 [administrative segregation]. All these told me that things were not right.

The Governor is able to have a significant influence both on prisoners' inclination and on their ability to contravene the 'routine expectancies' (Young 1987) of everyday life in prison. In exercising that influence, Governors make a series of moral decisions and policy choices, because 'more than one version of sustainable "order" has been shown to be possible' (Sparks *et al.* 1996: 320).

One element in providing legitimacy and a well-ordered prison is through the provision of positive regimes. A Governor used this metaphor to describe the balance between security and regimes:

> I often think back to a metaphor I read about in which prison is compared to a car. You have got to keep people in when the car is moving for their safety, and the safety of the general public. But the purpose of a car is to get people to a particular destination. Destinations will vary but progressive movement is what they are about. I like that metaphor because it is a constant reminder that prisons should be about taking people forward, but in a safe and secure manner, according to the rules.

Governors highlighted the need to get the core elements of the regime right – the accommodation, food, clothing, canteen and visits:

> I always give the example of a hotel and what you have to do to keep the customers happy. It's the same for us – it's about hot meals, clean laundry and something to do. All right, it's a bit more complicated than that but I still maintain that if we get the food, laundry, canteen, visits and association right, 99.9 per cent of prisoners will cause no problems.

In addition to these core elements, Governors emphasised the need to provide a constructive, purposeful and balanced regime if prisons were to be more than just 'human warehouses':

> Governors will be working actively to create a regime which, as far as it can, depending on the type of prison we're dealing with, will be varied, interesting, constructive and would be a regime which gives them something that they can use to move them towards release or to help them to recover their lives and operate effectively when they're released.

> You have got to provide some sort of meaningful regime. You have got to manipulate the money and get the people to provide it, both the hours out of cell and things for them to do when they are out.

Governors are often regarded by staff as the regime 'innovator', who seeks to introduce new ideas:

> I was told that I must be the man who would do midnight cricket. And when I said, 'Why would I do midnight cricket?', the Principal Officer said, 'We've had everything else. There's only midnight cricket left.' And the idea was that the Governor was there to invent new ways of helping young people or prisoners move along.

A common theme emerging from all the interviews was that a key role for the Governor was ensuring that prisoners and staff viewed the operation of the prison as being legitimate, just and fair; and that the security, order and regime were held in balance. Governors used a number of terms to describe this aspect of their role – 'balancing', 'mediating', 'harmonising' and 'shaping' – but the most frequently used term was 'regulating'. They referred to it as the 'professional part' of their job and as being specific to the prison environment:

> I still subscribe to the notion of the Governor who is regulating – the Governor is the regulator, leave aside your innovation, leave aside planning whatever – just regulating relationships, group dynamics, planning whatever. Regulating dangerous individuals, trying keeping a healthy community where people have confidence, largely anyway, that they are being treated fairly, decently and even in reasonably safe conditions.

> I think any Governor, any person who has governed a prison, will immediately know that managing the ever-present tensions takes up a lot of their working day.

> The reality is that I see the Governor as the buffer. The Governor has to weave between all functions. He has to mediate between all functions.

One of the main ways that Governors regulate the operation of a prison is through the decisions they reach. These decisions enable Governors to send clear messages to staff and prisoners:

> I suppose you'd call them balancing acts, and we like to talk in management terms of prioritising, of competing demands, and we've got plenty of those. But I'd much rather use the image of balancing acts, of taking decisions around whose interests are served in this area, which decisions would give benefit to which clientele, who should have priority in that situation.

It has been pointed out that 'like virtually all conceptualisations of social relations, order is a matter of degree' (Wrong 1994: 9). Governors indicated that they could achieve security and order through excessive control but that to do so would make their prisons punitive, restrictive, oppressive and over-controlled. They pointed out that oppressive confinement and repressive brutality and intimidation had no place in a modern prison system. One Governor gave this example:

> What people forget is that morality and human rights and what is acceptable today will have an impact on what the prison is like. Take two examples, drugs and keeping control. If there was no personal contact on visits and no temporary release there would be very few drugs inside but that is not acceptable. If I kept everyone locked up with no association and no work, I would have no problems keeping order, but today that is not acceptable. It used to be, but not today.

None of the Governors advocated the maintenance of order through strict enforcement of rules alone and all Governors have to decide for themselves where the balance should rest:

> I think your aim as Governor, always, is to have a stable, consistent, lawful prison and that means you spend a lot of time trying to balance the three elements of security, custody and care and constantly trying to make sure that one doesn't impinge on the others to such a great extent that it destabilises.

Other Governors used an example of where security and regime came into conflict as an area in which they could influence the balance within their institution:

> The POA said that officers had to be able to walk into the [sex offender] programme rooms now and then to ensure that no potential threats to security existed. The psychologists said that any interruptions would impact on group dynamic and confidentiality. They all came to me to argue the point. I had to decide and knew whatever I decided would send a clear message on how I saw the prison going in the future.

There was a commonly held understanding amongst Governors that most prisoners have a precise sense of what they can and cannot legitimately expect from life inside and it is only when this 'legitimate expectation' is met that order and safety can result. Regulating the prison in such a way as to deliver these elements was a central theme in good governance, according to Governors. In the absence of this sense of a just community, not only would the rights of prisoners be gravely under-mined but also the security of the prison and safety of staff and prisoners would be put at risk.

In reality prisons differ to a 'significant extent' in values such as respect, humanity, relationships, trust, fairness, order, well-being and decency' (Liebling and Arnold 2002: 5). The challenge for Governors is to regulate their institutions in such a way that they ensure that these positive values are embedded in the culture, and are adhered to by both staff and prisoners. Ensuring that the operation of the prison is seen as being legitimate is far from easy when 'every instance of brutality, every casual racist joke and demeaning remark, every ignored petition, every unwarranted bureaucratic delay, every inedible meal, every arbitrary decision to segregate or transfer without giving clear and well founded reasons, every petty miscarriage of justice, every futile and inactive period of time – is delegitimating' (Sparks and Bottoms 1995: 60).

Governors have to be seen to be acting legitimately (in terms of formal rules) at all times, and in ways that demonstrate fairness and provide meaningful rationales for the exercise of their power. This was particu-larly the case when conducting adjudications:

> People are looking for clues, staff and prisoners are looking for clues about how the prison is being run, what is important, what is not important, what is acceptable, not acceptable. It is a simple mechanism for gauging what is important and what is not in prison, is adjudications, and that is at several levels in respect of managing the prison.

> The importance I attach to adjudications, because that is the one central activity in a Governor's life where there is a public statement that the Governor is able to make about the standards, the values that he or she will expect of all the parties in the community. And that is actually speaking publicly to the institution. I mean that is a very interesting opportunity to do that and also a formal opportun-ity for the process of reparation to be seen to be taking place actually.

Prison officers possess a considerable degree of discretion in carrying out their job (Hawkins 1976; Fleisher 1989; Earley 1993; Liebling and Price 2001; Conover 2001). In the absence of detailed and unambiguous directions, a prison officer is confronted on a daily basis with 'numerous dilemmas' (Sykes 1958: 130; Morris and Morris 1963: 209). These dilemmas surround the interpretation of rules and regulations: whether a prisoner should be put on a disciplinary charge; what is appropriate behaviour; what is a reasonable amount of property in a cell; who to unlock from a cell first; who can have a shower when. Governors indicated that they needed to ensure that the behaviour of their officers was appropriate. This involved Governors having to prevent unnecessary adjudications; undue searches; inconsistent treatment; staff picking on particular prisoners; varying access to gym, canteen, showers and time out of cell. Governors need to stop prisoners being humiliated or feeling powerless, as well as ensuring that abuse does not take place and prisoners are not subjected to mind games and 'wind-ups' by staff. A Governor gave this example:

> However good the regime and conditions, if officers are abusing prisoners there will be trouble. I don't mean by that physically abusing prisoners, but in the way officers talk to prisoners and respond to their requests, the way they deliver the mail, what they say when unlocking in the morning and when locking up at night.

Governors are able to limit the discretionary room of their prison officers by resolving dilemmas that officers have to cope with. They are able to do this by designing detailed rules, regulations and routines that help to clarify what is expected in specific circumstances (Etzioni 1965). In addition, Governors can seek to influence how officers use their discretion by creating an 'interpretative framework' for dealing with day-to-day issues which arise in the officers' encounters with prisoners, and by establishing clear standards and expectations, as these Governors make clear:

> The Governor's job is to set the tone and pace of the establishment is the way in which I always describe it. I think the tone is about all the concepts that I would want to see in a well-run prison. The tone is about things like inside justice. The tone is about dignity, the way in which we treat each other, not just the way we treat the prisoners but the way in which we treat each other as staff.

> I think that one of the most important things that a Governor does, much more important than being a good finance manager, being a good personnel manager ... is set a moral standard for the establishment. He dictates the way the prisoners are treated.

Regulating the interface between uniformed staff and prisoners is made the more complicated because of the imbalance of power between them, the nature of a closed institution and the often-conflicting values and beliefs. Governors spoke of having to balance the interests, expectations, demands and perceptions of these various groups within their prisons:

The all important thing to me is for the Governor to make sure that he actually has the balance between the managers, the staff, and the prisoners absolutely right, so that the prisoners feel safe and are satisfied that we are giving them a fair deal, the staff feel safe and feel that they are having a good deal and the managers therefore actually also feel safe because we are a stable environment without too much problem.

The differing perspectives of staff and prisoners becomes most explicit when staff safety is perceived as being at risk:

It has happened to me a few times. A prisoner has assaulted a member of staff and the staff have moved the prisoner to the seg. At what point do I let him up? The staff want to keep him down there, the prisoner has done his time in CC [cellular confinement]. Everyone – the staff and the cons – are watching to see what you will do. You've got to balance lots of things in deciding what to do.

Governors saw the way in which prisoners' complaints were dealt with as being particularly important. While there will always be a danger that officers perceive that a Governor is appeasing prisoners by 'giving in' to their demands, Governors indicated that they had always to bear in mind the importance of achieving and maintaining legitimacy:

I need to always bear in mind the bigger picture even if it does make me unpopular with staff sometimes. What they forget is that prisoners are often right about things – take for example something that happened a few weeks ago. There has been a problem with the laundry and getting clean kit to the wings on time. We should have sorted it but for whatever reason we let it slip. The prisoners on B wing decided to refuse to go away [return to their cells] until they got clean kit. I went and talked to them and agreed with the points that they were making and said that we would sort it out. For me that was about doing what was right but some of the officers thought that I had given in to their demands and showed weakness.

One of the most sensitive areas is how a Governor deals with an allegation against a member of staff. All eyes in the prison focus on the Governor and watch to see what the Governor does with the complaint:

If one of the prisoners makes an allegation, what do you do? Do you suspend the officer, call the police, get someone to investigate, see the prisoner? It is not easy and probably has caused me most anguish since I came here. It sends messages, whatever you do sends messages out there. All sorts of things go through your mind. If the prisoners think you are doing nothing they will kick off. If you suspend the officer the POA will storm in and there may be a vote of no confidence. As you know, I'm not joking. My last Governor had a demo in the yard because the prisoners thought someone had been hit and the Governor was doing nothing about it. You've got to balance things, try and do what you think is right and stick with it. I've suspended a few staff since I've been here – there was a culture that it was OK to clip the lads around the ear. They now know that I will not put up with that crap.

Governors also regulated their establishments by maintaining a high profile and by acting as a role model. Governors believe that they are seen as the embodiment of what the establishment stands for and that staff and prisoners mirror their behaviour and approach:

> ... people actually trust what you do, not what you say or what's written down in the policy ... and if your examples are bad, then it makes it very difficult for people to give of their best. And it encourages people who might want to behave in an inappropriate way to do exactly that. Similarly the converse is true, if the example is good, then it will encourage people who would want to follow that example to be able to do it. And it discourages people from doing the opposite.

Governors spoke of the need to establish a physical presence in their prisons. This aspect of the work involves more than visiting areas of the prison to do auditing and monitoring. It was about finding out what was going on and ensuring that standards were being upheld:

> I said clearly that everyday I'm in the prison I have to go on the landings. No ifs, no buts. I don't care who's visiting. I don't care what meetings are on – I have to be visible. The primary function of a Governor is about being visible ... I walk round everywhere at least once, maybe twice, once in the morning and once in the afternoon, and aim to be at the hotplate. I will know then that I will see every prisoner at [this small category C prison] because I will be there and they will walk past me. I just think that's the real, first practical element at looking at being a governing Governor ... It allows you to set the tone, allows people to see you, allows you to gauge the feeling about the place, allows you to set proper standards, allows staff to see that you'll go where they may think it's difficult, and that's just a basic fundamental of governing. You cannot govern an establishment from behind a desk.

Maintaining a high profile also enabled governors to talk to staff and send messages about their standards and beliefs:

> I think it's very important that you are seen round the prison, that people know what your views are . . . staff should be aware of what the Governor is, or what his views are, what his standards are, and what sort of formal and informal measures, or should I say informal sanctions, are acceptable.

The amount that a Governor interacts with prisoners, the manner of the interaction and the language used, all send messages about how the Governor sees the community behaving:

> The fact is people do as you do. That the role model that you portray is very important. And that is delivered personally by the individual who is in charge.

> Someone once described, very accurately in my view, the Governor's role as being someone who is on stage, somewhat of a performer. From the moment he walks in the gate, he is under constant focus from his staff who watch very closely his reactions to certain things and I think that's right. Governors . . . are frequently tested to gauge their reaction to see what they will tolerate.

Walking around the prison allows Governors to communicate key messages but it also brings with it a potential danger. Governors do have to be wary of what they say and do as their actions and words can be misinterpreted, as one Governor recollected:

> Everything you do as Governor sends messages about where the line should be drawn. They all look to you for a signal about what will be tolerated and what won't. You've got to be very careful about what you do and say and what decisions you take. An off the cuff remark can have a major impact. I remember the time I told my security PO [principal officer] that one workshop did not have good tool security because of the windows. The next thing I knew the works were boarding up the windows. It didn't matter that it had been like it for years. The Governor had said something so it needed sorting. Didn't matter about the poor sods in the workshop having to work without natural light!

Many of these regulating functions can be described in today's vocabulary as manifestations of 'risk management'. Governors have to identify risks, assess those risks and then decide what level of risk is acceptable, on a daily basis. Governors gave these examples of where balancing risks became critical:

> Let me give you a recent example of what I mean by the delicate balance. I got kosher security info that there was a knife on the wing. So what do you do? One answer is to target who we think has got it and shove him in the seg. Fine but he's unlikely to keep the blade in his cell and someone else may get their hands on it, so we would have to wait for more intelligence. Or do you bang up the entire wing till it's found and manage the reaction from the lads when they finally get unlocked? Or do nothing and wait for it to be used? There are lots of other ways to manage that situation as you know but that gives you an idea of the sort of decisions we have to take . . . You use your experience, advice from others and often a gut feeling for what is the right thing to do.

> The doctor told me the other day that a red band [trusted prisoner who is given a responsible job] in the kitchen was HIV positive. You then have to think it through, the risks, and the possible consequences. Do you leave him there or do you move him?

Underpinning all aspects of a Governor's work is the need for the Governor to understand how prisons work; how the different aspects of a prison are intertwined; how a decision about one issue will have implications in another; and how the differing stakeholder groups will perceive decisions. This is what Governors call 'jailcraft'. Many Governors in the study highlighted its importance:

> I view jailcraft as knowing the ins and outs of a prison. Of being able to walk in all lines of that prison. Of being able to move up and move down at a whim, depending on who you are talking to. Of being able to gauge the atmosphere within a prison, not just gauging the atmosphere of whether there's tension, but gauging the actual atmosphere when you are talking to an inmate. The vibes coming from that inmate. Knowing what you can say and what you can't say. Knowing how you should bring him down. Knowing that if you say the wrong thing it is going to bring him up. That is jailcraft.

Stakeholder power and impact

The days of the prison fiefdom are long gone and Governors are now no longer free to do things according to whim. The present study confirms earlier findings that a Governor's ability to do things is dependent on a complex network of power-relations between stakeholders: '. . . although the governor is in overall charge of the institution and its various parts, he or she must satisfy a number of masters over a wide range of issues' (Vagg 1994: 110).

These stakeholders include a larger number of people and groups than ever before: prison staff; Prison Officers Association (POA); prisoners; administrators at Prison Service Headquarters; area managers; local bodies and organisations (such as YOTs and DATs); Boards of Visitors; politicians; pressure groups; lawyers; prisoners' families; media; and the public. These stakeholders confront one another as actors in a dynamic play of conflict, compromise, and mutual influence, what Giddens terms the 'dialectic of control in social systems' (Giddens 1984: 16). The situation has been described in the following way: 'Power is not untrammelled, and governors are routinely in negotiation with others – uniformed staff, central administration, prisoners, Boards of Visitors, and so on' (Sparks et al. 1996: 136).

Governors pointed out that, today, their ability to deliver depends increasingly on the relative power of stakeholders and their willingness to use that power to enact or subvert the Governor's plans and activities.

The interviews with Governors indicated that the relationship between Governors and the centre (Headquarters and its 'field' representative, the area manager) is a complex, and sometimes a tense one. In the past, Governors were in a position in which they were either unable, or unwilling, to comply with centrally prescribed policies. They were able to ignore, manipulate or interpret policy directives. Governors still have 'implementation discretion', like all operational senior managers, which allows them to develop courses of action that contradict or violate central policy prescriptions (Ingram 1990 and Winter 1990). Operational realities, and the need to deal with the contradictions that present themselves in Governors' daily work, are not easily reconciled with central prescription. The tension, between the Governors' desire to run their prisons as they would wish, and the Prison Service administrators' belief that all prisons should be managed in a consistent manner, continues to be a dominant one.

Governors also emphasised that at establishment level, the nature, character and culture of a prison has a huge impact on what they are able to do, how they manage and how quickly they are able to deliver changes. Challenging the status quo and achieving fundamental change requires existing patterns of behaviour, attitudes and expectations to change. This, in turn, requires that the existing ethos and equilibrium of a prison be disturbed, a process which can encounter resistance, both passive and active, from staff and prisoners.

Incoming Governors quickly become conscious that their freedom of action is constrained. They have to be particularly aware of what

Giddens (1984) refers to as the 'sense of place'. Each prison staff culture is distinct in terms of its memories, folklores, identities, and enmities (Garland 1990). It is the product of complex connections between everyday activities of individuals, the larger trajectory of their biographies, and the special features of each prison. This is especially true of older prisons that are small and bounded communities, and where many of the staff have been there for an extended period. Prison officers are therefore intimately aware of the history, traditions, and culture of the place, and significant events that, in the past, have helped to shape the culture and the 'way' things are done in their prison. One Governor explained the importance of understanding the relationship between local culture and change in this way:

> I've worked in many prisons over the years and I can honestly say that the culture was very different. I did things in one which I would never have got away with in another . . . The staff vary a lot – some of that has to do with the power of the POA, how long staff have worked there and the style of previous Governors . . . That affects what you can do. Changing anything at [an old training prison] was a huge bloody trauma. The POA would come in and say, 'Back in 1890 Governor so and so tried that and it didn't work, so let's not bother trying again.' Whereas at [a new local prison] there was no real history, so everything was new and certainly in the early days the staff were up for trying out new things.

The power and ability of the POA to resist change at a national Prison Service level, as well as at each prison, is legendary and well founded. Historically, the focus of the power struggle has been between Governors and uniformed staff, as the often-vitriolic industrial relations situation demonstrates (see Stern 1987: 78–83). Governors made clear that where the POA is particularly strong a Governor's ability to drive forward change would be more limited:

> I must say it's been a battle here over everything. The POA are antediluvian in their approach. They want nothing changed. They argue over the smallest things and we have so many 'failures to agree'. I've worked hard to try and get a good relationship but for the POA it's about objecting to everything. I'm sure if I said that door was blue, they'd argue it was red.

Line managers below the Governor, particularly senior and principal officers, are responsible for the daily implementation of the Governor's policies. This group is in a strong position therefore to impact on the level of implementation and the routine treatment of prisoners. As one

Governor put it: '. . . officers identified what they regarded as a flaw in the management chain which sometimes altered the Governor's intentions, preventing them from being translated into action. In other words, middle managers were thought to modify the Governor's policies' (Leonard 1999: 62).

Life in a prison is a continuous process of negotiation between the various actors, and power is not a thing which is possessed by one group of actors (prison staff) and directed at another (prisoners) but something which is in a constant state of negotiation between the two groups (see Sykes 1958; Morris and Morris 1963; Sparks *et al.* 1996; Bosworth 1999; Liebling and Price 2001; Godderis 2006). Governors were quick to make clear that prisoners were far from being a malleable and passive group, and that they frequently exercised power. They gave examples where prisoners had demonstrated their power by collectively protesting over food; regime time changes; visits arrangements; the time that television is turned off; the quality of the laundry; temperature in cells; and suspected brutality by prison officers. These protests are usually met with some success, in that Governors indicated that they would take such collective complaints seriously. Governors gave examples of individual prisoner protests that they had to deal with: movement to another prison; parole results; what personal possessions can be held in cells; adjudication results; and change of category. These individual protests tended to meet with a less sympathetic response from Governors.

Governors highlighted the fact that they needed to get prisoner agreement, or at least acquiescence, to maintain the daily routine in their prisons. They relied on prisoners for intelligence information; to cooperate with the regime; and on prisoner labour to undertake routine tasks. Prisoners act therefore as agents as well as subjects (Bosworth and Carrrabine 2001; Godderis 2006) and are able, to some extent, to influence how prisons operate. The same is not true for all prison systems. The development of Supermax prisons in the USA, for example, has to a great extent designed out the scope for prisoners to have any influence whatsoever (King 1999).

Governors highlighted the power of prisoners, as a group, to thwart or delay change. Governors spoke of having to negotiate with prisoners or to 'bribe' them into accepting changes to the regime:

I remember well the change over to private firms taking over the canteen and bringing in a bagging system. That was potentially a difficult change to manage, something which prisoners were concerned about and something that would have led to much grief if we didn't handle it well. As it happens I gave them all an extra phone card and quarter of an ounce of tobacco and there was no problem.

Most people would think prisoners do what they are told. Well, you and I know for a fact that's not true. There is no such thing as absolute power; it's about relative power. Take for example when I tried to extend the working day in the shops . . . Then the prisoners started; wanting more pay for a longer day. I couldn't bloody believe it. We put a few of the ringleaders in the block [segregation unit] but there was still a groundswell of feeling . . . and we had to rethink it all.

This view reinforces findings of an earlier study which concluded that 'most prisoners find the ability to express their agency and to resist. Few prisons are run by coercion' (Bosworth 1999: 131).

Multiple and conflicting roles

Merton hypothesised that each social status (an individual's position in the social system) involves not only a single associated role but also 'an array of associated roles' (Merton 1957: 369). This 'role-set' consists of the complement of role relationships which persons have by virtue of occupying a particular social status. Governors spoke of having a number of related and overlapping roles, instead of having a single role. To speak of the Governor's role is therefore misleading, in that there appears to be no single role but rather a 'role-set' associated with the office of Governor. The Governor has internal (prison) roles in relation to staff and prisoners, and at the same time external (Prison Service) roles in relation to Headquarters and the broader community.

As a result of the environmental changes described in Chapter 4, the relative importance of the various roles that the Governor is expected to undertake is changing:

The reality of taking on the role of the Governor is that it is changing and you need to keep up with how it is procedurally prescribed, culturally prescribed, socially prescribed, and organisationally prescribed.

One of the themes to emerge from the research is that there is some disagreement amongst prison stakeholders over the Governors' current role, what they should do and the way they should govern. At times, different stakeholders ('role senders' – Yukl 1994) can make incompatible demands on the Governor, creating role conflicts (Kahn 1964). Conflicts may involve a difference of opinion over the relative priority of two roles (for example, internal manager or external figurehead), or the manner in which a role is carried out (for example, ensuring justice by doing adjudications themselves or by checking the records of adjudications completed by others). Sometimes role conflict occurs simply because of the range of expectations placed on the Governor, as this quote suggests:

> It's a difficult one. It's difficult sometimes knowing what you should be doing as we wear so many hats. Everyone wants a piece of you as Governor and they all want you to do different things.

Role expectations can also be inconsistent with objective task requirements. This is especially the case when the nature of the task has changed, while the norms and beliefs about the proper exercise of the role have remained the same:

> I get a little frustrated at times as you are pulled in so many different directions. Area office want you to do the papers and write reports. My staff want to see me around the place and to be able to see me about their personal problems. Prisoners want me to do their apps [applications to have an interview with the Governor]. The area manager told me to do adjudications, and wants me to represent him at meetings at Headquarters. And on top of that the local community want me to cut ribbons and speak at the WI [Women's Institute]. Well, you can't do the bloody lot, can you? You have to make choices.

The conflict between the organisational demands to operate as the general manager of the prison, and the expectations of the staff and prisoners who adhere to a more traditional view of how Governors should use their time, creates tension for Governors. In Giddens' (1990) terminology, there is a tension between 'place based' (traditional figurehead, highly visible, direct contact with prisoners) and 'non-place based' (modern manager) structures and systems. Governors pointed to a number of specific examples where their traditional and modern roles came into conflict:

> I am finding it harder and harder to achieve a balance between what I need to do to keep the area manager happy and what staff and prisoners expect me to be doing as Governor. This is not some semantic difference, it is a real issue for many of us – do the paperwork or get around the prison. Spend time in the prison or go to outside meetings. Talk with staff and prisoners or write a report on something for area. I exaggerate but there are real tensions.

> Uniformed staff still, particularly those more experienced uniformed staff, still view their own Governor in the traditional sense. That he

is the master of all you survey and he is the really important one in the prison that you have got to worry about. It's changing – some of the younger staff are seeing the Governor in a wider concept, as someone that should be giving support and guidance – should be giving them support and guidance – and a much more modern managerial role of the Governor.

Faced with potentially conflicting views about their roles, Governors indicated that they have either to conform to expectations from as many role senders as possible, or risk being labelled as non-conformist or a bad Governor. The current research suggests that Governors each take up the roles as they see fit, in the context of the various expectations placed upon them. This always leads to some variation between Governors.

Variations in management style and approach

Governors do very similar work, as one Governor put it:

I think there will be a pretty good slam of commonality between what they are doing as Governors and what I'm doing as a Governor. I'd hazard a guess that there's probably about 80 per cent overlap – I don't know. The critical bit is the bit on the margin but what I do outside of very interesting interviews with Shane Bryans et al. is do what everybody else is doing, which is flog through the paperwork, translate the paperwork and intention and policy and instructions into managerial action.

How they do that work depends on the style and approach of each Governor. Individual Governors approach their work with a complex array of concepts, theoretical models, experience and knowledge:

We are all different and we have all got our own styles and ways of doing it . . . different individuals will do that differently because of their styles.

The interviews indicated that Governors have different management styles and approaches with regard to whether power was shared and with whom; how visible they were in the prison; what they spent their time doing; and how a prison should be organised and run. A Governor's approach and style can be influenced by a number of factors: background, ideology, training, experience and needs of a particular post (Margerison 1991; Salaman 1992; Mumford 1997). From the current study it is possible to identify variations in the approaches adopted by Governors.

Some Governors adopted a more 'autocratic approach' and their responses indicated that they sought to dominate staff, as well as prisoners. These Governors exercised personal power and seemed to share decision-making with few others. A number of interviewees spoke of their prisons in a way that conjured up images of a prison fiefdom reminiscent of a medieval barony:

> Some people would call me autocratic I suppose but it is more about setting standards and making sure they are met. I'm the Governor and I'm in charge. My officers and prisoners know that. They know I make the decisions and I am responsible for everything that happens in my prison . . . Yes, I do go around bollocking people but I see that as part of my job.

> It is no different to when I was in the army. I am the commanding officer and people do what I tell them or else. I don't hold fucking debates, I make up my mind and tell people. My dep expects me to tell him what to do and that goes all the way down . . . Everyone in this prison knows what is expected of them and gets on with it.

Most Governors interviewed indicated that they adopted a more 'shared-power approach' – one where the staff are empowered but the Governor remains in control. This approach seemed to place less emphasis on the use of detailed written orders and more on 'trusting' officers to exercise their discretion, according to the ethos and standards set by the Governor. Governors who adopted this approach would often consult staff and prisoners before making decisions:

> I can't tell you when I last issued an order . . . It's very easy. I could just walk in and say do that and it would be done. It would be done without question but what I need to know is that it is being done when I'm not there. You have to encourage, you have to remind, you have to persuade people that there is a better way to do it or you want something else to happen, but you have to explain why you want it to happen and the part that plays in a bigger picture, so that they have got a framework in which to operate.

> I don't always feel comfortable with the paramilitary uniformed bit. Society has moved on and so have people's expectations. I just couldn't get away with some of the things I saw my old Governors doing to staff. These days we need to involve more, consult more and get people to see why we want things done. It's more about asking and encouraging than telling.

One of the main factors that differentiated Governors in terms of their style was the degree to which they got involved in the detailed operation of the prison. Some Governors were more 'hands on' and spoke of being involved in the smallest detail of the running of the prison. Examples given included doing cell inspections; checking keys at the key safe and money in the cashier's office; and allocating all the incoming mail at a daily meeting. Others adopted a high-level, strategic approach focusing more on long-terms plans than day-to-day operational issues:

> I quite often go and help out with rub down searches during labour movement or go and serve the food on the hotplate . . . It helps me to remember what all this is really about.

> I see my role as a strategic one, it is about direction and planning not about the day-to-day operations of [a large local prison]. My senior team, especially the dep, run the routine things and to be honest I don't understand the detailed mechanics of what keeps this place going. My dep was promoted from PO [principal officer] to the governor grades so knows what makes this place tick and I leave that to him.

What was common to both groups was the belief in the need to maintain a personal presence in the prison. As one former Governor put it: 'We must recognise that prisons are not perfect organisations of efficiency, fairness and justice. Because of this, the governor's awareness of his prison must rest on more than a vicarious knowledge' (Gadd 1988: 8).

While the desire to be visible was common to all Governors, in reality Governors varied in the extent to which they visited all areas of the prison, and what they saw as the purpose of the visit. Some Governors did a traditional daily 'tour' of the prison; others were more focused and conducted inspection visits according to a rolling schedule. This individualistic approach can be compared to the US Bureau of Prisons, which is prescriptive and requires that: 'when they tour, [Wardens] must actively seek out information, not just passively walk around' (Henderson and Phillips 1989: 16).

Governors also indicated that the length of time that they had been in post, the 'phase of governorship', as one Governor put it, influenced the way they did the job. The longer that Governors had been in post the more willing they were to trust other people to do routine work, and the less need they felt to impose themselves on daily decision-making. After a long period in post, Governors believed that staff understood their approach and could be expected to make decisions in accordance with their standards. In the early days of a governorship, Governors appeared keen to establish themselves and maintain a high visibility to ensure that staff knew what was expected and to set standards:

> I suppose it is about the stage in the governorship. Here I am still very much about trying to set standards and picking up things that I think are not right and trying to say to people, this is not right, this is what we need to do to set it right . . . I like to know what's going on and why it's going on. At [my last prison] in the latter days, then I suppose I was slightly different. I would have much more of a routine day because the staff there were empowered so I had complete confidence that, in a sense, nothing would go wrong or happen, with any significance, without me hearing about it. That's not the case here. It's still very much this is the problem and the Governor will sort it out, so we are still in the very early days I think.

In the past, there was no 'the Prison Service way of doing it' embedded in the socialisation or training of Governors. A book or manual on 'how to govern a prison' does not exist and there is currently no prescription on style or 'mould' into which Governors must fit. To a great extent Governors seem to develop their own 'how to govern' template from seeing other Governors operating, their role models, and experience early in their service.

The issue of compatibility between the Governor's style and what is needed in an institution at a particular time has been the subject of some debate. A number of examples were recounted by Governors of where incoming Governors had adopted very different approaches and styles to their predecessors or were not the 'type' of Governor that the staff wanted. As a result, Governors have been known to suffer 'status degradation' (Garfinkel 1956) or have been moved from their post (Finkelstein 1996). A recent report highlighted the matter in this way:

> Feltham's Board of Visitors noted that Mr Clifford walked the ship, and was regularly seen around the establishment. In that way, the message went out to everyone that he was going to be 'hands on'. But his personal style was not to everyone's taste, and it may not have been right for this critical time in Feltham's history. He was a forthright man, who had a tendency to talk down to staff, and to be long on criticism while short on praise . . . In an establishment where staff morale was so low, what was needed was a Governor who was able to get staff on his side. The anecdotal evidence was that this was an area in which Mr Clifford did not succeed. (Keith 2006: para. 40.7)

Institutional influences

Governors frequently made the point that while prisons were substantially the same with regard to rules and regulations, they could vary dramatically in terms of their local culture and working practices. This is in contrast to earlier studies that adopted an ideal-type notion to prisons that saw them as everywhere substantially similar (Sykes 1958; Goffman 1968).

The characteristics of each prison (size, age, stage of development, architecture and category) were highlighted during the interviews as having an impact on the way Governors govern. The size of a prison, in terms of the number of staff and prisoners, can dictate how the Governor spends his or her time:

> I think you have got to look at the size of the establishment before you can actually come to a view on the role and work of the Governor ... I think Governor 3 prisons are still of a size and non-complexity that an energetic Governor can run by dint of their own personality ... I think once you move up to the next level of establishment, to a Governor 2 establishment, then the Governor, as a manager, has to be reverting to being a team player. You are working through systems. In small prisons, the Governor is clearly the dominant force, both physically in terms of being able to get round it and in terms of having the hand on most key decisions. You move up then to the next level ... you need the systems to run it.

The physical structure, architecture and area the prison occupies also had an impact on what a Governor is able to do. Governors pointed out that they have far more contact with staff and prisoners in smaller establishments, as they are able to maintain a presence in all areas of the institution on a daily basis. In larger establishments Governors said that they have to rely on other means to ensure that key messages about standards and culture reach the staff and prisoner population:

> Here for instance you can't go right round the establishment in the morning because it is too big, unless you just walk. If you want to stop and talk to people, you can't do it. So I don't get around [this prison] daily like I did at [a small local prison].

It is not only the size of the establishment that dictates the ability of a Governor to visit all areas; it is also the physical layout, as one Governor made clear:

The amount that you can do yourself in any gaol differs. It wasn't difficult at [a small YOI] – if I wanted to get round the gaol and be seen in all the wings, I could do that in an hour and a half very easily. I couldn't do that [at this large local prison]. If I was at Pentonville, for all the size in terms of prison numbers at Pentonville, like almost twice the number we've got here, I could do it in 15 minutes, because Pentonville has only got a traditional Victorian four wings and a lot of prisoners on each of the wings. It's all contained literally within a very short site and you can actually physically get round the site in no time.

The challenge for Governors of prisons which are not of a traditional panopticon design is how best to maximise their presence across a geographically spread-out institution. One Governor had clearly appreciated the social meaning of modern prison architecture:

At [a large local prison of a panopticon design] it was easy. I would stand on the centre first thing in the morning, at lunch and teatime and everyone would know that the Governor was there. I could see all the landings on all the wings but more importantly all the staff on duty that day and all the prisoners could see me. They seemed to find it reassuring to know that 'the old man' was there. Whereas here [a campus-style training prison] it's a nightmare. I could spend all morning walking about and only see a few staff and prisoners. So I thought about it and now I always head for the times and places when people will see me. You know, in the gate first thing in the morning to see the staff coming on duty; or standing on the yard when labour movement is going on. All the prisoners walk by and see you there.

Governors are able therefore to compensate for a prison's physical layout by adjusting their way of working. Overcoming the constraints of prison architecture is possible as 'ultimately the problem is not one of architecture. It is a problem of philosophy' (Casale 1989: 98).

Another factor highlighted by Governors as determining the work that they did was the stage of development of the prison:

There are certain things which, at certain stages, depending on what you feel about where the organisation is, you spend more time on.

If the jail is going through a difficult time, whether it be a rocky time operationally, then clearly your approach has to be different than if it's going through a difficult time financially. If it's the former you will probably be about the prison more and be visible. If it's

153

financial difficulties you will be in an office poring over a bloody calculator. So I think it is different depending where you are.

If you have just taken over perhaps a big local prison whose culture needs sorting out, then I think one spends an enormous amount of time and energy trying to shift the culture and redirect that place rather than looking at other stuff.

Ideology, ethics and values

The degree to which their ideologies, ethics and values inform and direct Governors' work is an issue which has received little attention. Chapter 5 described the Governors' espoused ideologies – the values, beliefs and goals that underpin their daily work. The interviews suggest that, based on their ideologies, Governors appear to develop what Sykes (1958: 35) refers to as a 'philosophy of custody' in order to inform the way they exercise their discretion and run their institutions. Governors seem to develop this 'philosophy of custody' as a means of coping with the ambiguity and uncertainty of centrally imposed goals and tasks (Street *et al.* 1966; DiIulio 1987; Boin 1998) and because 'prisons are a minefield of difficult moral issues' (Lewis 1997: 62). This 'philosophy of custody' was often not explicit in the interviews but rather a subconscious operating philosophy that seemed to underpin and guide their daily work.

Governors in the study made the point that you cannot have 'value-free' governance but that values should inform daily activities and decision-making:

The governance of prisons cannot be reduced to the 'value-free' promotion of economy, efficiency, effectiveness. It's got to be about more than just getting more for your money or the achievement of key performance indicators. It's about promoting human rights and keeping potential harm to a minimum. Governors must know where they stand and keep to their principles.

I think that Governors have a duty to think about the legitimacy and propriety of things before rushing to do them. We must ask ourselves, 'Is this the right thing to do?' And we must be prepared to make a stand on some things. After all, I believe that we are the last bastion in protecting prisoners' rights.

Commentators have taken a similar view and suggested that:

Prisons and other institutions retain one major difference, they operate within an intensely moral arena ... Good Governors provide a strong sense of what their values are – what is acceptable and what is not ... Governors must have the capacity to project a strong moral framework in their unique institutions. This is more than rule setting or passively requiring standards to be observed. (Acheson 2003: 12)

Governors revealed that they face ethical dilemmas on a daily basis. They may be required to make decisions that involve a breach of acceptable behaviour or the rules (Zinn 1993); a choice between equally unsatisfactory alternatives (Davis and Aroskar 1978); competing values and loyalties (Loewenberg and Dolgoff 1988); and conflicting ethical values (Walker 1993). These examples provided by Governors indicate types of ethical issues that can arise:

What you stand for comes out in different ways. I had to decide the other day where to spend a bit of money we had. It came down to a choice between spending it on the visits room or the staff locker room. Not a life and death matter but made me think about things.

Should I break the rules if I morally think it the right thing to do? You know what I mean – do I let someone out for a funeral even though they do not fit the criteria? Well, I am old enough in the tooth to do what I think is right. Not everybody does that these days. I guess the ambitious Governors do everything by the book, which is probably why I am still a Governor and not an area manager.

I was doing adjudications the other day and had to decide whose evidence to believe – the prisoner or the officer. Did I believe the prisoner who has a criminal record or the officer who has a responsible job? It's something Governors have to do all the time.

A number of Governors spoke passionately about their belief that they had a duty to prevent physical and mental damage to prisoners. This duty was grounded in morality and ethics rather than in any managerial requirement to prevent abuse:

So I think the role of the Governor is far greater than just managing an institution. It's far greater than just being managerially responsible. It has a social dimension as well. I see my job as making sure that people are not abused. I do not mean physically abused, even though that is always a danger, but mentally abused and taken advantage of. You know, being unlocked later than everyone else or having smaller portions of food or letters not arriving. That sort of thing.

155

Overcrowding, for example, created 'value conflict' for a number of Governors:

> I am finding it much harder to get the right balance between what is right for individual prisoners and what I am being told to do. These days, with pressures on numbers and space it is all about moving people around. But it causes problems, for example, what about the prisoner who is in the middle of a course or training programme? What about the prisoner who wants to come back here for a local discharge? Do I do what is right for the prisoner or what I am being told to do by the Prison Service?

Moral conflict can also be seen as resulting from the drive to introduce managerialism (see Chapter 4) into the Prison Service. A number of Governors spoke of the potential conflict between running an efficient machine-like bureaucracy which 'processed' prisoners, reduced costs and achieved targets, and their commitment to treat prisoners as individuals with needs that should be met. The management of any penal institution carries with it the moral duty to remember that it holds individuals and that it is not about processing 'units'. One Governor put it in this way:

> Actually it is more than bureaucracy. It's more than the administration process. It's not just about having a nicely administered prison. Because I'm sure it's perfectly possible to conceive of very nice concentration camps that would have been very clean and all the paperwork was done, and all the rest of it, but actually, probably were achieving their purpose, but not the humanitarian sort of thing. So I see, in that sense, management and administration as neutral. That they are what you have to do to achieve a particular end, but the end in fact could be making widgets. It is how the Governor exercises his discretion that influences the culture and what the place is really like and that depends on his values and beliefs.

The managerialist culture did not fit readily with some Governors' caring and reforming ideas and was seen by some as an attempt to change their orientation, value base and ways of working. The language and tools of managerialism (for example, managing director instead of Governor, strategic and business planning, units as a term for prisoners) have been criticised as being inappropriate for use in a caring profession (Wilson 1995). One Governor was moved to write:

> Values and policies to which Governors have long been committed, are now derided as soft-headed and soft-hearted ... one conse-

quence of the trend towards pragmatism is that we have become accustomed to seeing efficiency as the *only* goal . . . I believe that one of the reasons for Governors' depression is that many of us do not share the values underlying current policies. Nor do we believe that those policies are in the best interests of victims, potential victims, offenders or their families. (Godfrey 1996: 13)

This view from Governors endorses the suggestion from a number of academics who noted that new managerialism in the Prison Service was seen by its critics as eroding the traditional moral (including reformative) commitments of institutions in favour of an exclusive concern with *process* and measurement (Sparks *et al.* 1996). The professional and vocational values that underpinned the motivation of many Governors on joining the Prison Service are coming into conflict with the more managerial approach found today, thereby creating a degree of 'institutional dissonance' (Rutherford 1994: 160).

Many Governors embraced the changes (for various reasons – survival, self-promotion, belief in the new way), while others suggested that they were waiting silently for the pendulum to swing back in the other direction. A few Governors were subjected to 'robust management' as a result of their views and approach. A small number of senior Governors who were not well disposed to the changes left their governing posts (some willingly, others less so), either on early retirement or because they were given non-operational posts. One Governor described his dilemma in this way:

I love governing and it's why I joined the Service but to be frank, the pressure is starting to get to me. The performance management stuff and the paperwork, it's not the same as it was and I'm not convinced that it is the right way forward. I'm looking to move on and spend my last few years behind a desk somewhere shuffling papers.

Whatever their correctional and managerial orientation, Governors in the study shared an espoused commitment to protect prisoners' rights, ensuring that no brutality takes place; preserve life, minimising the number of suicides; and provide decent living conditions. Most achieve this; a few do not. The Prison Service continues to be faced with criticism of the conditions in a number of its prisons (see, for example, CPT 1996, 2000 and 2002; HM Chief Inspector of Prisons 1997a; annual reports of HM Chief Inspector of Prisons) and the lack of care of some prisoners (Wilson and Fowler 2004; Keith 2006).

A myriad of moral and ethical concerns will continue to surround the governance of our prisons. Governors will remain at the forefront of recognising that the moral foundation of our prisons involves moving from the safety of a scientific, objective analysis of prison issues towards the more uncomfortable, and likely more obscure, ethical questions about how we choose to treat those individuals that we confine (Godderis 2006: 265).

This chapter has given an indication of some of the reality of governing. What Governors do, and what they are able to achieve, is the result of the interaction of a range of personal, organisational and prison-specific factors. The simple conception that Governors are free agents able to do and achieve what they want is no longer, even if it ever was, a reality. No Governor receives, or is able to impose, a template of how that prison should be governed or what they can hope to deliver, on taking over a prison. The myriad stakeholders, the idiosyncrasy of Governors, and the architecture of prisons all combine to make each period of governance distinct and inherently unpredictable.

Chapter 7

Prison governance – some conclusions

Variations on a theme – a typology of Governors

Earlier chapters identified the origins, backgrounds and career paths of current Governors, described their motivation for doing the job and the ideologies which influence the way they do their work (Chapter 5), emphasised work elements common to Governors as a group and the uniqueness of each Governor and environment (Chapter 6). During the research it became apparent that groups of Governors shared common beliefs, ways of operating, and approaches to prison governance – what Reiner refers to as 'distinctive constellations ... that can be seen as variations around central themes' (Reiner 1991: 303).

While prison sociology has been criticised for contenting itself with producing 'anodyne typologies' (Sparks *et al.* 1996: 81), typologies can be meaningful if categories are constructed with careful thought (Doty and Glick 1994). Common themes found amongst Governors can be viewed as 'ideal types' in the Weberian sense (Weber 1949: 84). Ideal types are models of what are logically possible permutations but are, at the end of the day, generalisations, fictitious and unlikely to be encountered in a pure form in the real world. Governors, after all, are individuals with distinct attributes and unique histories. That said, the ideal types can provide helpful comparators and benchmarks, when considering prison governance in its many forms.

Each ideal type of Governor can be defined by pedigree (origins, ideology, career path), period (when they joined the Service), place (where they have governed), and approach (management style, way of operating). Using these themes, four ideal types of Governors suggest themselves from the research: general managers; chief officers; liberal idealists and conforming mavericks.

General managers joined the Prison Service in the 1980s or 1990s. They joined on a fast-track scheme, in response to job advertisements describing the role in managerial terms. General managers can best be described as coming from an upwardly mobile working-class background. They tend to have a degree that is managerial, such as business studies, rather than a vocational degree. Their motivation for joining tended to be 'instrumental' and focused on the material aspects of the job such as pay, status, security and career prospects. General managers define their values and beliefs in managerial terms. For them it is less about a moral mission to reform prisoners and more about ensuring that key performance indicators are achieved. Individual prisoners, and their needs, are not particularly high on their agenda, as they adopt an 'actuarial approach', in which prisoners are dealt with according to group criteria. They tend to work more in large prisons where other managers deal with the daily operational grind. General managers see themselves as chief executives of a company, supported in their work by a number of departmental or functional managers. They feel comfortable chairing meetings, studying financial spreadsheets and dealing with papers. The main focus of general managers is running an 'efficient, economic and effective' prison that achieves its KPIs and runs as smoothly as possible. They concentrate on performance measures, focus on tangible achievements and adopt a short-term orientation – the annual business cycle. Their emphasis is on quantifiable results not qualitative improvement. The difficulties associated with prisons can, according to the general manager, be dealt with by a sophisticated and professional management approach. The general manager is the very model of a modern prison Governor.

Chief officers have spent most of their working career in the Prison Service and have been promoted through the ranks. Their pedigree is working-class; they enjoy the epithet 'man of the people' and pride themselves that they have made it to the top – the 'working-class lad made good'. Chief officers tend to have lower levels of formal education but do not see that as a disadvantage. Many have obtained educational qualifications, including degrees, whilst working in the Service. They have a wealth of prison-specific operational knowledge gained in the officer grades and are always keen to recount the experiences of their days in uniform – 'I've tried it, been there and done it.' Their decision-making is heavily reliant on previous experience. Chief officers espouse no particular ideology but are keen to ensure that Manuals, Orders and Instructions are read and implemented to the letter. Their philosophy is centred on doing as instructed, and achieving a disciplined, well-ordered and clean prison. There is less interest in longer-term strategic issues than on daily operations. They maintain a high level of physical presence in the prison and define their management style as 'management by walking about'. They are more comfortable on the landings than they are chairing business meetings. Because of their in-depth operational knowledge they micro-manage. Chief officers can be more autocratic and confrontational in their style and tend to be less inclusive, as they believe they 'know best'. They enjoy the authority that the role of Governor brings and the status of representing the prison at external functions.

Liberal idealists joined the Prison Service in the 1970s or early 1980s. They did so with a sense of vocation and out of a desire to reform and rehabilitate prisoners. They were mostly recruited directly from university, with a vocational degree in one of the social sciences, and tend to come from a more middle-class background than other Governors. Liberal idealists spent their early career working with prisoners, often as Borstal housemasters or wing governors. These formative experiences were carried into their later career and they maintain the optimism that constructive work can be done with prisoners, provided appropriate resources are available. Underpinning their work is a desire to make prisons into constructive and purposeful places. In order to do so, they spend much of their time cultivating a vision, undertaking strategic planning and engaging stakeholders, including prisoners, in the process. They adopt a longer-term perspective and focus more on cultural change than short-term performance improvement. Operational daily management is left to others and they look to their deputy to be the operational head of the prison. They see managerialism, and its manifestations, as a distraction from the real purpose of the job and consider recent changes as undermining their professional expertise. Prison officers can view liberal idealists as social reformers who do not appreciate the 'hard end' of the business and who often take the prisoners' side over theirs. They prefer to work in prisons that are focused more on training and reform, rather than on containment and processing of large numbers of prisoners. Liberal idealists tend to have a wider view of the criminal justice system, are interested in penal theory and get involved in criminal justice system non-governmental organisations (such as the Howard League, Centre for Criminal Justice Studies, Prison Reform Trust and Penal Reform International).

Conforming mavericks can come from any of the other ideal types but are a distinct group in that they challenge the status quo. They conform to the extent that they need to, in order to be able to be creative and developmental. Conforming mavericks tend to be entrepreneurial, to want to try new ways of working and are willing to 'push the boundaries'. The system tolerates their individuality because they produce high-profile and pioneering schemes and ways of operating. They conform to the extent that their prisons achieve most of their KPIs, and they adhere to most of the requirements imposed by Headquarters.

Conforming mavericks are confident in their abilities, are highly focused and well motivated. Their prisons become the focal point for official visitors because of their innovative ways of working and examples of 'best practice'. They also tend to be more charismatic than other Governors, are able to articulate publicly their values and belief systems and demonstrate what they are trying to achieve. Conforming mavericks gravitate to niche areas of the Service, often produce eye-catching initiatives and court publicity. The latter may be for their own aggrandisement or out of a genuine belief that their 'good practice' should be replicated elsewhere. They are very much energetic evangelists, who have the power to transform an institution either because of a single programme or because of their 'spirit'. However, because they push the boundaries, conforming mavericks are vulnerable to criticism and censure if things go wrong. Conforming mavericks are also the group that are most likely to leave the Prison Service because they become disillusioned, frustrated or feel that their talents are not being put to best use.

It is unlikely that any one Governor will fit the totality of an ideal type. Individual, and often contradictory, factors surrounding Governors are more likely to make each of them a hybrid of one of the ideal types. The structuring process of identifying ideal types does however provide an opportunity to understand the range of variation of Governors and their approaches, styles and philosophies.

There continues to be a variation between the types, defined by operating philosophies and approaches, as well as their mode of entry to the Service and the era in which they joined. A clear trend was identified in the shifting balance between the ideal types. General managers are increasingly replacing liberal idealists, as the work takes on an increasingly managerial flavour. Conforming mavericks are disappearing as diversity, variation and the Governor's ability to shape the prison regime is being curtailed. The number of chief officers is growing as the Service comes to value people who will ensure compliance with orders and instructions.

Changes to Governors' work and approach

A Governor writing over 25 years ago suggested that, despite organisational changes, the essence of a Governor's work would always remain the same: 'There [will] . . . still [be] the same prisoners to be dealt with and the same problems, even if slightly altered by the advance (or otherwise) of civilisation. Prisoners still have to be provided with food and beds and put to work; their families have to be catered for by visits and communication made with the public and friends' (Miller 1976: 187).

While Governors were unanimous in their view that the fundamental task of Governors remains the same, they were clear that some elements of their work were substantially different to that undertaken by their predecessors:

> In terms of running the establishment I think it is vastly different.

> It has changed beyond all recognition. Quite genuinely beyond all recognition.

> You've got to understand all sorts of things previous Governors would have had no idea about.

One study concluded: 'A transformation has thus occurred in the role of the prison governor, changing from that of a feudal baron-cum-house-parent to that of a corporate manager' (Genders and Player 1995: 205).

A long-term dynamic, which James and Raine refer to as 'administrative processing' (James and Raine 1998: 47), has led to more complex procedures and bureaucracy, within which Governors have to operate. This mass of regulations of which Governors spoke – international prescriptions relating to basic human rights, Prison Service Orders and Instructions, performance-measuring, KPIs and Prison Service Standards – is significantly greater than earlier Governors had to endure. The work has become far more rule-based as a result.

Governors also pointed to the increase in the complexity of their role, a result of having to take on a broader range of responsibilities. They highlighted the requirement to manage finances, to be involved in personnel management, and to undertake longer-term planning as being additional areas that they had to take on:

> The job has changed in respect of the content of our work. As things like finance and personnel issues have been devolved to Governors, so the workload has increased enormously. People used to make the decision about finance for us. They used to make the decision about how many staff we would have, to make the decision of how much overtime we would work.

Governors today not only manage multi-disciplinary teams, they also have to manage contractual relationships with a number of service providers from the private, public and voluntary sectors. Those contractors deliver a range of services that traditionally were provided in-house. A Governor may well be managing contracts for the provision of education, catering, maintenance, library, canteen, laundry, visitors' centre, probation, offending behaviour programmes, and drug treatment, each of which may be with a different organisation:

Life is very different today. I no longer just manage direct delivery of services. I have to manage other organisations managing those services. It gets very time-consuming drawing up the specifications, awarding contracts and then monitoring the delivery of the service.

My head of activities calculated the other day that we have five different contractors working here and 26 different voluntary-sector organisations coming in. That makes things bloody complicated, I can tell you.

Governors now have to undertake partnership working with local bodies, such as Drug Action Teams, Primary Care Trusts, Crime Reduction Groups and victim groups:

I've had to devote much more time in recent years to working outside of the prison. I sit on a number of local bodies and local government groups. It is a new way of working but a way that Governors have to get used to.

As budgets were reduced Governors said that they had to generate new sources of funding, rather than relying simply on an allocated budget from Headquarters. The effect was to stimulate some innovation, although this remained at the level of the 'individual rather than service initiative' (James and Raine 1998: 42). Governors, like public-sector managers in education and healthcare, undertook increasing amounts of 'entrepreneurial activity'. (See Boyett 1996 for a discussion of the 'public-sector entrepreneur'.) Some Governors set up innovative joint working with private-sector and voluntary-sector organisations and in some cases established joint ventures with private-sector firms to run workshops and vocational courses in prisons (Davies 1995; Flynn 1995; Simon 1999).

Governors were of the view that their job had moved away from 'traditional governing' and had become more managerial:

I think that my observations have been pretty much consistent with the view that, over 20 years, Governors have migrated somewhat from being 'Governor the other bit' 90 per cent of the time and 'Governor procedural bit' 10 per cent of the time. They've probably got to the point where it's 90 per cent the procedural manager, and 10 per cent the Governor bit.

We are much more concerned now with processes and about managing as opposed to governing and it just takes up so much of your time.

The present study therefore supports previous findings that have highlighted the fact that the Governor's work has taken on a stronger managerial flavour:

> The idea of the 'governing governor', who holds a tight rein on the prison, is constantly about the establishment, and does his own troubleshooting, is now largely defunct ... The 'Number One Governor', these days, is more often to be found chairing institutional meetings, attending headquarters functions, composing reports, or devising budgets. (Vagg 1994: 113)

> [Managerialism] made the governor focus more on performance indicators, measures, business planning and budgets than ever before. The main result of this has been a reduction in the direct management of prisoners by governors. Governors have been forced to limit the amount of time they spend conducting adjudications, hearing applications and touring the prison. The days of the 'hands on' governor who knew the names of all their prisoners and staff are long gone. (Bryans and Wilson 1998: *xx*).

Governors pointed to one of the consequences of introducing managerialist processes as being the proliferation in the amount of paperwork in prisons. As one commentator put it: 'Governors increasingly need good time-management skills in order to deal with the vastly increasing amounts of paperwork which threaten to become their false *raison d'être*' (West 1997: 35). The production of performance reports, audit documents and action plans, together with having to read weighty and detailed Instructions and Orders has, according to Governors, added to the administrative burden they face:

> It's a constant battle – the paperwork. I could spend 12 hours a day, seven days a week trying to keep on top of the paperwork. There is so much of it these days. Huge manuals to read, letters to do, reports to write, complaints to deal with. I could spend my whole day in the office and never see the end of it.

In particular, Governors made it clear that paperwork was increasingly making them more remote from staff and particularly prisoners, and less aware (from direct personal contact) of what was happening in their prisons:

> I do feel that I am becoming more and more remote both from prisoners and from the front-line staff as well.

The danger is, as you know, you become increasingly deskbound . . . what you don't do is get out and talk to prisoners and staff. But one thing I have always been quite clear about is you do not run a prison from sitting behind your desk in an office. You can lose touch very quickly with reality, if that's the way you operate.

Governors view the new governance structure as, in reality, having been not so much about giving them the freedom to manage but rather about creating new mechanisms that do exactly the opposite. This desire to control Governors has manifested itself in typical bureaucratic mechanisms such as elaborate written rules and regulations; using distortion-proof instructions; setting objective measures of performance; and intensively monitoring their performance. Some thought that the introduction of private-sector practices and management techniques would free Governors from traditional bureaucratic control. The reality has been somewhat different: '[W]hat might appear at first sight to be a de-centralising agenda, the management techniques introduced to monitor better performance of new corporate and individual operatives in the penal field, arguably strengthened the authority of the "new" system at the centre rather than weaken it' (Ryan 2003: 75).

Governors point to the more corporate approach to planning, introduced in recent years, together with auditing to ensure adherence to detailed orders and instructions, as resulting in less scope for them as individuals to shape their prisons, as they would wish.

The current reliance on written rules and regulations within the Prison Service is seen by many Governors as a substitute for managerial discretion and professional judgement, and has led to 'an obsessive emphasis on merely following the rules' (Freeman 1999: 49). This approach is at odds with the view of many Governors who believed that they should keep considerable 'operational discretion' (Berman 1980: 211). As one Governor put it:

I get the feeling that Headquarters would like to go back to the Du Cane days when the DG [Director General] knew exactly what was going on in every prison at any one time because it was set down in detailed rules . . . Governors would simply be administrators making sure things happened when they should and to the set-down standard.

Governors made clear that the job now is more about managing the delivery of a service and meeting laid-down standards:

I consciously set out to say I must improve this because it won't pass the standards audit. It has sort of redirected my focus and made me look at things I might not have looked at . . . My work now is much more about meeting laid-down standards and pushing up perform-ance to hit my KPTs. Before it was much more creative and thoughtful. Today I feel much more like a small cog in a wheel than someone who can design the machine.

The 'clawing back' of power and decision-making to the centre has, according to some Governors, reduced their discretion. For example, Governors are no longer the ultimate operational commanders in emergencies and have limited freedom to shape the prison regime:

Any Silver [the title of the Governor in charge of a prison during an incident] will tell you that, though he may have to take a quick decision without consultation, the process is designed to ensure that he submits plans which are 'approved' by Gold [an area manager based at Headquarters].

I think that another thing which is again a shift in the distance one has travelled managerially is the regime of a prison. The regime of the prison was determined by the Governor, largely on kind of almost personal whim and personal belief. There were no standards. There were no business plans. And there was really very little resource management. So that the extent to which industries were or were not developed, education was or was not developed, was very much a matter of the local culture, what had happened over time, and there was really no kind of formal management of it. Things are different now – there are orders on what offending behaviour programmes I can run, what education I must provide, what I must do in my workshops.

Similarly, Governors said that they are no longer the ultimate dispenser of their budget, as it can be cut or reallocated by the area manager at any time. The award of contracts for drug programmes, education, canteen and works service takes place on national or area level and the decisions do not rest with the Governor. Other budgets are 'ring-fenced' so Governors cannot reallocate the money to other areas, or have been removed completely from the Governor's control (such as the budgets for healthcare and education).

The 'professional structure' in which Governors were assumed to know what was best for their institutions and their prisoners has changed. The new status assigned to area managers has created a tension for some Governors and has made them feel devalued, as their autonomy has increasingly been curtailed. The rigorous application of standards and instructions meant that some Governors were increasingly alienated from the Prison Service as they perceived their status as professional practitioners was being undermined (see for example Godfrey 1996 and Wilson 1995 and 2000).

In short, the current study has revealed that there has been a significant shift in power away from individual Governors. Governors are today told what resources are appropriate for their prisons (by 'management consultancy reviews' commissioned by, and reporting to, area managers); how those resources should be used (ring-fenced budgets for various areas such as offending behaviour, education, healthcare); what the regime should consist of (PSO on regime elements such as education, physical education, offending behaviour programmes); what rewards and privileges should be made available to prisoners (the PSO on Incentives and Earned Privileges); and what level of performance is expected (Prison Service Standards). 'Robust' line management then intensively monitors Governors, ensures that they do not deviate from laid-down procedures and holds them to account for the performance of their prison. Should line management fail to identify any shortcomings, a number of external bodies are now able to scrutinise and challenge a Governor's decision (Ombudsman, courts, NGOs).

The Prison Service has not in the past sought to impose, or to socialise Governors into, a 'common mould' (Waddington 1983). The opportunities for the socialisation of Governors into a corporate mould are limited, with few training events for Governors and infrequent meetings of Governors as a group. The Prison Service has, in the past, tolerated differences of style and approach. As one Governor put it:

If you put all Governors in a room, you will still see that there is a difference between us. There is no company man approach. We do not dress the same. We do not come from the same backgrounds. We have different social characteristics. We do things in a different way. It is not like McDonald's, where there is a manual that tells you how to manage, what to wear and what to believe. To me that's a good thing.

Governors suggested that this approach might be changing:

... in recent years we have started to get more corporate. A certain type of person is being appointed as Governor and we are all under pressure to do the same things and in the same way.

The changing nature of the work, the need to conform to a prescribed managerial image and increasing pressures on the holder of the office of Governor, are having an effect on the style of governing. There is less room in the Prison Service today for the flamboyant, charismatic and independent Governor of the past. Governors suggested that they continue to bring to the post their own individual biographies, personal attributes and values, but that today the scope for individualism is significantly reduced:

> I think it is fair to say that probably there was a time where you could govern through sheer strength of character. If you had a particular style and you were a very strong-willed person, and perhaps a very charismatic person, then probably you could get away with managing by character and personality, largely anyway, so long as you got things right. I don't think that people can get away with that sort of style nowadays . . . the old sort of archetypal Captain on the Bridge bit is totally redundant. I think that style of management has long gone.

> I think the Prison Service has probably said goodbye to the solely charismatic Governor, at least people who depended on charisma to govern. Governors today are very similar, and we all do the same things. It's a pity really not to have some of the colour and eccentricity that those old Governors had.

Governors are now expected to be competent and professional managers who plan and deliver a public service within a set budget and to laid-down standards. They are expected not to be insubordinate, free-thinking, or openly challenge the current approach to prison management. As one commentator put it: 'Departmental officials look for strong but "obedient" field leaders in order to maintain cohesion' (Boin 1998: 210). Governors said that they are less willing today to ignore, or fail to comply with, written instructions. This is partly because the chances of their delinquency being found out are higher (through the more intensive monitoring and audit infrastructure), but also because of the increased frequency with which action (often disciplinary) is taken against those found not to be compliant. It has been suggested that 'disciplinary excesses to which public sector workers have been subjected since the 1980s have made corrosive and disabling inroads into the willingness of public service professionals to use their discretion to take risks in the public interest' (Carlen 2001: 14). Some Governors shared this perspective:

> You don't have the freedom you once had to be critical. It's like New Labour, no one wants to hear a dissenting voice. Prison Service conferences are set-piece events and 'troublesome' Governors are disappeared.

> There is a feeling of paranoia around at the minute. Governors are all paranoid that they will be the next one to be investigated or

moved from their post. I am old in the tooth enough to see what is going on. They want 'yes men' to govern according to the book, not Governors who will take a risk or ignore instructions which they think are not in the best interest of their prison.

The continuing significance of the Governor

Historically there have been immensely powerful Governors who have single-handedly determined the course of a prison for long periods of time (for examples see Jacobs 1977; DiIulio 1987; Taylor 1993; Pisciotta 1994; Kantrowitz 1996). Previous studies have suggested that Governors have a fundamental impact, either by contribution or default, on how a prison is run (Sparks *et al.* 1996; HM Prison Service 1997a, West 1997; Bryans and Wilson 1998; Boin 1998; Carlen 2001). It would be reasonable to speculate that the importance of the role of Governor would have significantly diminished with the increased control, direction, regulation and monitoring of Governors' work described earlier.

For a variety of reasons, however, Governors made clear that they remain significant and influential players in the prison landscape. As one commentator put it:

> Governors are the most important individual influence on what a prison is like, even though no governor can any longer be the nearly autonomous agent he or she once was, equally able to create either charismatic and meaningful establishments or ill-functioning islands determined by whim. The prison community is their resource and the quality of life within it is their product. (West 1997: 32)

The present research supports such a view and Governors recognised the continuing importance of their role:

> I think the prison is about the Governor and that the character of the establishment, the atmosphere in the establishment and the professionalism of the establishment all still radiate from the Governor himself.

> The sudden and complete transformation by a change of Governor, which has always been my experience, means that a Governor should never underestimate her or his influence. And I spent quite a lot of my career pretending that it wasn't true, and only latterly accepting that that is true.

> . . . there are so many obvious examples of that, where an establishment will go one way or another depending on who is in charge of it.

A Prison Service director has reached the same conclusion about the continuing importance of the Governor's role:

> Aside from the Director General as an individual, the Governor of the establishment is the key role in the Service, beyond any doubt in my view. More important than area managers, he's more important than directors, he's more important than policy people at Headquarters by a factor of thousands of per cent in terms of what happens on the ground in their establishment. So if you want to deliver, if you really want to do things, then you've got to get Governors on your side, and tuned up to do it.

Governors pointed to a number of reasons for the continuing importance of their role: the nature of the custodial institution itself; the historical vestiges in the role; the level of discretion that Governors still exercise over individuals; and the need for someone to regulate the operation of a prison on a daily basis.

Prisons have a number of characteristics that make them complex institutions in which to manage. Distinctive features of the prison that point to its managerial complexity include: the power disparity between staff and prisoners (the dialectic of domination and subordination is very different from that which subsists in the 'open parts of society' (Cohen 1985)); the level of deprivation (liberty, movement, access to goods and services, sexual relations with partners); the high levels of surveillance (in cells, toilets, showers, meetings with family); the limits which are placed on freedom of choice (daily timetable, regime, food); and the requirement that prisons encompass the whole of the lives of their inmates for 24 hours a day, 365 days a year. Perhaps the most significant feature is the dynamic that is created because prisoners are detained against their will. There is always the potential for prisoners to be disruptive, unless prompted and encouraged to conduct themselves well, as one Governor commented:

> You have a totally diverse range of people in your institution which you have to manage, and I include staff in that. You have no control over your client group at all. You get what you get ... So we have got a totally diverse client group that we have to manage. And the fact that they are not volunteers I think is also the other big difference. You could take the military analogy quite a long way, but then you come down at the end to the crunch that none of ours are volunteers. So you have got a potentially 100 per cent hostile group being managed, which has got to be unique. They do not want to be here. And that must be a unique challenge for the person in charge.

Prisons therefore exercise considerable power and influence over the individuals held within them. This power can be used for positive purposes or it can be abused. The Governor, as head of the institution, continues to have the ability to influence how that power is exercised and the purposes to which it is put. That has not changed over time. The external controls and monitoring have increased but on a daily basis it is still the Governor who signals what is and is not acceptable behaviour, the way prisoners should be treated and what restrictions are reasonable. Where the Governor does not exercise that power, some other individual, or group of individuals, will set the standard and decide what is acceptable behaviour.

> Prisons are very coercive environments. Even today the Governor should visit the punishment cells, visit the hospital, I mean areas of vulnerability, is my kind of general point. Areas where there is sensitivity, where things can go wrong, where abuses can occur. So health care, segregation . . . A good Governor understands that . . . I think it is also important for the Governor to go into what one might call the dark corners. Things like the boiler house, and the store rooms. To see all parts of the prison and make sure that things are working right. If people know the Governor is watching then they will do what is right but if they know that he is not watching or that he does not care then it is a slippery slope to abusive behaviour.

The Governor's role has developed over time, as Chapters 2 and 3 describe. As it did so, the role became vested with a certain amount of mythology, symbolism and power.

> The role or the office of Governor is vested with mythology and power because it has to be, I suppose . . . We have enormous power over people's lives.

> It comes back to the sort of symbolism of the role . . . It is a total institution. There is a lot of implied danger within it. It's a risk business. It's very people-orientated and complex. Those all make it such that the head is vested with more symbolism than, say, a general manager of a factory.

Much of that symbolism and mythology remains with the post today, and contributes to the significance that people attribute to the holder of the office of Governor. One manifestation of this mythology is the way in which prisoners and staff consider the Governor to be the ultimate source of power and authority. This is surprising given that a superstructure above the Governor makes many decisions and allocates resources; most Governors now have little to do with individual prisoners and their problems (those Governors who do adjudications and visit their segregation units have some direct contact with 'troublesome' prisoners but most prisoners see little of the Governor and have even less personal contact); and decisions about individual prisoners (such as temporary release, category change or segregation) are often decided on by other managers. However, for most prisoners and staff it is still the Governor who can make a difference in their lives and it is to the Governor that they turn to address their requests and concerns.

To some extent prison staff have been complicit in maintaining the 'mythology' that surrounds the Governor. They encourage prisoners to believe that Governors remain powerful. This mythologising enables staff to use the Governor as a way to manage their interaction with prisoners – for example, by saying that 'the Governor won't let us', 'it's the Governor's fault', 'the Governor changed the rules', 'if the Governor finds out I'll be in trouble'.

Prison officers also still expect Governors to attend social events, speak at funerals, visit sick staff, and sort out domestic issues (debts, marriage problems, housing matters). They expect to be able to have private meetings with Governors and that they will take an interest in their personal lives. Few senior managers in the business world would face similar expectations.

While Governors' powers have been directed and constrained in many ways, their residual power remains extensive. Governors still exercise considerable discretion in how to exercise their power on a daily basis. Policy instructions, despite their proliferation to cover a greater number of areas, can never be so comprehensive as to cover all eventualities in what is a complex operational environment. Many rules, instructions and orders remain sufficiently 'open textured' (Twining and Miers 1982: 213) to provide considerable scope for interpretation by the Governor:

> On the one hand, we are not short of instructions, you know; this office is full of cupboards which are full of manuals; but whether those instructions fully meet, fully advise, fully structure, fully guide Governors in order to make the decisions on a day-to-day basis, I'm very doubtful of that. I mean, it's down to you as the Governor to deal with ambiguity.

> I think by and large as long as you are within the Prison Rules and the broad guidelines that we get within the specific functions, there is still a colossal amount of both autonomy and flexibility in how you govern a prison.

It can also be argued that NPM itself has enhanced the importance of Governors by making them accountable for the total operation of their prisons (budget, staffing, prisoners and achievement of KPTs). The Governor is now both managerially and institutionally powerful, despite being more closely line-managed and monitored:

> There are still very few heads of large organisations where so much responsibility, authority and power is vested in a single role.

> So I think we still, as a Service, believe that Governors have to be powerful people, run on varying lengths of lead, but with the area manager hanging very firmly on to the other end of that lead these days.

The prison environment remains one of great ambiguity in terms of its conflicting purposes. The Prison Service as a 'Weberian bureaucracy is ill-equipped for correctly translating vague and conflicting goals into integrated action' (Boin 1998: 66). Coming up with policies that allow Governors to achieve all official penal goals in a uniform, efficient and politically acceptable manner is an 'impossible job' (DiIulio 1990 and Hargrove and Glidewell 1990). It falls to the Governor to interpret the aims, purpose, and goals of imprisonment. Governors must still balance competing priorities in the light of a proliferation of objectives and tasks, which go way beyond Governors' functional and financial capacity to deliver (Carlen 2001). A Governor in the study explained it in this way:

> I think primarily we are talking about, not totally, but a fairly unique institution . . . If you look at the stakeholders, the interest groups that you are trying to satisfy, I doubt if there are many organisations as complex as the Prison Service and often contradictory constituents as stakeholders. And in that sense, I think it's more complex, less clear in its aims, contradictory in some areas so that you are facing often in more directions than you've got faces. That gives it a bit of a uniqueness and I think that's to some extent too because of the lack of clarity in that and I don't think it can be clarified. I think it's intrinsically complex and contradictory and, because of that, you're doing much more as a Governor. People look to you as the Governor to put it all into context, to explain things and to put the pieces of the jigsaw together.

Social systems that may appear stable and permanent are, in reality, in a dynamic state of 'perpetual reconstruction' (Hatch 1997). Prisons are volatile institutions that can quickly degenerate into a state of disorder. In their daily work Governors must exercise their judgement to manipulate the various aspects of the regime in order to ensure security, order and justice on the one hand, and reform, rehabilitation and reintegration on the other. As one commentator put it, 'There can be no simple and invariant solution to all problems of order and legitimacy. Prisons are mercurial institutions' (Rock 1996: 349).

The implementation, on a daily basis, of all aspects of centrally prescribed policy is not feasible and Governors have to decide the degree and speed of implementation.

> We get so many manuals and instructions these days that you can't do everything. I have a look at them and decide what is most important and what can be left for later. It is only when standards audit come that you realise you should have implemented something a long time ago.

Governors continue to have a role in assessing and managing risk. Judgements have to be made about what level of risk is acceptable for any given purpose or in any particular situation; what factors should be taken into account; and what weight should be given to those factors. Whatever the process for risk assessment, Governors continue to have to make the final decision on the risk posed by an individual in various circumstances such as Home Detention Curfew; release on temporary licence; the size of an escort to court or hospital; employment location; segregation; transfer; and security category. Governors saw risk management as a key element in the continuing importance of their role:

> There is no scientific way of doing a risk assessment when you are working with people and especially cons. You might be able to do a proper risk assessment with a gas boiler or oil rig but with prisoners it's different. You can try and be objective and use all the modern assessment techniques but at the end of the day it's a human judgement – my judgement in many cases. There will always be a risk when you are working with prisoners. That's the nature of the beast – they are unpredictable and cannot be relied upon to do what you expect. After all, that's why most of them are in here.

Prisons continue to direct the lives of prisoners to a level of intimate detail. The rules cannot cover every situation and eventuality, so prison officers have to exercise considerable discretion in dealing with prisoners (Liebling and Price 2001), what Mathiesen (1965) referred to as the distribution of 'benefits and burdens' by staff. Governors in the study confirmed that view and made clear that staff, in exercising considerable discretion, had a real impact on individual prisoners. Governors believed that they had a central part to play in setting the boundaries for the compromise and accommodation which daily takes place between staff and prisoners. As a consequence, Governors pointed out that an important aspect of their work remains setting the boundaries for the exercise of the prison officers' discretion and establishing what is and is not acceptable behaviour.

Prison management theory

Underlying the current research was a belief that in order to develop a better understanding of the prison environment, researchers need to focus not only on prisoners and prison officers and their social systems, but also on how prisons are managed. This book contributes to the emerging field of prison management literature in that it focuses on the discourse of a powerful group in penal institutions (Abercrombie *et al.* 1980). Governors' discourse can be characterised as born of 'grounded professionalism based on their accumulated knowledge, their practical experience and their personal judgement' (Adler and Longhurst 1994: 156) and, as such, can shine an important light on how our prisons are managed.

Prison management models differ in relation to the body of rules, regulations and routines according to which a prison is managed. Such models tend to vary between the extreme ends of *laissez-faire* and 'strictly disciplinarian' (Cressey 1958) and represent a choice made among various means of inmate governance (Sykes 1958). Prison management models also suggest a difference in a second dimension: the formal structure, administrative routines and organisational culture (Cressey 1959 and DiIulio 1987). The military-type command structure with its formal system of control occupies one end of the continuum and the decentralised decision-making structure is positioned at the opposite end.

The approach adopted in prisons in England and Wales can best be described (using Barak-Glantz's (1981) classification) as a 'bureaucratic-lawful' prison management model, in which the operation of the prison is directed by detailed rules and regulations, and breaches of which can be challenged internally and externally. A few prisons (Special Security Units, Special Control Units, large local prisons) adopt a more 'controlled' approach, in which prisoners have a restricted and controlled existence. An even smaller number of prisons (Grendon therapeutic prison and some therapeutic units within other prisons) have elements of 'shared-powers' in which aspects of running the prison are shared by management and prisoners. While an increasing number of prisons have independently recognised the value of prisoner involvement in the running of regimes (see Solomon and Edgar 2004 for a discussion of the work of prisoner councils) the level of prisoner involvement is far from that envisaged in an absolute 'shared-powers' model.

No Governor spoke of 'inmate-control' as a basis for running his or her prison. Some did however point to inheriting prisons in which there were 'no-go' areas for staff and where some wings were 'run by prisoners'.

Within this 'bureaucratic-lawful' prison management model, Governors suggested that there was some level of variation depending on the Governor's personal style, approach and values; the history of the prison and its culture; the type of prisoner held; the views and relative power of stakeholders (POA, prisoners, area manager, Independent Monitoring Board); current Prison Service policy; views of the inspectorate; and the external environment.

It falls to Governors to create 'some sort of management model' (Boin 1998: 9) that is appropriate for them and their prisons. Governors pointed to various administrative features that were available to them to manipulate, including type of prisoner/staff relationships; discretion afforded to prison officers; regimentation of regime; degree to which rules are implemented and rigidly enforced; response to prisoner rule-breaking and disruption; level of prisoner consultation, participation in decision-making and ability to exercise choice. Governors emphasised in particular that the use of different administrative features should depend on the particular environment, the category and function of the prison and on what level of 'control' is needed at a particular moment in time. For example, there were times when a 'control model' approach was considered more appropriate (in the aftermath of a series of escapes; where there were high levels of disorder; where particularly dangerous prisoners were held; or when a new prison or regime was being established). This suggests that there is no single best management approach to the running of prisons, which is contrary to findings in other jurisdictions (see for example DiIulio 1987). The current research suggests therefore that a 'contingent model' of prison management is the dominant feature of prison governance in England and Wales.

Sui generis revisited

There has been a long-held view that governing is a unique and distinct professional occupation. The previous Governors' union incorporated in its logo the words *sui generis*. Their current representative body, the Prison Governors Association, maintained in its submission to the 2001 Prison Service Pay Review Body that the role remained 'unique and special' (Prison Governors Association 2001a: 9). However, given that there have been important changes to the role and work of Governors', can the claim that the work of a Governor is *sui generis* be justified today?

The work of Governors is now more managerial, with greater emphasis on financial, personnel, strategic and performance management aspects of the work. Governors, like their counterparts in other jurisdictions (see Wright, K. 1994 and Hunter 2001 on American wardens), have moved from being 'specialists' to being 'generalists' but have retained a significant specialist element within their role. Governors were united in their view that this specialist aspect involved regulating the operation of the prison, managing emergent tensions and the interface between staff and prisoners, and creating a working balance of the various forces and influences operating in their prisons. In order to do this Governors adopted a pragmatic approach to governing, whereby they 'muddle through' (Lindblom 1959) in an attempt to find the right balance and feasible solutions to practical issues that arise on a daily basis. Governors reinforced earlier findings (for example, Matthews 1999) in that they saw themselves as having to effectively balance and regulate the use of space, time and the quality of relationships in order to create a 'good' prison.

The reality is that Governors must not only be competent in technical areas (such as financial management, incident command, conducting adjudications) but also must have an appreciation of, and be able to manipulate, the 'softer' elements of a prison (such as culture, emotions, tensions, expectations) in order to regulate its daily operation. This aspect of a Governor's role – jailcraft – has remained constant over the years. A Governor described governance in this way:

> I think the very title Governor implies a key role which is multi-faceted . . . as a Governor I need to be financially very astute, politically aware, able to manage the dissonant balance between the needs and expectations of trainees and the needs and expectations of staff and the needs and expectations of society. That triangular balance is very interesting. One needs to set standards for normal behaviour within the institution, in other words so that a community of this size is actually able to function in a positive, meaningful way for everybody, not to stagnate and not to have a period of attrition in the relationship between the various key players who will vary from day to day. I also need to . . . balance their justifiable expectations.

Contemporary prison governance is still about creating a safe and secure establishment, which has a positive ethos, and in which staff and prisoners are able to make a contribution to the community. This involves the Governor crafting prison culture (both prison staff and prisoner subcultures); and understanding how to blend the various approaches to maintaining order. It entails demonstrating clear values and beliefs in order to make clear what is, and is not, acceptable behaviour and setting appropriate boundaries. It is about guarding against abuse of power and ensuring that staff exercise their authority legitimately and fairly. It requires imparting respect for the rights of others among both staff and prisoners, as well as ensuring that the rules are applied in a fair and reasonable manner. It involves exercising power and decision-making based on a firm moral foundation. It necessitates effectively channelling the extreme emotions and feelings of prisoners and managing relational and discretionary elements of the prison environment. It is about providing a range of constructive activities and promoting participation in those activities. It involves representing the establishment outside the walls and managing the boundaries with external stakeholders. But above all, it is about creating hope and providing the opportunity for personal growth amongst staff and prisoners, in what is a potentially damaging environment.

Governors' ability to do this is linked to the quality of relationships that they form and develop with other people, and the way they exercise their authority. Governors must create and nurture shared ownership of, and commitment to, driving the establishment forward. Governors must recognise the potential in their senior team, and use it to empower and develop all staff. This requires visible leadership of both staff and prisoners, particularly where decisions need to be made in complex and difficult situations.

While the nature of some of the work that Governors undertake has changed, Governors were of the view that aspects of their role were very similar to those of their predecessors:

> The leadership issue has not changed. The responsibility issue has not changed. It's just that the tools used have become more complex, and the pitfalls are far greater, but the actual role I don't think has changed. I'm sure it's not changed.

> The work has changed. There is no doubt that in terms of the things you have to spend time on now as a Governor, that has shifted around ... if I differentiate the role and the work, I think the role probably hasn't changed.

The distinctiveness of the working environment, historical vestiges in the role and the need to exercise a balancing and regulating function, all contribute to making the Governor's role critical to the successful operation of today's prisons. The issue, though, of whether that role is *sui generis* remains a debatable one. There is no doubt that features of

179

imprisonment described earlier make prisons distinct environments in which to manage. But many other working environments are also distinct and require specific knowledge, skills and experience in order to work within them. To justify the assertion that the Governor's role is *sui generis* it would be necessary to demonstrate that there is no other comparable role.

Governors base their assertion that their role is unique on a number of features: the amount of power, influence and authority that still rests with the Governor; the uniqueness and complexity of the environment in which it is exercised; the breadth and range of responsibilities; the ability and requirement to switch between management and command roles; the level of involvement they must have with the detailed operation of the institution (requiring technical expertise); and the intensity and coercive nature of prisons, which require balancing the control of prisoners with their protection. They point to the need to regulate and balance the daily operation of a prison, and the requirement to demonstrate clear moral and ethical standards, as the unique element in their role:

> The Governor's role as regulator is, perhaps, the role which has changed the least over the years. It is also the role that is specific to the total institution of the prison.

While there have been some attempts to eradicate 'qualitative, profes-sional and discretionary judgement from operational decisions' (Carlen 2001: 11), and to make Governors operate within narrower and less flexible boundaries, Governors stated that they still need to use their power, authority and discretion in a way that protects the individual and mitigates the negative aspects of the closed institution. One Governor described it in this way:

> I think the worst of it is that those who don't realise that they have a greater task to perform get sucked into the managerial model. They end up doing trivial things. And whilst they are doing these things they lose sight of what they are supposed to be doing. The net result is that the establishment will start to drift and they drift inevitably. You can't actually take your hands off the steering wheel and expect not to hit something eventually. It is absolutely vital that the governing Governor stays there and keeps it on track and understands that that is his or her role. And it isn't anybody else's job. You can't hand it over to the area manager. You can't hand it over to [the deputy director general] although I am sure he would like to direct everybody. You can't hand it down to your deputy. It is recognising that nobody else can do that job. I think, most

importantly, recognising what that job is and what the distractions are around.

Governors saw their continuing significance as the 'soul and conscience' of the prison. Their values and principles were embodied within all that they did and were the benchmark for measuring everything that happened in the prison. For them it was about ensuring that 'The pursuit of values such as justice, tolerance, decency, humanity, and civility [are] part of any penal institution's self-consciousness – an intrinsic and constitutive aspect of its role' (Garland 1990: 292).

There will always be a tension that exists between control from above in the form of rules, regulations and directives, that reduce the governor's autonomy, and the need for flexibility and personal influence in managing prisons, because of the very nature of penal institutions. So long as this remains the case, the work of a prison Governor will remain a form of management that is *sui generis*. It is in the Governor's role as custodian of values and ethos, regulator and creator of balance, managing in a potentially damaging and hostile environment, that the *sui generis* aspects of the Governor's role remain most clearly manifest.

Chapter 8

Prisons, governance and research – looking to the future

Implications for policy and practice

Over 40 years ago, in the classic volume *The Prison: Studies in Institutional Organisation and Change*, Cressey (1961) suggested that administrators and other policy makers do not find theoretical works too helpful for their job. Giddens suggests that research can reconstitute and alter the field of practice where the research is absorbed back into discourse and practice (what he call the 'double hermeneutic', Giddens 1989: 289). This section highlights areas where the present research has implications for policy and practice. In doing so it is hoped that the current research will contribute to bridging the divide between theory and practice (Petersilia 1996).

The changes in recent years to the Governor's role and work, identified in this study, have resulted in confused expectations over what Governors should be doing. This lack of clarity is compounded as existing rules, regulations, orders and instructions require that Governors personally undertake a host of duties, some of which have their basis in history rather than in the contemporary prison world. There is a need for the Prison Service to set out in clear terms what it expects of today's Governors and then amend orders and instructions accordingly, in order to enable Governors to focus on their core work.

Despite the pressure to move from 'management by presence' to 'management by information', Governors were emphatic in their belief that prisons could not be effectively governed from sitting behind a desk. It is only by making personal contact with staff and prisoners, by visiting the less-frequented areas of a prison, by looking and listening to the interaction between staff and prisoners, and by speaking with visitors to the prison, that Governors can get a real appreciation of what is happening in their institution. In spending less time 'walking the landings' there is a danger that Governors will lose the 'feel' for their establishments and will no longer sense when things are not right. While Governors now have detailed information of the performance of various aspects of their prison's operation (from other managers, audits, internal monitoring, and prisoner request complaints forms) all of these are open to omission, manipulation and distortion. Governors who seldom leave their office run the risk of becoming isolated and removed from the reality of the prison's routine operation, and are no longer able to detect and prevent abuse and unfair treatment. These conclusions support earlier findings on the importance of the head of the institution being visible, interacting with the stakeholders and monitoring personally what is happening in their establishment groups (Mactavish 1997; National Institute of Corrections 1997; Boin 1998; Bryans and Wilson 1998). It is important therefore for the Prison Service to put in place support mechanisms for Governors to enable them to have sufficient time to continue to 'walk the landings'.

Governors spend a relatively short period of time in each prison they govern. It was reported that 44 prisons have had four or more Governors, or acting Governors, in charge in the last five years (Lyon 2003: 3). Only 17 of the 42 Governors interviewed for this study were still governing a prison at the end of 2003. One Governor highlighted the issue:

We all seem to move around so quickly these days. There cannot be so few good Governors that they are moved from crisis to crisis . . . it cannot be good for the prison.

The impact on a prison of a change in Governor can be enormous. A prison will need to adjust to the Governor's personal style, understand the new priorities, and cope with the Governor's lack of local knowledge. Stakeholders will need to develop relationships and trust with the new Governor. While these issues may not be a problem in stable institutions, in more troubled prisons frequent changes in Governor can be extremely damaging. Frequent changes of Governor 'allowed those resistant to change to fight rearguard actions, slow down the pace of change and, if we are not careful, send establishments into reverse' (Newell, M. 2003: 26). The ability of a Governor to make lasting changes and embed those changes in the prison culture takes time. Governors suggest that it takes at least a year to identify issues, build relationships and understand the culture, another year to develop, resource and implement change, and a third year to establish and embed a long-term strategy:

I think Governors should be made to stay in post for at least five years. It takes that long to sort somewhere out and to make the changes last. There are too many people who look at Governing as a stepping stone for promotion or who want bigger prisons or more money. Prison officers can see right through that sort of Governor and the place may look as though it has changed but as soon as he goes it's back to where it was.

The PGA takes a similar view, as does a former Chief Inspector of Prisons and a recent report on the Prison Service:

The Prison Service should look to encouraging Governors to remain in post for longer periods of time by reviewing promotion and pay arrangements. As one former Governor put it: 'It is time to change the stories so that longevity becomes the norm rather than the rare exception.' (Newell, T. 2003: 22)

The Prison Service ... moves its commanding officers, or prison governors, around far too often, leaving them in post for much too short a time. (Ramsbotham 2003: 36)

Governors should remain in post for longer ... and succession planning should be robust enough to take that into account. (Keith 2006: para. 38.3)

The Prison Service should ensure that Governors remain in post for longer periods and provide incentives for those that do so, if it wants to achieve real change in its institutions.

Governors currently feel that they are unable to influence policy. The research indicates that this is one reason for Governors not implementing policy as it was intended. By involving Governors at the policy formulation stage, the Prison Service would reduce the 'appreciative gap' between those who formulate policy and those who have to implement it. This will help to achieve 'like-mindedness' among members of the organisation and reduce the gap between policy and its implementation (Sabatier and Mazmanian 1983).

Prison governance has evolved a body of practice, a way of going about things, which has been generally responsive to changes in the internal and external environment. The individual Governor is initiated into this practice and learns much of the substance of his or her work through a process of on-the-job apprenticeship, rather than through formal training courses, textbooks or college teaching. The 'rules' of how to do the job are not so much the product of design but the product of countless long-forgotten experiments that achieved practical results. Others relate to the 'art' of the job: the hints, tips and clues which

Governors learn to read, understand and use to their advantage. The learning and knowledge that underpins 'jailcraft' has, in the past, been passed from generation to generation through the experience and training that prepared people to govern. Governors made clear that this sort of experience and training is critical, as there is very little written material to help them better understand their role and how to perform it. There is a need for the Prison Service to review the way in which it will facilitate this passing of knowledge from generation to generation of Governors, as there is currently no written tradition of doing so.

With more practitioners undertaking academic study that is relevant to operational policy and practice, there is a need to consider how the findings can be transferred into the operational domain. Readily accessible, understandable and relevant research findings will help to establish a written tradition of learning, which currently does not exist amongst Governors. The dissemination of the research material that is currently being generated is an issue that the Prison Service has yet to systematically take forward.

Changes to the work, competing priorities, and pressures of robust performance management have all contributed to increasing the level of stress that Governors endure. Some Governors also reported conflicts over values and ideology, especially in relation to the impact of managerialism. If the Prison Service is to effectively exercise its duty of care to Governors it will need to monitor their stress levels and ensure that appropriate action is taken to support them in their work. If Governors are not functioning properly, it is unlikely that their prisons will be operating effectively.

What next? Suggestions for further research

The research that formed the basis of this book was based on a sample of Governors in post in the late 1990s. Not all Governors at the time were interviewed and the turnover of Governors has proved to be very high since the research was conducted. The views of Governors may have changed since the fieldwork was completed, as the continuing structural changes (such as the creation of NOMS, a new Director General, continued rise in the prison population) will have had an impact on Governors and their work. A new study would be able to chart further changes to the work and perspective of Governors.

The current study has, for the most part, focused on Governors' views about their work. While self-report data has a respectable place in criminology (see, for example, Hirschi *et al.* 1980 and Graham and Bowling 1995), it has been pointed out that 'groups of social actors in specific settings produce discourses that reflect and construct their social interest' (Adler and Longhurst 1994: 31). As managers often do not act in ways that they claim to act (Watson 1996), the 'espoused' theories of Governors about what they do, and their role, may differ from reality. Research based solely on managers' accounts of what they do is necessary but not sufficient. There is a need to analyse how they act, through, for example, participant observation (Lawton 1998), and future researchers should consider such a methodological approach. A study using different methodologies (such as observation or work diaries) may also shed some light on different aspects of a Governor's work, which were not revealed in their oral accounts. Such research would also indicate whether what Governors said they did was borne out in their day-to-day work.

The study has provided one snapshot of prison governance and, like many research studies, has left many questions unanswered, in particular, questions relating to situational and environmental impacts on a Governor's work; the role of the senior team; gender issues; and the relationship between a Governor's ability and the performance of his or her prison.

Situational and environmental issues were raised by a number of Governors in this study as having an impact on what they did and how they did it. For example, it is now widely accepted that different dispositions of power and practice exist in juvenile and women's institutions, compared to adult male institutions (see for example, Street *et al.* 1966; Carlen 1983; Manderaka-Sheppard 1986; Willmott 1999). It has also long been recognised that the social structure of female prison communities differs from male prison communities, and that this will have an impact on the way they should be managed (Ward and Kassebaum 1965; Willmott 1999; Carlen 2002; De Cou 2002). These areas require further study and suggest a number of research questions: Do different environments exist within one organisation? What impact does the type of prison, size of prison, category of prison, or stage of a prison's development have on the way it should be managed? Do different prison environments have different job demands that require different competencies of their Governors? Can the Governor of a high-performing dispersal prison successfully govern an open prison? Does the Governor of a small training prison need the same skills as the Governor of a large local prison that is 10 times its size?

Many Governors spoke of the importance of the senior team and pointed out that it was only through their ability to develop and work within a strong senior team that they were able to deliver change. Management theorists support this view and suggest that organisational success has as much to do with the functioning of a high-performance team as it does with the head of an organisation (see for example, Johnson 1995; Bennis and Townsend 1996; Owen 1996; and Obeng 1997), a view highlighted in reports on the Prison Service: 'The selection of the Management Team in particular, is of paramount importance' (Learmont 1995b: para. 2.31); 'Governors have to rely on their senior management team for many things' (Keith 2006: para. 40.1). If this is true, then the selection and appointment of a senior team within a prison will have as much impact on the health of that prison as the appointment of a Governor. Further research looking at prison governance from a team perspective is therefore needed, as 'insufficient attention has been paid to the development of management groups within prisons' (Newell, T. 2003: 21).

The majority of Governors are male (86 per cent), which was reflected in the interview sample for this study. Recent management researchers have argued that female senior managers do things differently from their male colleagues, and adopt distinct styles and approaches (see for example, Collinson and Collinson 1989; Sheppard 1989; Kanter 1993; Owen 1996). While the role of females in criminal justice professions has received some research attention in the USA (Wilson 1982; Moyer 1985; Pollock 1986; Zimmer 1986; Farnworth 1992; Heidensohn 1992; Martin and Jurik 1996; McMahon 1999), female Governors in this country, like their male counterparts, have been the subject of very limited study. One small study that has taken place suggested that 'governing was somehow 'different' for men and women and made different demands of them ... they brought different skills to the job' (Cawley 2001: 49 and 53). Further research is needed to identify any difference between male and female Governors in what they do, the way they do it and the outcomes they achieve.

The issue of institutional failure and governance has also not been adequately explored. A number of research questions present themselves in this area: Can a good Governor govern a poorly performing prison? Can a poor Governor govern a high-performing prison? What relationship is there between organisational failures (such as high-profile escapes, deaths in custody, major disturbances) and the Governor of the prison concerned?

Some final thoughts – governing in the future

It follows from earlier discussions that Governors today are somewhat less mythical, and more managerial, than their predecessors. Prisoners and staff are often heard mourning the loss of the highly visible, charismatic and powerful Governors of the past and compare them favourably to the more office-bound managers who now occupy the Governor's chair. There will invariably be further changes to the Governor's role in the future. As Ryan puts it: 'The profound changes which have transformed the delivery of our penal services will not be the last' (Ryan 2003: 106).

Many Governors expressed concern that future changes to their role and work will be shaped by bureaucrats at Prison Service Headquarters, who have as their continuing quest the constraint and restriction of Governors' discretion, their aim being to achieve a uniform prison system, in which Governors would simply become administrators, implementing set-down policy (as is the case with Governors in French prisons – see Vagg 1994). This organisational tension centres around the balance between uniformity and diversity (how much diversity in prison conditions or treatment can properly be sustained or tolerated in a legitimate society); and the mechanism of accountability (the balance between political, administrative and legal methods of holding prisons and their Governors to account).

The debate about uniformity manifests itself in the degree to which Governors should have the freedom to govern without being dictated to by the centre. Unchecked fragmentation has in the past led to a lack of cohesion, inflexibility, variety in thinking and differentiation of practice. A more integrated and controlled approach, it is argued, will ensure more consistency and higher performance levels. Advocates of this more integrated approach point to the Federal Bureau of Prisons (FBOP) in the USA, where a tight control of wardens led to the implementation of policy in a consistent, effective and legitimate manner (Fleisher 1989; DiIulio 1994a, Roberts 1994; Boin 1998). The FBOP has built a comprehensive enforcement machine that prevents any idiosyncratic behaviour or deviant activity by wardens. In 1996 Bureau policy consisted of some 9,000 pages and 260 Standards (Boin 1998: 197, note 28). One commentator found that 'despite the many other differences that one could easily enumerate (physical distance from FBOP central office, architecture and physical plant, nature and extent of prison industry operations, accreditation status), the operational uniformities were profound' (DiIulio 1994a: 166).

A warden moving from one federal facility to another will find 'all systems in place' because 'bureau policy structures everything we do' (warden quoted in Boin 1998: 109), and 'if you see the FBOP shield on the front gate, then whether it's Talladega, Memphis, or Bastrop you know how things run inside' (warden quoted in DiIulio 1994a: 165).

Indeed, many of the changes in this country had their genesis in the FBOP approach. A former Director General of the Prison Service made clear his view that the FBOP was 'a model of how I wanted our prisons to be run' (Lewis 1997: 72–73).

A high level of integration can have a number of drawbacks, including overcontrolled behaviour and a unity of approach that does not permit alternative ways of doing things. When individuals who are less inclined to allow dissent, experimentation and variation dominate integrated systems the organisations may develop into unhealthy totalitarian institutions (Wolin 1960 and Perrow 1986). To opponents, this highly integrated approach creates an image of a prison system operating as though it were in a controlled and value-free environment. What would be recognised and rewarded in such a system is the efficient, economical and trouble-free management of establishments. This would best be achieved through the use of comprehensive and detailed procedures, which were applied in an impersonal and automatic manner. The removal of all discretion would lead to the reduction of the uncertainties of human contact and human judgement. Comprehensive auditing and monitoring would allow failures of compliance with the system to be instantly recognised and blame laid immediately on the Governor, with no room for argument or excuses. The Governor concerned would then be removed for poor performance and the establishment performance-tested. Faulkner paints a bleak picture of what this managerial future could look like:

All that matters is what can be counted or measured; questions about how people think or feel, the character of their relationships, the extent to which there is a spirit of confidence, respect for human dignity and decency or a sense of compassion or mutual trust and understanding are reduced to tick-boxes concerning the completion of processes or procedures, compliance with requirements or indicators of failure. (Faulkner 2001: 100)

This is not to argue that many of the recent developments are without merit. Attempts to deliver minimum standards across the prison estate are to be welcomed. Prisoners are today less subject to the vagaries of individual Governors and their staff. There is greater consistency and a better understanding of what is needed to drive up performance. Clearer and more robust line-management of Governors has contributed to improved performance and will no doubt continue to do so in the future.

While the level of system integration has increased, and the work of a Governor has changed in recent years, the current research suggests that the nature of the prison environment is such that it will always require an on-site gubernatorial figure to exercise discretion and ensure that a balance is maintained. One Governor put it in this way: 'Prisons are intensely human situations in which there can never be enough rules to cover every eventuality. Rules are likely to inform knowledgeable individuals engaged in discourse but, where none exists or they do not cover the presenting situation, accommodations must be reached between the individuals so that the prison can run' (Leonard 1999: 30).

It is generally accepted that the complete control of the behaviour of 'street-level' managers is beyond central control, even if it is the goal (Lipsky 1980). Rather than seek to control and dictate everything that a Governor does, a more constructive approach would be to view discretion as 'inevitable, necessary and desirable' rather than problematic (Handler 1986: 11). This view has been reinforced by a number of commentators on the prison system: 'Headquarters must also be able to create and establish consistent policies and practices between prisons . . . But these policies and practices need to take account of the practical requirements of running a prison. They need to help the ultimate aim of the Service, not shackle the establishments into uniformity and inappropriate procedures' (Woolf and Tumim 1991: paras 12.69 and 12.71).

There are some signs that the Prison Service is starting to move away from unnecessary central prescription and that it is trying to achieve a better balance between mandatory standards and operational discretion (see for example the decision to do away with central prescription on training and security – HM Prison Service 2003b: 23). On the other hand, Governors are increasingly having less control over processing financial and human resources and procurement transactions (see, for example, a discussion on the impact on Governors of the creation of shared service centres – *Guardian*, 31 May 2006, '"All under one roof" philosophy put to the test').

Prisons are more than just bricks and mortar and will remain 'complex and dynamic social organisations' (James *et al.* 1997: 173). Prison governance will not get any simpler, and if the recent past is any indication, is likely to become even more complex, requiring greater use of professional judgement and discretion. Governors will still shape a prison and dictate by their action, or inaction, the safety, stability, security and justice within that prison. A good Governor will still encourage a positive approach to looking after prisoners with humanity, safeguarding prisoners' rights, minimising the negative aspects of imprisonment and providing prisoners with the opportunity to obtain skills and tackle their offending behaviour. Poor Governors will still let their prisons 'very rapidly deteriorate into unruly places that can only encourage further delinquent behaviour' (Dunbar and Langdon 1998: 32).

Prisons will continue to be 'complex institutions, difficult to manage' (Simon 1999: 218) and managing them will continue to be 'an exceptionally complex task' (Faulkner 2001: 301). Exactly what a Governor should do to achieve a healthy prison will remain a little elusive. As a result, governing a prison will remain an exciting, demanding and complex responsibility that requires enormous dedication and commitment. What is clear is that Governors will increasingly be held accountable for all that happens in their institutions, even though they are responsible for matters that they cannot wholly control. As a recent report pointed out:

President Truman had a sign on his desk in the Oval Office which read: 'The buck stops here'. The sign had been made at a reformatory in Oklahoma, where it had been on the desk of the Warden. The Warden was right. In prison, the buck does indeed stop with the Governor. If there are systemic failings in a prison, the Governor is accountable for them. (Keith 2006: para. 40.1)

Governors are key actors in prisons and it is only by understanding how prisons are governed, and by whom, that we will have a better insight into how our prisons operate. It has been suggested that: 'Just as early Roman history was measured by its consulships, so prison history can be measured by its Governors' (Rock 1996: 11). During the course of the research nothing has suggested that the same will not be true in the future.

Typical management structure in a prison

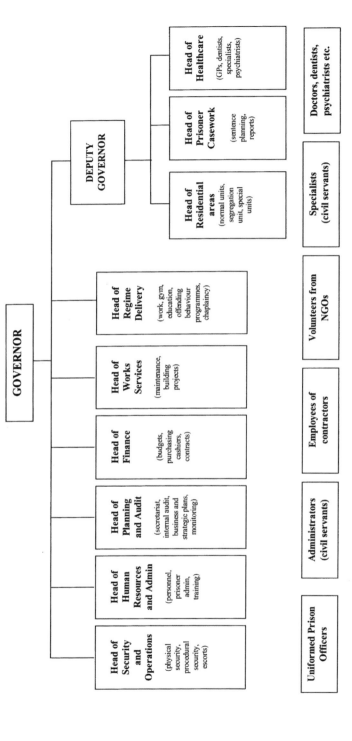

References

Abbot, B. and Bryans, S. (2001) 'Prison Governors', in S. Bryans and R. Jones (eds), *Prisons and the Prisoner: an introduction to the work of Her Majesty's Prison Service*. London: The Stationery Office.

Abercrombie, N., Hill, S. and Turner, B. (1980) *The Dominant Ideology Thesis*. London: Allen and Unwin.

Acheson, I. (2003) 'Moral Management', *Prison Report*, 61: June, 12–13.

Adler, M. and Longhurst, B. (1994) *Discourse, Power and Justice – towards a new sociology of imprisonment*. London: Routledge.

Advisory Council on the Penal System (1968) *The Regime for Long Term Prisoners in Conditions of Maximum Security* (The Radzinowicz Report). London: HMSO.

Anderson, R. (1878) *The Prison Acts 1877 and 1865 and The New Rules*. London: Shaw and Sons.

Babington, A. (1971) *The English Bastille – A History of Newgate Gaol and Prison Conditions in Britain 1188–1902*. London: McDonald.

Banks, C., Mayhew, P. and Sapsford, R. (1975) *Absconding from Open Prisons*. London: HMSO.

Barak-Glantz, I. (1981) 'Towards a conceptual schema of prison management styles', *The Prison Journal*, 60 (2): 42–60.

Barclay, A. (1988) 'Initial thinking on the role of the Governor under Fresh Start', *Prison Service Journal*, July: 5–6.

Beck, U. (1992) *Risk Society*. London: Sage.

Bell, J. (1996) *Doing your Research Project*. Buckingham: Open University Press.

Bennis, W. and Townsend, R. (1996) *Reinventing Leadership*. London: Judy Piatkus.

Berman, P. (1980) 'Thinking about Programmed and Adaptive Implementation: Matching Strategies to Situations', in H. Ingram and D. Mann (eds), *Why Policies Succeed or Fail*. Beverly Hills: Sage.

Blake, W. (1927) *Quod*. London: Hodder & Stoughton.

Boin, A. (1998) *Contrasts in Leadership: An Institutional Study of Two Prison Systems*. Delft: Eburon.

Boin, A. and Rattray, W. (2004) 'Understanding prison riots: Towards a threshold theory', *Punishment and Society*, 6 (1): 46–65.

Bosworth, M. (1999) *Engendering Resistance: Agency and Power in Women's Prisons*. Aldershot: Ashgate.

Bosworth, M. and Carrabine, E. (2001) 'Reassessing resistance: race, gender and sexuality in prison', *Punishment and Society*, 3: 501–515.

Bottomley, K. (1973) *Decisions in the Penal Process*. London: Robertson.

Bottoms, A. (1995) 'The Philosophy and Politics of Punishment and Sentencing', in C. Clarkson and R. Morgan (eds), *The Politics of Sentencing Reform*. Oxford: Clarendon Press.

Boyett, I. (1996) 'The Public Sector Entrepreneur – a definition', *International Journal of Public Sector Management*, 9 (2): 36–51.

Boyne, G., Farrell, C., Law, J., Powell, M. and Walker, R. (2003) *Evaluating Public Management Reforms*. Buckingham: Open University Press.

Brayfield, A. and Rothe, H. (1951) 'An index of job satisfaction', *Journal of Applied Psychology*, 35: 307–311.

Brown, J. (1996) 'Police research: some critical issues', in F. Leishman, B. Loveday and S. Savage, *Core Issues in Policing*. Harlow: Longman.

Brunacini, A. (1985) *Fire Command*. Quincy, MA: National Fire Protection Association.

Bryans, S. (1996) 'The Market Testing of Prisons: Ideology, Economics and Reality', *Prison Service Journal*, 104: 37–43.

Bryans, S. (1999) 'Management Training and Development in the Prison Service', *Prison Service Journal*, 121: 23–28.

Bryans, S. (2000a) 'Governing Prisons: An Analysis of who is governing prisons and the competencies which they require to govern effectively', *The Howard Journal*, 39 (1): 14–29.

Bryans, S. (2000b) 'The managerialisation of prisons – efficiency without a purpose?', *Criminal Justice Matters*, 40: 7–9.

Bryans, S., Martin, C. and Walker, R. (eds) (2002) *Prisons and the Voluntary Sector: A Bridge into the Community*. Winchester: Waterside Press.

Bryans, S. and Jones, R. (eds) (2001) *Prisons and the Prisoner: an Introduction to the Work of Her Majesty's Prison Service*. London: The Stationery Office.

Bryans, S. and Walford, J. (1998) 'Leadership in the Prison Service', *Prison Service Journal*, 119: 11–13.

Bryans, S. and Wilson, D. (1998) *The Prison Governor: Theory and Practice*. Leyhill: Prison Service Journal Publications.

Bryans, S. and Wilson, D. (2000) *The Prison Governor: Theory and Practice* (2nd edn). Leyhill: Prison Service Journal Publications.

Carlen, P. (1983) *Women's Imprisonment*. London: Routledge and Kegan Paul.

Carlen, P. (1990) *Alternatives to Women's Imprisonment*. Buckingham: Open University Press.

Carlen, P. (2001) *Governing the governors: telling tales of managers, mandarins and mavericks*, Future Governance Paper 5. London: Economic and Social Research Council.

Carlen, P. (ed.) (2002) *Women and Punishment: the Struggle for Justice*. Cullompton: Willan Publishing.

Carter, P. (2004) *Managing Offenders, Reducing Crime – A new approach*. London: Prime Minister's Strategy Unit.

Casale, S. (1989) *Women Inside: The experience of women remand prisoners in Holloway*. London: The Civil Liberties Trust.

Cawley, K. (2001) *A Crisis of Identity? Role Conflict and Managerial Styles Amongst Female Prison Governors* (unpublished thesis). Cambridge: Institute of Criminology Library.

Chandler, A. (1962) *Strategy and Structure: Chapters in the History of the Industrial Enterprise*. Cambridge, MA: MIT Press.

Chaplin, B. (1982) 'Accountable Regimes – what next?', *Prison Service Journal*, October: 3–5.

Chaplin, B. (1986) 'What happened to Accountable Regimes?', *Prison Service Journal*, October: 8–10.

Cheney, D., Dickson, L., Fitzpatrick, J. and Uglow, S. (eds) (2001) *Criminal Justice and the Human Rights Act 1998* (2nd edn). London: Jordans.

Chesterton, G. (1856) *Revelation of Prison Life; with an Enquiry into Prison Discipline and Secondary Punishments*. London: Hurst and Blackett.

Clarke, J., Cochrane, A. and McLaughlin, E. (1994a) 'Mission Accomplished or Unfinished Business? The Impact of Managerialisation' in J. Clarke, A. Cochrane and E. McLaughlin (eds), *Managing Social Policy*. London: Sage.

Cohen, S. (1985) *Visions of Social Control: Crime, Punishment and Classification*. Cambridge: Polity Press.

Cohen, S. and Taylor, L. (1972) *Psychological Survival: The Experience of Long-term Imprisonment*. London: Penguin.

Collinson, D. and Collinson, M. (1989) 'Sexuality in the Workplace: The Domination of Men's Sexuality', in J. Hearn, D. Sheppard, P. Tancred-Sheriff and G. Burrell (eds), *The Sexuality of Organisation*. London: Sage.

Conover, T. (2001) *Holding the Key: My Year as a Guard in Sing Sing*. London: Scribner.

Conrad, J. (1960) 'The Assistant Governor in the English Prison', *British Journal of Criminology*, X (4), April: 245–261.

Cook, A. (1914) *Our Prison System*. London: Drane's.

Council of Europe (1969) 'The Status, Selection and Training of governing grades of staff of penal establishments', *Third Report of Sub-Committee No. VI of the European Committee on Crime Problems*. Strasbourg: Council of Europe.

CPT (1996) *Report to the Government of the United Kingdom on the visit to the United Kingdom carried out by the European Committee for the Prevention of Torture and Inhuman or Degrading Treatment or Punishment from 15 to 31 May 1994*, CPT/Inf (96) 11. Strasbourg: Council of Europe.

CPT (2000) *Report to the Government of the United Kingdom on the visit to the United Kingdom carried out by the European Committee for the Prevention of Torture and Inhuman or Degrading Treatment or Punishment from 8 to 17 September 1997*, CPT/Inf (2000) 1. Strasbourg: Council of Europe.

CPT (2002) *Report to the Government of the United Kingdom on the visit to the United Kingdom carried out by the European Committee for the Prevention of Torture and Inhuman or Degrading Treatment or Punishment from 4 to 16 February 2001*, CPT/Inf (2002) 6. Strasbourg: Council of Europe.

Crainer, S. (ed.) (1996) *Leaders on Leadership: Twelve Reflections on the Theme of Leadership*. Corby: Institute of Management Foundation.

Crawley, E. (2003) *Doing Prison Work: The public and private lives of prison officers*. Cullompton: Willan Publishing.

Creighton, S. and King, V. (2000) *Prisons and the Law* (2nd edn). London: Butterworths.

Cressey, D. (1958) 'Achievement of an Unstated Organizational Goal: An Observation on Prisons', *The Pacific Sociological Review*, 1: 43–49.

Cressey, D. (1959) 'Contradictory Directives in Complex Organisations: The Case of the Prison', *Administrative Science Quarterly*, 4 (1): 1–19.

Cressey, D. (ed.) (1961) *The Prison: Studies in Institutional Organization and Change*. New York: Holt, Rinehart and Winston.

Crewe, I. (1974) 'Studying Elites in Britain', in *British Political Sociology Yearbook I: Elites in Western Democracy*. London: Croom Helm.

Cullen, E. and Newell, T. (1999) *Murderers and Life Imprisonment: Containment, Treatment, Safety and Risk*. Winchester: Waterside Press.

Cullen, F., Lattessa, E., Burton, V. and Lombardo, L. (1993a) 'The Correctional orientation of prison wardens: Is the rehabilitative ideal supported?', *Criminology*, 31(1): 69–92.

Cullen, F., Lattessa, E., Kopache, R., Lombardo, L. and Burton, V. (1993b) 'Prison Wardens' Job Satisfaction', *The Prison Journal*, June: 141–161.

Culley, M., O'Reilly, A., Millward, N., Forth, J., Woodland, S., Dix, G. and Bryson, A. (1999) *The 1998 Workplace Employee Relations Survey*. London: Department for Trade and Industry.

Curtis, R. (1987) 'Local Financial Budgets', *Prison Service Journal*, January: 23–24.

Davies, M. (1995) 'Prisons as social firms: the way forward for prison industry?', in *A Good and Useful Life: Constructive Prison Regimes*. London: Prison Reform Trust.

Davis, A. and Aroskar, M. (1978) *Ethical Dilemmas and Nursing Practice*. New York: Appleton.

De Cou, K. (2002) 'A gender-wise prison? Opportunities for, and limits to, reform', in P. Carlen (ed.), *Women and Punishment: the Struggle for Justice*. Cullompton: Willan Publishing.

Desveaux, J. (1995) *Designing Bureaucracies: Institutional Capacity and Large-Scale Problem Solving*. Stanford: Stanford University Press.

DiIulio, J. (1987) *Governing Prisons: A comparative study of correctional management*. New York: Freedom Press.

DiIulio, J. (1989) 'Recovering the Public Management variable: lessons from schools, prisons, armies', *Public Administration Review*, 49 (2): 127–133.

DiIulio, J. (1990) 'Managing a Barbed-Wire Bureaucracy: The Impossible Job of Corrections Commissioner', in E. Hargrove and J. Glidewell (eds), *Impossible Jobs in Public Management*. Lawrence: University Press of Kansas.

DiIulio, J. (1991) 'Understanding Prisons: The New Old Penology', *Law and Social Inquiry*, 6 (1): 65–99.

DiIulio, J. (1994a) 'The Evolution of Executive Management in the Federal Bureau of Prisons', in J. Roberts (ed.), *Escaping Prison Myths: Selected Topics in the History of Federal Corrections*. Washington: American University Press.

DiIulio, J. (1994b) 'Let 'em rot', *Wall Street Journal*, 26 January.

Donahue, J. (1989) *The Privatisation Decision: Public Ends, Private Means*. New York: Basic Books.

Doty, D. and Glick, W. (1994) 'Typologies as a Unique Form of Theory Building: Towards Improved Understanding and Modelling', *Academy of Management Review*, 19 (2): 230–251.

Douglas, M. (1986) *Risk*. London: Routledge.

Driscoll, A. (1982) 'Commandant's introduction', *Senior Command Course Instructions*. Rugby Prison Service Library.

Duffee, D. (1980) *Correctional Management – Change and Control in Correctional Organisations*. Project Heights, Ill: Waveland Press.

Duguid, S. (2001) 'Theory and the Correctional Enterprise', in D. Wilson and A. Reuss, *Prison(er) Education: Stories of Change and Transformation*. Winchester: Waterside Press.

Dunbar, I. (1985) *A Sense of Direction*. London: Home Office.

Dunbar, I. and Langdon, A. (1998) *Tough Justice: Sentencing and Penal Policies in the 1990s*. London: Blackstone.

Earley, P. (1993) *The Hot House: Life Inside Leavenworth Prison*. Des Plains: Bantam Books.

Ericson, R. and Haggert, K. (1997) *Policing the Risk Society*. Oxford: Oxford University Press.

Etzioni, A. (1965) 'Organizational Control Structure', in J. March (ed.), *Handbook of Organizations*. Chicago: Rand McNally Publishing.

Evans, R. (1987) 'Management Performance and Information', *Prison Service Journal*, April: 9–12.

Evans, R. (1990) 'Management Models and Performance Monitoring in the Prison Department', *Prison Service Journal*, Spring: 2–8.

Evans, R. and Marsden, D. (1985) 'Accountable Regimes at Featherstone Prison 1981–1984', *Prison Service Journal*, April: 4–6.

Fancourt-Clayton, G. (1958) *The Wall is Strong: The Life of a Prison Governor*. London: John Long.

Farnworth, L. (1992) 'Women Doing A Man's Job: Female Prison Officers Working in a Male Prison', *Australian and New Zealand Journal of Criminology*, 25: 278–296.

Farrington, K. (1992) 'The Modern Prison as Total Institution? Public Perception Versus Objective Reality', *Crime and Delinquency*, 38: 6–26.

Faugeron, C. (1996) 'The Changing Functions of Imprisonment', in R. Matthews and P. Francis (eds), *Prisons 2000 – An International Perspective on the Current State and Future of Imprisonment*. Basingstoke: Macmillan.

Faulkner, D. (2001) *Crime, State and Citizen: A Field Full of Folk*. Winchester: Waterside Press.

Feeley, M. and Simon, J. (1992) 'The New Penology: Notes on the Emerging Strategy of Corrections and Its Implications', *Criminology*, 30 (4): 449–474.

Feeley, M. and Simon, J. (1994) 'Actuarial Justice: The Emerging New Criminal Law', in D. Nelken (ed.), *The Futures of Criminology*. London: Sage.

Ferlie, E., Ashburner, L., Fitzgerald, L. and Pettigrew, A. (1996) *The New Public Management in Action*. Oxford: Oxford University Press.

Finkelstein, E. (1993) *Prison Culture – an inside view*. Aldershot: Avebury.

Finkelstein, E. (1996) 'Status degradation and organizational succession in prison', *British Journal of Sociology*, 47 (4): 671–683.

Fitzgerald M. and Sim J. (1982) *British Prisons* (2nd edn). Oxford: Basil Blackwell.

Flanagan, T., Johnson, W. and Bennett, K. (1996) 'Job satisfaction amongst correctional executives: a contemporary portrait of wardens of state prisons for adults', *Prison Journal*, 76(4): 385–397.

Fleisher, M. (1989) *Warehousing Violence*. London: Sage.

Flin, R. (1996) *Sitting in the Hot Seat: Leaders and Teams for Critical Incident Management*. Chichester: John Wiley and Sons.

Flynn, N. (1995) 'Making workshops work', *Prison Report* 30: 26–27.

Forsythe, W. (1990) *Penal Discipline, Reformatory Projects and the English Prison Commission 1895–1939*. Exeter: University of Exeter Press.

Foucault, M. (1979) *Discipline and Punish: The Birth of the Prison*. London: Peregrine.

Fox, L. (1952) *The English Prison and Borstal Systems*. London: Routledge and Kegan Paul.

Freeman, R. (1999) *Correctional Organisation and Management – Public Policy, Challenges, Behaviour and Structure*. Boston: Butterworth Heinemann.

Gadd, T. (1988) 'A little touch of Harry in the night', *Prison Service Journal*, July: 7–9.

Garfinkel, H. (1956) 'Conditions of Successful Status Degradation Ceremonies', *American Journal of Sociology*, 61: 420–424.

Garland, D. (1990) *Punishment and Modern Society*. Oxford: Oxford University Press.

Garland, D. (2001) *The Culture of Control: Crime and Social Order in Contemporary Society*. Oxford: Oxford University Press.

Garrity, D. (1964) 'Some implications of prison organisation for penal objectives', *The Howard Journal*, xi (3): 166–179.

Genders, E. and Player, E. (1989) *Race Relations in Prisons*. Oxford: Clarendon Press.

Genders, E. and Player, E. (1995) *Grendon – A Study of a Therapeutic Prison*. Oxford: Clarendon Press.

Giddens, A. (1984) *The Constitution of Society*. Cambridge: Polity Press.

Giddens, A. (1989) 'A reply to my critics', in D. Held and J. Thompson (eds), *Social Theory of Modern Societies: Anthony Giddens and His Critics*. Cambridge: Cambridge University Press.

Giddens, A. (1990) *The Consequences of Modernity*. Cambridge: Polity Press.

Giddens, A. (1991) 'Structuration Theory: Past, Present and Future', in C. Bryant and D. Jary (eds), *Giddens' Theory of Structuration: A Critical Appreciation*. London: Routledge.

Godderis, R. (2006) 'Dining in The symbolic Power of Food in Prison', *Howard Journal*, 45 (3): 255–267.

Godfrey, D. (1996) 'The Morale of Prison Governors: Some Reflections', *Prison Service Journal*, 104: 12–15.

Goffman, E. (1968) *Asylums: Essays on the Social Situation of Mental Patients and Other Inmates.* London: Penguin.

Graham, J. and Bowling, B. (1995) *Young People and Crime,* Home Office Research Study 145. London: Home Office.

Gravett, S. (1999) *Coping with Prison – A Guide to Practitioners on the Realities of Imprisonment.* London: Cassell.

Grew, B. (1958) *Prison Governor.* London: Herbert Jenkins.

Gruenberg, B. (1980) 'The Happy Worker: An analysis of educational and occupational differences in determinants of job satisfaction', *American Journal of Sociology,* 86: 247–271.

Gunn, J., Robertson, G., Dell, S. and Way, C. (1978) *Psychiatric Aspects of Imprisonment.* London: Academic Press.

Gunn, J., Maden, T. and Swinton, M. (1991) *Mentally Disordered Offenders.* London: HMSO.

HM Chief Inspector of Prisons (1997) 'Jail conditions dreadful, says chief inspector', *Independent,* 16 October: 4.

HM Prison Service (1984) *Management in the Prison Service* (Circular Instruction 55/1984).

HM Prison Service (1986) *Manpower* (Central Manpower Management Team, P6 Division).

HM Prison Service (1987) *Fresh Start* (Bulletin No. 8).

HM Prison Service (1988) *The Prison Service Statement of Purpose* – announced at the Governors' Conference November 1988 and included in *HM Prison Service (1989) Report of the Work of the Prison Service April 1988–March 1989*, CM 835.

HM Prison Service (1989a) *Regime Monitoring Handbook.*

HM Prison Service (1989b) *Review of organisation and location above establishment level* (a report by PA Consulting Group).

HM Prison Service (1992) *Report of the Work of the Prison Service April 1991–March 1992*, CM 2087. London: HMSO.

HM Prison Service (1993a) *Personnel and finance: devolution of Manpower responsibilities* (Circular Instruction 10/1993).

HM Prison Service (1993b) *New arrangements for establishment contracts, corporate objectives and establishment annual reports* (Instruction to Governors 24/1993).

HM Prison Service (1993c) *Prison Service financial strategy* (Notice to Staff 106/1993).

HM Prison Service (1993d) *The preparation of strategic development plans* (Instruction to Governors 33/1993).

HM Prison Service (1993e) *We Are An Agency Now.*

HM Prison Service (1993f) *The Prison Service and the Citizen's Charter.*

HM Prison Service (1993g) *Industrial Relations Procedural Agreement* (Notice to Staff 78/1993).

HM Prison Service (1994a) *Criminal Justice and Public Order Act – Pay and Industrial Relations sections* (Notice to Staff 450/1994).

HM Prison Service (1994b) *Corporate Plan 1994–97.*

HM Prison Service (1994c) *Devolution* (Advice to Governors 26/1994).

HM Prison Service (1994d) *Staff Survey.*

HM Prison Service (1994e) *Operating Standards.*

HM Prison Service (1995) *Incentives and Earned Privileges* (Instruction to Governors 74/1995).

HM Prison Service (1996a) *Management Structures: Guidance for Establishments* (Advice to Governors 5/1996).

HM Prison Service (1996b) *Management Development Project.*

HM Prison Service (1996c) *Area Manager Review.*

HM Prison Service (1997a) *Prison Service Review.*

HM Prison Service (1997b) *Staff Handbook.*

HM Prison Service (1997c) *Becoming a prison governor: the accelerated promotion scheme.*

HM Prison Service (1998) *Annual Report and Accounts, April 1997–March 1998*.

HM Prison Service (2000a) *Staff Survey*.

HM Prison Service (2000b) *HM Prison Service Performance Standards Manual*.

HM Prison Service (2000c) *Annual Report and Accounts April 1999 to March 2000*, HC 622. London: The Stationery Office.

HM Prison Service (2000d) *The Judge at Your Gate* (Information and Practice Guidance Note).

HM Prison Service (2001a) *Annual Report and Accounts April 2000 to March 2001*, HC 29. London: The Stationery Office.

HM Prison Service (2001b) *Staff Survey*.

HM Prison Service (2002) *Annual Report and Accounts April 2001 to March 2002*, HC 957. London: The Stationery Office.

HM Prison Service (2003a) *Prison Performance Ratings*.

HM Prison Service (2003b) *Annual Report and Accounts April 2002 to March 2003*, HC885, London: The Stationery Office.

HM Prison Service (2004a) www.hmprisonservice.gov.uk.

HM Prison Service (2004b) *HM Prison Service (Public Sector Prisons) Annual Report and Accounts April 2003–March 2004*. London: The Stationery Office.

HM Treasury (1989) *Review of the unified Prison Service Grade 1 and Regional Director posts in the Prison Service of England and Wales and Scotland*. London: HM Treasury.

Halsey, A., Heath, A. and Ridge, J. (1980) *Origins and Destinations: family, class and education in modern Britain*. Oxford: Oxford University Press.

Hammersley, M. and Atkinson, P. (1983) *Ethnography, Principles in Practice*. London: Routledge.

Handler, J. (1986) *The Conditions of Discretion: Autonomy, Community, Bureaucracy*. New York: Russell Sage Foundation.

Harding, C., Hines, B., Ireland, R. and Rawlings, P. (1985) *Imprisonment in England and Wales – a concise history*. London: Croom Helm.

Harding, R. (1997) *Private Prisons and Public Accountability*. Buckingham: Open University Press.

Hargrove, E. and Glidewell, J. (eds) (1990) *Impossible Jobs in Public Management*. Lawrence: University Press of Kansas.

Hatch, M. (1997) *Organisation Theory*. Oxford: Oxford University Press.

Hawkins, G. (1976) *The Prison: Policy and Practice*. Chicago: Chicago University Press.

Hay, W. and Sparks, R. (1992) 'Vulnerable prisoners: risk in long-term prisons', in A. Bottomley, A. Fowles, and R. Reiner (eds), *Criminal Justice: Theory and Practice*. London: British Society of Criminology.

Heidensohn, F. (1992) *Women in control? The Role of Women in Law Enforcement*. New York: Oxford University Press.

Henderson, J. and Phillips, R. (1989) 'Ensuring a Safe, Humane Institution Through the Basics of Corrections', *Federal Prisons Journal*, 1 (1): 15–19.

Hibbert, C. (1957) *The Road to Tyburn*. London: Longmans Green.

Hirschi, T., Hindelang, M. and Weiss, J. (1980) 'The Status of Self-report Measures', in M. Klein and K. Teilman (eds), *Handbook of Criminal Justice*. Newbury Park: Sage.

Hobhouse, S. and Brockway, F. (1922) *English Prisons Today*. London: Longmans Green.

Hofstede, G. (1996) *Cultures and Organizations: Software of the Mind*. London: McGraw-Hill.

Hofstede, G. (1998) 'Identifying Organizational Subcultures: An Empirical Approach', *Journal of Management Studies*, 35: 1–12.

Home Office (1858) *Rules and Regulations for the Government of The Convict Prisons*. London: HMSO.

Home Office (1865a) *Regulations for Government of Prisons*. Beverley: Kemp and Son.

Home Office (1865b) *Convict Prisons – Standing Orders*. London: HMSO.

Home Office (1883) *Report of the Committee Appointed to Inquire into the Position and Prospects of Convict Wardens and Broadmoor Assylum Attendants* (The Rosebery Committee). London: Home Office Library.

Home Office (1891) *Report of the Committee Appointed to Inquire into the Hours of Duty, Leave Pay and Allowances of the subordinate Officers in the Convict and Local Prisons and of the Officers of the Broadmoor Criminal Lunatic Assylum* (The De Ramsey Committee). London: Home Office Library.

Home Office (1894) *Standing Orders for the Government of Convict Prisons*. London: HMSO.

Home Office (1895) *Report from the Departmental Committee on Prisons* (The Gladstone Report), CM. 7702. London: HMSO.

Home Office (1923) *Report of the Departmental Committee Appointed to Inquire into the Pay and Conditions of Service at the Prisons and Borstal Institutions in England and Scotland* (Stanhope Committee), Cmnd. 1959. London: HMSO.

Home Office (1947) *Report of the Commissioners of Prisons and Directors of Convict Prisons for the Year 1946*, Cmnd. 7271. London: HMSO.

Home Office (1958) *Report of the Committee on Remuneration and Conditions of Service of certain grades in the Prison Service* (The Wynn Parry Report). London: Home Office.

Home Office (1969) *People in Prison, England and Wales*, Cmnd. 4214. London: HMSO.

Home Office (1972) *Report of the Working Party on the Recruitment of Prison Governors*. London: HMSO.

Home Office (1974) *Organisation and Staffing Structures for the Management of Prison Service establishments – Report of Management Review Team*, Prison Management Review Third Stage – Volumes 1 and 2. London: Home Office.

Home Office (1981) *Prison Governor Grading – a report of a review of governor grade posts in penal establishments in England and Wales*, Report No. PD 8/1981. London: HMSO.

Home Office (1984a) *Management Structure in Prison Department establishments – report of the Review Team*. London: HMSO.

Home Office (1984b) *Managing the Long-Term Prison System: The Report of the Control Review Committee*. London: HMSO.

Home Office (1990) *Crime, Justice and Protecting the Public*, Cmnd. 424. London: HMSO.

Home Office (1991) *Custody, Care and Justice: The Way Ahead for the Prison Service in England and Wales*, CM.1648. London: HMSO.

Home Office (1995) *Senior Management Review of the Prison Service Agency*. London: Home Office.

Home Office (1997) *Home Affairs Committee Second Report: The Management of the Prison Service (Public and Private)*, Vol. 1 and 2. London: HMSO.

Home Office (2000) *Statistics on Race and the Criminal Justice System*. London: Home Office.

Home Office (2001) *Statistics on Women and the Criminal Justice System*. London: Home Office.

Home Office (2004) *Reducing Crime – Changing Lives*. London: Home Office.

Hough, M. (1996) 'People Talking about Punishment', *The Howard Journal*, 35 (3): 191–214.

Houston, J. (1995) *Correctional Management – Functions, Skills and Systems*. Chicago: Nelson-Hall.

Hudson, B. (2003) *Justice in the Risk Society: challenging and re-affirming justice in late modernity*. London: Sage.

Ignatieff, M. (1978), *A Just Measure of Pain: the Penitentiary in the Industrial Revolution 1750–1850*. New York: Columbia University Press.

Ingram, H. (1990) 'Implementation: A Review and Suggested Framework', in N. Lynn and A. Wildavsky (eds), *Public Administration: The Art of The Discipline*. Chatham: Chatham House Publishers.

Irwin, J. (1970) *The Felon*. Englewood Cliffs, NJ: Prentice Hall.

Irwin, J. (1980) *Prisons in Turmoil*. Chicago: Little Brown.
Irwin, J. and Cressey, D. (1962) 'Thieves, Inmates and the Inmate Culture', *Social problems*, 10: 142–155.

Jacobs, J. (1977) *Statesville: The Penitentiary in Mass Society*. Chicago: Chicago University Press.
Jacobs, J. (1983) *New perspectives on Prisons and Imprisonment*. Ithaca: Cornell University Press.
James, A., Bottomley, A., Liebling, A. and Clare, E. (1997) *Privatising Prisons: Rhetoric and Reality*. London: Sage.
James, A. and Raine, J. (1998) *The New Politics of Criminal Justice*. Harlow: Longman.
Johnson, M. (ed.) (1995) *Managing in the Next Millennium*. Oxford: Butterworth Heinemann.
Joint Prison/Probation Accreditation Panel (2002) *Third Report 2001–02*. London: Home Office.
Jones, R. (2000) 'Digital Rule: Punishment, Control and Technology', *Punishment and Society*: 5–22.

Kahn, R. (1964) *Organizational Stress: Studies in Role Conflict and Ambiguity*. New York: John Wiley and Sons.
Kanter, R. (1993) *Men and Women of the Corporation* (2nd edn). New York: Basic Books.
Kantrowitz, N. (1996) *Close Control: Managing a Maximum Security Prison (The Story of Ragen's Stateville Penitentiary)*. Guilderland: Harrow and Heston.
Keith, Mr Justice (2006) *Report of the Zahid Mubarek Inquiry* (Mubarek Report), HC 1082. London: The Stationery Office.
Keegan, J. (1987) *The Mask of Command*. London: Jonathan Cape.
Kelly, J. (1967) *When the gates shut*. Harlow: Longmans.
Kemshall, H. (2003) *Understanding Risk in Criminal Justice*. Buckingham: Open University Press.
King, R. (1999) 'The rise and rise of supermax: An American solution in search of a problem?' *Punishment and Society*, 1(2): 163–186.
King, R. and Elliott, K. (1977) *Albany: birth of a prison – end of an era*. London: Routledge and Kegan Paul.
King, R. and Morgan, R. (1980) *The Future of the Prison System*. London: Gower.
Klare, H. (1960) *Anatomy of Prison*. London: Penguin.
Kotter, J. (1990) *A Force for Change: How Leadership Differs from Management*. New York: Free Press.

Lambert, E., Hogan, N. and Barton, S. (2002) 'Satisfied Correctional staff: A Review of the Literature on the Correlates of Correctional Staff Job Satisfaction', *Criminal Justice and Behavior*, 29 (2): 115–143.
Laming, Lord (2000) *Modernising the Management of the Prison Service: an Independent Report by the Targeted Performance Initiative Working Group, chaired by Lord Laming of Tewin CBE*. London: Home Office.
Larken, J. (1992) 'The command requirement and OIM qualification', quoted in R. Flin, *Sitting in the Hot Seat: Leaders and Teams for Critical Incident Management*. Chichester: John Wiley and Sons.
Lawton, A. (1998) *Ethical Management For The Public Services*. Buckingham: Open University Press.
Leach, T. (2000) 'Effective Practice: Some Possible Pitfalls', *Vista*, 5 (2): 141–149.
Learmont, General Sir John (1995a) *Review of Prison Service Security in England and Wales and the escape from Parkhurst Prison on Tuesday, 3 January 1995* (The Learmont Report). London: HMSO.

Learmont, General Sir John (1995b) *Review of the Implementation of the Recommendations contained in Sir John Woodcock's Report on the Escape from Whitemoor Prison on Friday, 9 September 1994*. London: Home Office.

Lee, J. (1966) 'Managing to Govern', *Prison Service Journal*, 5 (20).

Leech, M. and Shepherd, J. (eds) (2003) *The Prisons Handbook 2003–2004* (7th edn). Manchester: MLA Press.

Leggett, K. (2002) 'Excellent Organisations have Strong Cultures', *Prison Service Journal*, 139: 22–25.

Lennon, J. (2003) 'Penal Case Law', in M. Leech and J. Shepherd (eds), *The Prisons Handbook 2003–2004* (7th edn). Manchester: MLA Press.

Leonard, P. (1999) *What Drives Staff/Prisoner Relationships? An Exploration of the Influences Governors Have On Relationships Between Prison Officers and Prisoners* (unpublished thesis). Cambridge: Institute of Criminology Library.

Lewis, D. (1997) *Hidden Agendas – Politics, Law and Order*. London: Hamish Hamilton.

Liebling, A. (1992) *Suicides in Prison*. London: Routledge.

Liebling, A. (1995) 'Vulnerability and Prison Suicide', *British Journal of Criminology*, 35(2): 173–187.

Liebling, A. and Arnold, H. (2002) 'Evaluating Prisons: The Decency Agenda', *Prison Service Journal*, 141, May: 5–9.

Liebling, A., Muir, G. and Rose, G. (1997) *An Evaluation of Incentives and Earned Privileges: Final Report*. Cambridge: Institute of Criminology.

Liebling, A. and Price, D. (2001) *The Prison Officer*. Leyhill: Prison Service Journal Publications.

Lindblom, C. (1959) 'The Science of Muddling Through', *Public Administration Review*, 39: 517–526.

Lipsky, M. (1980) *Street-Level Bureaucracy: The Dilemmas of the Individual in Public Services*. New York: Russell Sage Foundation.

Livingstone, S. and Owen, T. (1999) *Prison Law* (2nd edn). Oxford: Oxford University Press.

Lodge, D. (1984) *Small World*. London: Secker and Warburg.

Lucken, K. (1998) 'Contemporary Penal Trends: Modern or Postmodern?', *British Journal of Criminology*, 38 (1): 106–123.

Lygo, Admiral Sir Raymond (1991) *Management of the Prison Service* (The Lygo Report). London: Home Office.

Lyon, J. (2003) 'Managing to work in Prisons', *Prison Report* 61, June.

Mactavish, M. (1997) 'A Correctional Leadership Practices Model', *Corrections Today*, 59(1): 60–61, 70.

Manderaka-Sheppard, A. (1986) *The Dynamics of Aggression in Women's Prisons*. London: Gower.

Mann, M. (ed.) (1984) *The International Encyclopaedia of Sociology*. New York: Continuum.

Margerison, C. (1991) *Making Management Development Work*. Maidenhead: McGraw-Hill.

Marriage, H. and Selby, M. (1983) 'Operational assessment in the South East Region – a fresh approach to the management of institutions', *Prison Service Journal*, 52: 11–13.

Marsh, A., Dobbs, J., Monk, J. and White, A. (1985) *Staff attitudes in the Prison Service – an enquiry carried out on behalf of the Home Office*, Office of Population Censuses and Surveys, Social Survey Division. London: HMSO.

Martin, S. and Jurik, N. (1996) *Doing Justice, Doing Gender: Women in Law and Criminal Justice Occupations*. Thousand Oaks, CA: Sage.

Maslow, A. (1954) *Motivation and Personality*. New York: Harper and Row.

Mathiesen, T. (1965) *The Defences of the Weak: A Sociological Study of a Norwegian Correctional Institution*. London: Tavistock.

Matthews, R. (1999) *Doing Time: An Introduction to the Sociology of Imprisonment*. Basingstoke: Macmillan Press.

Matthews, R. (2003) 'Rethinking penal policy: towards a systems approach', in R. Matthews and J. Young (eds), *The New Politics of Crime and Punishment*. Collumpton: Willan Publishing.

Matthews, R. and Francis, P. (eds) (1996) *Prisons 2000: An International Perspective on the Current State and Future of Imprisonment*. Basingstoke: Macmillan.

May, Mr Justice (1979) *Committee of Inquiry into the United Kingdom Prison Services – Report* (The May Report), Cmnd. 7673. London: HMSO.

May, T. (1993) *Social Research – issues, methods and process*. Buckingham: Open University Press.

McCarthy, J. (1981) Governor of Wormwood Scrubs, Letter to the Editor, *Times*, 19 November.

McCleery, R. (1961) 'The governmental process and informal social control', in D. Cressey (ed.), *The Prison: Studies in Institutional Organization and Change*. New York: Holt, Rinehart and Winston.

McConville, S. (1981) *A History of English Prison Administration – volume 1, 1750–1877*. London: Routledge and Kegan Paul.

McConville, S. (1995) *English Local Prisons 1860–1900, next only to death*. London: Routledge.

McGowen, R. (1995) 'The Well-ordered Prison: England 1780–1865', in N. Morris and D. Rothman (eds), *The Oxford History of the Prison – The Practice of Punishment in Western Society*. Oxford: Oxford University Press.

McLaughlin, E. and Muncie, J. (1994) 'Managing the Criminal Justice System', in J. Clarke, A. Cochrane and E. McLaughlin, *Managing Social Policy*. London: Sage.

McMahon, M. (1989) *Women on Guard: Discrimination and Harassment in Corrections*. Toronto: University of Toronto Press.

McShane, M. and Williams, F. (1993) *The management of correctional institutions*. New York: Garland Publishing.

McWilliams, B. (1992) 'The Rise and Development of Management Thought in the English Probation System', in R. Stratham and P. Whitehead (eds), *Managing the Probation Service: Issues for the 1990s*. Harlow: Longman.

Merton, R. (1957) *Social Theory and Social Structure*. New York: Free Press.

Miller, A. (1976) *Inside Outside – the story of a Prison Governor*. London: Queensgate Press.

Miller, W. (1973) 'Ideology and Criminal Justice Policy: Some Current Issues', *Journal of Criminal Law and Criminology*, 64: 141–162.

Mintzberg, H. (1973) *The Nature of Managerial Work*. New York: Harper and Row.

Mintzberg, H. (1983) *Structures in Fives: Designing Effective Organizations*. Englewood Cliffs: Prentice Hall.

Mintzberg, H. (1989) *Mintzberg on Management – Inside our strange world of organisations*. New York: The Free Press.

Morgan, R. (2002) 'Imprisonment: A Brief History, the Contemporary Scene, and Likely Prospects', in M. Maguire, R. Morgan and R. Reiner (eds), *The Oxford Handbook of Criminology* (3rd edn). Oxford: Oxford University Press.

Morris, N. (1974) *The Future of Imprisonment*. Chicago: The University of Chicago Press.

Morris, N. and Rothman, D. (1995) *The Oxford History of the Prison – the practice of punishment in Western society*. Oxford: Oxford University Press.

Morris, T. and Morris, P. (1963) *Pentonville – a sociological study of an English prison*. London: Routledge and Kegan Paul.

Mountbatten, Admiral, the Earl (1966) *Report of the Inquiry into Prison Escapes and Security*, Cmnd. 3175. London: HMSO.

Moyer, I. (ed.) (1985) *The Changing Roles of Women in Criminal Justice Systems: offenders, victims and professionals*. Prospect Hills, Ill: Waveland Press.

Mumford, A. (1997) *Management Development – Strategies for Action*. London: Institute for Personnel and Development.

Narey, M. (2001) 'Foreword', in HM Prison Service *Annual Report and Accounts April 2000 to March 2001*, HC 29. London: The Stationery Office.

Narey, M. (2003) *Speech to the Prison Service Conference*, 13 February, www.hmprisonservice.gov.uk.

National Audit Office (2003) *The Operational Performance of PFI Prisons*, HC 7000. London: The Stationery Office.

National Institute of Corrections (1997) *NIC Service Plan for Fiscal Year 1998: Training Technical Assistance*. Washington: US Department of Justice.

National Statistics (2001) *Living in Britain – results from the 2000 General Household Survey*. London: The Stationery Office.

Newell, M. (2002) 'Performance Management: Overused and Misunderstood', *Prison Service Journal*, 141: 10–14.

Newell, M. (2003) 'Holding the Line', *Prison Report*, 61: 26–27.

Newell, T. (2003) 'The Staying Power of Governors', *Prison Report*, 61: 21–22.

Obeng, E. (1997) *New Rules for the New World: Cautionary Tales for the New World Manager*. Oxford: Capstone Publishing.

O'Donoghue, E. (1923) *Bridewell Hospital: Palace, Prison, Schools: I, from the Earliest Times to the Reign of Elizabeth*. London: John Lane.

Osborne, D. and Gaebler, T. (1992) *Reinventing Government: How the Entrepreneurial Spirit is Transforming the Public Sector*. Reading, MA: Addison Wesley.

Owen, H. (1996) *Creating Top Flight Teams*. London: Kogan Page.

Oxford English Dictionary (1985) *Oxford English Dictionary* (2nd edn), vol. viii. Oxford: Clarendon Press.

Pakes, F. (2004) 'The Politics of Discontent: The Emergence of a New Criminal Justice Discourse in the Netherlands', *Howard Journal*, 43(3): 284–298.

Peak, K. (1995) *Justice Administration: Police, Courts and Corrections Management*. New Jersey: Prentice Hall.

Perrow, C. (1986) *Complex Organisations: A Critical Essay*. New York: McGraw Hill.

Petersilia, J. (1996) 'Improving Corrections Policy: The Importance of Researchers and Practitioners Working Together', in A. Harland, *Choosing Correctional Options That Work*. Thousand Oaks, CA: Sage.

Phillips, R. and McConnell, C. (1996) *The Effective Corrections Manager: Maximising Staff Performance in Demanding Times*. Gaithersburg, MD: Aspen Publishers.

Pilling, J. (1996) *Back to Basics: Relationships in the Prison Service*, Eve Saville Memorial Lecture (unpublished).

Pisciotta, A. (1994) *Benevolent Repression: Social Control and The American Reformatory-Prison Movement*. New York: New York University Press.

Polkinghorne, D. (1988) *Narrative Knowing and the Human Sciences*. New York: SUNY Press.

Pollitt, C. (1990) *Managerialism and the Public Services: The Anglo-American Experience*. Oxford: Blackwell.

Pollock, J. (1986) *Sex and Supervision: Guarding Male and Female Inmates*. Westport: Greenwood.

Power, M. (1997) *The Audit Society: Rituals of Verification*. Oxford: Oxford University Press.

Pratt, J. (2000a) 'Emotive and ostentatious punishment: Its decline and resurgence in modern society', *Punishment and Society*, 2 (4): 417–439.

Pratt, J. (2000b) 'The Return of the Wheelbarrowmen; or, The Arrival of Postmodern Penality?', *British Journal of Criminology*, 40: 127–145.

Priestley, P. (1989) *Jail Journeys – the English prison experience 1918–1990*. London: Routledge.

Priestley, P. (1999) *Victorian Prison Lives – English Prison Biography 1830–1914*. London: Pimlico.

Prison Department (1967) *Management Review of the Prison Service Organisation*. (Management Review Team Report).

Prison Department (1970) *Control of Manpower Resources* (Circular Instruction 80/1970).

Prison Department (1973a) *Responsibilities of Governors-in-charge and second-in-charge* (Circular Instruction 17/1973).

Prison Department (1973b) *Five day working week* (Notice to Staff 43/1973.

Prison Governors Association (2000) 'PGA Impact on Prison Policy', *Prison Governors Association Magazine*, 51: 8.

Prison Governors Association (2001a) 'Submission to the Prison Service Pay Review Body – August 2001', *Prison Governors Association Bulletin*, 155, 22 October.

Prison Governors Association (2001b) Letter from an anonymous Governor, *Prison Governors Association Magazine*, 53: 6.

Prisons Ombudsman (1996) *First Annual Report of the Prisons Ombudsman 1995*. London: Home Office.

Prisons and Probation Ombudsman (2003) *Towards Resettlement – Annual Report 2002–03*, CM 851. London: Home Office.

Prison Reform Trust (2001) *Prison Report 54*. London: Prison Reform Trust.

Pugh, R. (1968) *Imprisonment in Medieval England*. Cambridge: Cambridge University Press.

Raelin, J. (1986) *The Clash of Cultures: Managers and Professionals*. Boston, MA: Harvard Business School Press.

Ramsbotham, D. (2001) 'The State of our Prisons', *Prison Service Journal*, 137, September: 38–45.

Ramsbotham, D. (2003) *Prisongate: The Shocking State of Britain's Prisons and the Need For Visionary Change*. London: The Free Press.

Reaney, P. (1958) *A Dictionary of British Surnames*. London: Routledge and Kegan Paul.

Reichman, N. (1986) 'Managing Crime Risks: Toward an Insurance-Based Model of Social Control', *Research in Law, Deviancy and Social Control*, 8: 151–172.

Reiner, R. (1991) *Chief Constables – Bobbies, Bosses or Bureaucrats?*. Oxford: Oxford University Press.

Reiner, R. (2000) 'Police Research', in V. Jupp, P. Davies and P. Francis (eds), *Doing Criminological Research*. London: Sage.

Rich, C. (1932) *Recollections of a Prison Governor*. London: Hurst and Blackett.

Roberts, J. (ed.) (1994) *Escaping Prison Myths: Selected Topics in the History of Federal Corrections*. Washington: The American University Press.

Robson, C. (1993) *Real World Research*. Oxford: Blackwell.

Rock, P. (1996) *Reconstructing a women's prison – the Holloway Redevelopment Project 1968–88*. Oxford: Clarendon Press.

Ruck, S. (1951) *Paterson on Prisons – being the collected papers of Sir Alexander Paterson*. London: Frederick Muller.

Ruggles-Brise, E. (1921) *The English Prison System*. Basingstoke: Macmillan.

Rutherford, A. (1984) *Prisons and the Process of Justice*. London: Heinemann.

Rutherford, A. (1994) *Criminal Justice and the Pursuit of Decency*. Winchester: Waterside Press.

Rutherford, A. (1996) *Transforming Criminal Policy*. Winchester: Waterside Press.

Rutherford, A. (2000) 'Feeling good again about prisons', *New Law Journal*, January: 63–64.

Ryan, M. (2003) *Penal Policy and Political Culture in England and Wales*. Winchester: Waterside Press.

Sabatier, P. and Mazmanian, D. (1983) 'Policy Implementation', in S. Nagel (ed.), *Encyclopaedia of Policy Studies*. New York: Marcel Dekker.

Salaman, G. (ed.) (1992) *Human Resource Strategies*. London: Sage.

Sapsford, R. and Jupp, V. (1996) *Data Collection and Analysis*. London: Sage.

Savage, S., Charman, S. and Cope, S. (2000) *Policing and the Power of Persuasion – The Changing Role of the Association of Chief Police Officers*. London: Blackstone.

Selby, M. (1994) 'Gaols for Gaolers?', *Prison Report*, 98: 22–23.

Selznick, P. (1957) *Leadership in Administration: A Sociological Interpretation*. Berkeley: University of California Press.

Shaw, S. (1998) 'Prisons and the Human Rights Act', *Prison Report*.

Sheppard, D. (1989) 'Organisation, Power and Sexuality: The Image and Self-Image of women managers', in J. Hearn, D. Sheppard, P. Tancred-Sheriff and G. Burrell (eds), *The Sexuality of Organisation*. London: Sage.

Sheptycki, J. (1994) 'It looks different from the outside', *Policing*, 10: 125–133.

Shichor, D. (1999) 'Privatizing Correctional Institutions: An Organizational Perspective', *The Prison Journal*, 79 (2): 226–249.

Shorter Oxford English Dictionary (2002) *The Shorter Oxford English Dictionary*. Oxford: Oxford University Press.

Simon, F. (1999) *Prisoners' Work and Vocational Training*. London: Routledge.

Solomon, E. and Edgar, K. (2004) *Having Their Say – The Work of Prisoner Councils*. London: Prison Reform Trust.

Sparks, R. and Bottoms, A. (1995) 'Legitimacy and order in prisons', *British Journal of Sociology*, 46 (1): 45–62.

Sparks, R., Bottoms, A. and Hay, W. (1996) *Prisons and the Problem of Order*. Oxford: Clarendon Press.

Stanworth, P. (1984) 'Elites and privilege', in P. Abrams and R. Brown (eds), *UK society – work, urbanism and inequality*. London: Weidenfeld and Nicolson.

Stern, V. (1987) *Bricks of Shame: Britain's Prisons*. London: Penguin.

Stolz, B. (1997) 'Privatizing Corrections: Changing the corrections policy-making sub-government', *The Prison Journal*, 77: 92–111.

Street, D., Vinter, R. and Perrow, C. (1966) *Organization for Treatment: A Comparative Study of Institutions for Delinquents*. New York: The Free Press.

Suchman, M. (1995) 'Managing Legitimacy: Strategic and Institutional Approaches', *Academy of Management Review*, 20 (3): 571–610.

Sykes, G. (1958) *The Society of Captives*. Princeton: Princeton University Press.

Taylor, W. (1993) *Brokered Justice: Race, Politics, and Mississippi Prisons*. Columbus: Ohio State University Press.

Thomas, J. (1972) *The English Prison Officer since 1850 – a study in conflict*. London: Routledge and Kegan Paul.

Thomas, J. (1981) 'From Caprice to Anarchy: The Role of the English Prison Governor', *International Journal of Offender Therapy and Comparative Criminology*, 25 (3): 222–231.

Train, C. (1985) 'Management accountability in the Prison Service', in M. Maguire, J. Vagg and R. Morgan, *Accountability and Prisons – opening up a closed world*. London: Tavistock Publications.

Tumim, Judge S. (1996) 'Foreword', in P. Rock, *Reconstructing A Women's Prison: The Holloway Redevelopment Project 1968–88*. Oxford: Clarendon Press.

Twining, W. and Miers, D. (1982) *How to do Things with Rules* (2nd edn). London: Weidenfeld and Nicolson.

Tyndall, N. (1969) 'The application of managerial skills to the role of the directing staff of a modern prison', in Council of Europe, *The status, selection and training of governing grades of staff in penal establishments*, Third Report of Sub-Committee No. VI of the European Committee on Crime Problems. Strasbourg: Council of Europe.

Useem, B. and Kimball, P. (1989) *States of Siege: U.S. Prison Riots, 1971–1986*. Oxford: Oxford University Press.

Vagg, J. (1994) *Prison Systems: A Comparative Study of Accountability in England, France, Germany and the Netherlands*. Oxford: Clarendon Press.

Waddington, P. (1983) *The Training of Prison Governors – Role Ambiguity and Socialisation*. London: Croom Helm.

Waddington, P. (1999) 'Police (Canteen) Sub-culture: An Appreciation', *British Journal of Criminology*, 39 (2): 287–309.

Wagstaffe, S. (2002) 'There is Measure in all Things', *Prison Service Journal*, 141: 2–4.

Walker, K. (1993) 'Values, Ethics and Ethical Decision-Making', *Adult Learning*, 5 (2): 13–14.

Wall, D. (1998) *The Chief Constables of England and Wales – The socio-legal history of a criminal justice elite*. Dartmouth: Ashgate.

Walmsley, R., Howard, L. and White, S. (1992) *The National Prison Survey 1991: Main Findings*. London: HMSO.

Ward, D. and Kassebaum, G. (1965) *Women's Prison: Sex and Social Structure*. London: Weidenfeld and Nicolson.

Wasik, M. and Taylor, R. (1995) *Blackstone's Guide to the Criminal Justice and Public Order Act 1994*. London: Blackstone Press.

Watson, T. (1996) 'How do managers think? Identity, morality and pragmatism in managerial theory and practice', *Management and Learning*, 27 (3): 323–341.

Webb, S. and Webb, B. (1922) *English Prisons Under Local Government*. London: Longmans Green.

Weber, M. (1949) *The Methodology of the Social Sciences*. Glencoe, Minn: Free Press.

Webster's New Collegiate Dictionary (1973) *The New Webster Encyclopaedic Dictionary of The English Language*. Chicago: Consolidated Book Publishers.

West, T. (1997) *Prisons of Promise*. Winchester: Waterside Press.

Whitemore, R. (1995) 'Tasks and Duties of Superintendents and Wardens in Pennsylvania', *American Jails*, May/June: 53–58.

Williamson, D. (1986) *Evaluation of the Senior Command Courses 1983–1986*, (unpublished). Prison Service College Library.

Williamson, D. (1988) 'Training for Governing', *Prison Service Journal*: 13–15.

Williamson, D. (1991) *Report on training needs analysis for the Senior Management Programme*. London: HM Prison Service.

Willmott, Y. (1999) *Governing Women's Prisons – A Qualitative Study* (unpublished thesis). Cambridge: Institute of Criminology Library.

Wilson, D. (1995) 'Against the Culture of Management: A Personal Polemic to Re-invent The Governor', *Prison Service Journal*, 98: 7–9.

Wilson, D. (2000) 'Whatever happened to "the Governor"?', *Criminal Justice Matters*, 40, Summer: 11–12.

Wilson, D. and Reuss, A. (2000) *Prison(er) Education: Stories of Change and Transformation*. Winchester: Waterside Press.

Wilson, D. and Fowler, T. (2004) 'The Murder of Zahid Mubarek', *The Howard Journal*, 43 (1): 96–98.

Wilson, J. (1989) *Bureaucracy: What Government Agencies Do and Why They Do It*. New York: Basic Books.

Wilson, N. (1982) 'Women in the Criminal Justice Profession – An Analysis of Status Conflict', in N. Rafter and E. Stanko, *Judge, Lawyer, Victim, Thief*. Boston: Northeastern University Press.

Winter, S. (1990) 'Integrating Implementation Research', in D. Palumbo and D. Calista (eds), *Implementation and the Policy Process: Opening Up the Black Box*. New York: Greenwood Press.

Wolin, S. (1960) *Politics and Vision: Continuity and Innovation in Western Political Thought*. Boston: Little, Brown and Company.

Woodcock, Sir John (1994) *The Escape from Whitemoor Prison on Friday 9 September 1994* (The Woodcock Inquiry), Cmnd. 2741. London: HMSO.

Woolf, Lord Justice and Tumim, Judge S. (1991) *Prison Disturbances April 1990: Report of an inquiry by the Rt. Hon. Lord Justice Woolf and His Hon. Judge Stephen Tumim* (The Woolf Report), Cmnd. 1456. London: HMSO.

Wortley, R. (2002) *Situational Prison Control: Crime Prevention in Correctional Institutions.* Cambridge: Cambridge University Press.

Wright, K. (1994) *Effective Prison Leadership.* New York: Binghamton.

Wrong, D. (1994) *The Problem of Order.* Cambridge, MA: Harvard University Press.

Young, J. (1999) *The Exclusive Society.* London: Sage.

Young, J. (2003) 'Winning the fight against crime? New Labour, populism and lost opportunities', in R. Matthews and J. Young (eds), *The New Politics of Crime and Punishment.* Cullompton: Willan Publishing.

Young, P. (1987) 'The concept of social control and its relevance to the prisons debate' in A. Bottoms and R. Light (eds), *Problems of long term imprisonment.* Aldershot: Gower.

Yukl, G. (1994) *Leadership in organisations.* New Jersey: Prentice Hall.

Zimmer, L. (1986) *Women Guarding Men.* Chicago: University of Chicago Press.

Zinn, L. (1993) 'Do the Right Thing: Ethical Decision-making in Professional and Business Practice', *Adult Learning*, 5(2): 7–8.

Index